IRISH RISE

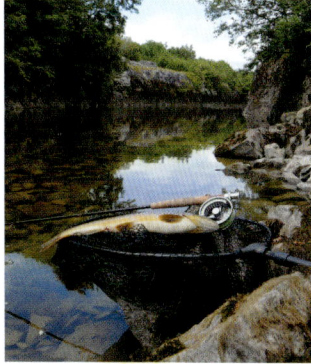

Also by Dennis Moss
Trout from a Boat (Merlin Unwin)

IRISH RISE

Reflections by Lough and Stream

DENNIS MOSS

Quiller

DEDICATION

Do locha aolchlocha na h-Éireann – Go h-álainn i gcónaí
To the limestone loughs of Ireland – Always beautiful

Copyright © 2010 Dennis Moss

First published in the UK in 2010
by Quiller, an imprint of Quiller Publishing Ltd

British Library Cataloguing-in-Publication Data
A catalogue record for this book
is available from the British Library

ISBN 978 1 84689 091 8

Printed in China

Quiller

An imprint of Quiller Publishing Ltd
Wykey House, Wykey, Shrewsbury, SY4 1JA
Tel: 01939 261616 Fax: 01939 261606
E-mail: info@quillerbooks.com
Website: www.countrybooksdirect.com

CONTENTS

ACKNOWLEDGEMENTS

Somewhere within, a seed is sown to initiate the stimulus to write a book about fishing experiences. Friends, colleagues, all have an active influence, but one man in particular proved to be the catalyst which made me put my reminiscences to paper. A very close friend for many years, perhaps he doesn't want to see me sit back and vegetate as he never ceased with his prompting to goad me into action. He is one who has also shown remarkable patience as it was his penance to read through the manuscript for this book. A man with a remarkable pool of knowledge and a mine of useful information when it comes to matters concerning fishery science. Thank you Vaughan Lewis for your friendship and positive support.

My thanks also to Andrew Flitcroft the editor of *Trout and Salmon* for writing the foreword to this book, and also for accepting my articles for publication in the said magazine. To Lawrence McCarthy (www.corribangling.com), a man with a tireless engine who would never consider failure as an option, thank you for your support and friendship. I would also like to thank the author Jon Beer; Tim Jacklin of the Wild Trout Trust; and Richard Davies for supplying some of the photographs which appear in this book. Also a special heartfelt thanks to all my Irish friends, particularly John Donlon, Tommy Carey, Enda Murtagh and close neighbours the Murphy family Kevin, Lana and the girls. I live in a beautiful part of the world, and to have such good friends and neighbours is a double blessing. Thanks also to Merlin Unwin and photographer Peter Gathercole for supplying the images of the flies for the Chapter Favourite Flies.

Finally a big thank you to my youngest son Duncan who has not only been a great help to me in areas concerning new technology, he has also been very supportive at a time when I needed it most.

FOREWORD

I haven't known Dennis very long, but in the time I've spent chatting to him over the phone I have realised what a huge amount of respect and liking I have for the man. He has intrigued and inspired me like no other – not only with the articles he has submitted for publication in *Trout and Salmon*, but with his thirst for knowledge, his willingness to share his experiences and his genuine interest in my own, and others', successes and failures.

I first met Dennis in person in the summer of 2009. He and his great fishing pal, Larry McCarthy, had invited me over to fish Lough Corrib. Inspired by the enormous wild trout they'd caught during caenis hatches on the lough, I couldn't possibly refuse the invitation. The memories from that trip will stay with me forever. It was not that I caught many fish – in fact I found the fishing tough – it was because I was taken to places and put in front of trout that I could only dream about. We fished reed-fringed bays among coots taking their first dip of the day, the oily ripple and soft dawn light broken only by the shoulders of huge brown trout supping on clusters of spent caenis. The number of fish I covered was too great to quantify, but a good many of them would, had they succumbed to my flies, have deserved a place behind glass, above my mantlepiece.

In those three days I saw only one other boat on the lough. Why? Because when others hang their rods up after the Mayfly hatch – resigned to the 'summer doldrums' – Dennis is in his element, hunting monster wild trout on his chosen method – the dry-fly.

Dennis's success is not down to luck – his approach is strategic, accurately timed and painstakingly executed. This, he would say, is the key to success. This spring alone he has caught ten wild lough trout over 4 lb, five over 5 lb, one over 6 lb and a fish over 8 lb – proof, if it were needed, that he is no ordinary angler. Fish like these are not caught by mistake – instead they are followed, observed and, when the time is right, ambushed.

Similarly, when Dennis puts his rod down to pen his thoughts, he will not do so without good reason. If you have read his articles in *Trout and Salmon* and his previous book *Trout from a Boat* (published in 2007) you will know that his words are born of vast experience in all forms of fishing. His theories on conservation and catch-and-release are backed with sound reasoning. Dennis is not backward in speaking his mind and he does so here, but this eclectic blend of opinions, thoughts, reminiscences and experiences will, I have no doubt, strike a chord with every passionate trout angler.

Dennis is a gentle, thinking angler, irrepressibly inquisitive and constantly curious. But put a rod in his hand and you will rarely have seen a man fish with such child-like enthusiasm and excitement. Truly admirable.

Andrew Flitcroft
Editor, *Trout and Salmon*

INTRODUCTION

Etch your name on an exposed piece of rock, and the inscription will last a lifetime.

Walk through a field of dew-laden grass, and the path of your traverse is recorded as the mantle of silver wash over the verdure of green is broken by every footstep. As time moves on the droplets of moisture trapped on the grasses evaporate. The silver mantle no longer exists, it fades as the water droplets become a gas and disperse, and as it fades all trace of your footsteps will be lost. In our journey through life some of our experiences will fade just like the footsteps in the dew-laden grass, and become lost to memory forever. And yet there are moments which do not fade, they are recorded in the natural computer we call a brain and remain as strong and as clear as the inscription on the exposed piece of rock. They will be important occasions: unique experiences: happy events: special moments which we hold onto and never wish to lose. These moments in time remain with us for our lifetime, and if we wish to recall them they are reflected back through the mirror of our mind.

This is a book about fishing, of my recollections and thoughts of a time spent by lake and stream.

1 Early Days – We All Have to Begin Somewhere

There has to have been a beginning, that defining moment when I first picked up a rod and cast a line, but I do not remember it. My earliest childhood recollections would be of fishing with my father on family picnics by the river. Fishing always seemed to be a part of my life – I just grew into it. Born into a family where my father and uncles shared an interest in country pursuits, it was no surprise that I would share those same interests. Having such an influence around one isn't a guarantee that we will take up the sport, but if we are interested it helps. For me the dye was cast; I have always wanted to fish.

There are many literary references by anglers who recall the capture of their first fish. This event is beyond my memory. However, I do remember the first fish to make a lasting impression on me. Roach and perch are the favourite first-time fish of many anglers, but it wasn't one of these species which I remember most vividly. The fish which made such an impact that I can remember the moment as clearly as yesterday, was a fish which pulled and felt heavy. For the first time as a small boy I had hooked a fish which pulled like the very devil, almost tearing the rod from my grasp. The weight and strength of the creature on the end of my line was simply unimaginable for a small boy used to catching tiddlers. It was so exciting. I couldn't just lift and swing the fish in I had to haul him from the bottom, and as hard as I lifted the fish seemed to pull back with greater strength. This tug of war was finally concluded, when my father put the net under an eel of about 2½ lbs.

I remember the detail of the event so vividly – baiting the hook with a lobworm and casting no more than a few feet over the marginal rush beds. I remember the red topped porcupine quill float coming to rest close to the reeds, and then after casting slumping backwards resting my back against an old willow. And then the waiting. Waiting was always the hardest part as young hands were impatient to move the bait and cast in again. Like all children I wanted to be doing rather than waiting, to relieve the tedium. Inevitably patience was the

River of my youth – the Evenlode Ascott-under-Wychwood

requirement to bring success, and I craved success, but I also craved to be doing something, anything would do. This wasn't to be, and my instruction was to leave the bait where it was, and so I waited. Then came my reward. The red tip of the porcupine float dithered and bobbed before sliding away, and on tightening I felt that heavy weight on the end of my line. To a boy fisher this was bliss.

As a boy I grew up in the Cotswold village of Ascott-under-Wychwood, and the River Evenlode which flows close to the village became my childhood piscatorial learning ground. The river was like a magnet to me, and I spent many

12

happy hours on the rain-fed waters of the Evenlode learning my craft. The Paddington to Worcester Great Western railway line runs through the Evenlode valley. The railway line was always a central feature to my fishing, as a lot of my favourite haunts along the river were in close proximity to the main line. I have fond memories full of nostalgia of that railway line, fishing the river to the sound of passing steam trains thundering along the track. In the evenings as dusk fell, the warm glow from the firebox of a passing engine would illuminate the surrounding embankment. One could follow the passage of the engine way off into the distance, not only through the noise made by the engine but also from the sight of the moving fireball charging along the line.

To fish the river below the village I had to pass over the main line at a level crossing which was operated from an adjacent signal box. The signal box was always manned, and whenever I returned from that part of the river I had to cross the line. One of the attendant signalmen would come to the entrance of the signal box to enquire if I had had any luck. As they were local village people and keen to show an interest, they would always congratulate me if I were to return with a good trout or a pike. Being kindly folk and knowing that I had crossed over the line to go fishing, they would look out for me on my return. Whenever I was late returning in the evening, which was usually the case in mid-summer, they would warn me if my father had been out looking for me and suggest I waste no time on my return journey. In fact at one time in my early teens, the late nights became so regular, they viewed my run for home as a matter of routine. During the summer months the signalmen used to look out for me, and saw my run for home as a sort of game. I don't know if they took bets on whether my father would find me first, but they were always sympathetic towards my position, that of a young boy mad keen on fishing, and out later than his parents allowed, wishing to avoid a good telling off if he could. Sometimes they would suggest that I take an alternative route home, so that I could avoid being caught. If the fish were feeding, then this would always cause me problems, as I was prepared to run the risk of my father's wrath and stay out much later than I should. Then the cat and mouse game was guaranteed to ensue. At least it provided amusement for the signalmen.

During spells of warm, settled weather, the fish would always feed better in the lower light levels and cooler temperature of the evening. As they came on to feed I would be lured into staying on well beyond my curfew time. It was difficult to leave, and very often I would stay on until I could no longer see the tip of my float in the hope that the monsters would become more confident in the growing darkness. Anticipation would build as the dusk crept in, and I would often take my best fish of the day as the light failed. As the gathering dusk grew deeper, and the darkness rolled in, blanketing the surrounding countryside in dark shadow, friendly features that were earlier so familiar took on a different guise. In the fading light my mind began to play tricks, firing a youthful imagination. Sinister shapes would loom out of the shadows, but it wasn't only the paranormal, ghosts and ghouls that the brain had to contend with, the fading light could also deceive the eye. It had the hypnotic effect of producing imaginary bites, as the float disappeared and then reappeared from the murk of gloomy light. But not all the bites were tricks of the mind. Sometimes the illusion would manifest itself as something real, and a big roach would roll over at the end of my line to reward my endeavours. A sweetener for the subsequent oral battering I would receive, if I were to be discovered before making the sanctuary of home and my bed. Whenever my father caught up with me, I knew that I would have to endure a good lecture about being out so late. As a parent he was concerned about my welfare, and although annoyed deep down he was relieved that he had found me. After the lecture, he would soften and at some time on our return journey he would enquire about the fishing. He had to – the self-same interest was within him also.

Those early years taught me a great deal about fish location, how they will move at different times of the year and how best to approach a swim to present a bait to the fish without them detecting my presence. This was my apprenticeship, learning about water craft, and once this knowledge had been attained it could be applied to any river or lake system. That small river not only provided me with a good grounding of how to locate and catch fish. As it was small I could easily see in if the light was good. There were swims where you could see the fish, and in time as I grew older this allowed me to be more selective. Without knowing it I had developed an approach where I purposely set out to catch the bigger fish, and being able to look in I had a good knowledge of where fish of a certain species were holding, so I could be more selective if I wished, and target a specific species. Also as a lot of the fishing was visual, I did a lot of stalking.

By doing this I could observe the reaction of fish to different baits, and determine which bait certain species of fish preferred. Although my methods and range of baits were basic, I was going through a learning curve, and although I did not know it at the time this knowledge would serve me well for when I later moved on to bigger and different waters. But while I fished the River Evenlode through boyhood and into my teens, my thoughts were not of the future, for the time being the river held enough interest to keep me occupied.

In those days I fished the summer through to mid-March for coarse fish, and from April to July for brown trout. The brown trout even then, was one of my favourite species to pursue – a highly desirable and elusive fish, requiring a mobile approach that differed from the more sedentary tactics employed for some of the coarse fish. Brown trout loved the fast runs and riffles. We fished for them to the sound of broken water running over stones, a sound accentuated in the quietness of late dusk on May or June evenings. The fluid noise which running water makes is such an evocative sound, and never was it more lovely than on those windless and quiet late spring evenings, when the birds had fallen silent, and we were just left with the music of the river.

Fishing the Evenlode for wild browns was a spring and early summer pursuit. Worms, minnow or a small spinner were the methods, and I became quite adept at fishing any one of them. Clear water was essential for the minnow. On a warm May or June evening it was a deadly bait, which the fish would find hard to refuse if presented properly. If the water held a little colour then the worm was hard to beat, and a rising or falling river was always a good time for the bait angler. Mill pools and the fast runs below old stone bridges were my favourite haunts. I would fish these areas until the light had all but gone. Many was the evening when as dusk was falling, I would feel that tap, tap on the line, only to discover that my trout was in fact a bat. This was a regular occurrence as the light fell, especially below the old stone bridges. Why they bumped into the line is open to conjecture. There is a school of thought that suggests they attack the line thinking that it is some type of insect, whilst there are some who would argue that they just randomly bump into the line while flitting around in the dark. I can't help feeling that once a bat hits a line it will come back and repeat the action. It is as if they have detected the line but cannot pinpoint it accurately enough to take it with their mouth, and therefore whilst flitting around the target they brush the line with their wings. This is just an observation but if you ever fish under lights you will notice that once a bat bumps into the line, it usually circles and comes back again. This would suggest to me that it isn't random flying, but I'm open to either argument.

We took some good trout to over 4lbs on bait, however one big trout in particular conjures up vivid memories. It was a big fish, but it wasn't just the size of the trout, as big as he was, which made him so memorable, it was the fact that I hooked and lost him no fewer than five times. He was a lucky fish, which because of his luck and his ability to escape I named Houdini.

He lived in pool directly above an old disused mill. His lie was in a small depression at the head of the pool in a confined area behind a worn buttress. Behind the stone buttress the bottom had been gouged out to a depth of about three feet and this was his favourite position. Here that old fish had lived unmolested for a number of years. There was a long run of shallows above his lie and the rest of the pool would have been around two feet deep. I never knew of his existence and neither did anyone else in the village. If they had, they would have fished for him and I would have heard about it. His whereabouts had remained unknown, until one day I quite by chance dropped a bait onto the shallows above the scour. The bed of the river was very stony above the lie, and it was difficult to keep the bait moving. However by gently easing the bait, it lifted and drifted down through the lie. When my line dropped into the scour, it checked, producing that tell-tale movement of a taking fish. As I struck the water exploded, and then something big and heavy raced down the run to the bottom of the pool about forty yards away. Just short of the sill which acted as an overspill he turned, and then raced back up towards his lie at a tremendous speed. As he reached his lie he leapt, throwing the hook at the same time. I could see the fish clearly as he leapt. He was big, far bigger that any trout I had seen or caught up until that time. Losing him left me feeling bitterly disap-pointed, but I knew where he lived. Given time and a good rest I was confident that we would renew our acquaintance again.

That fish, as I chanced my arm many times, and stayed out much later than I should in the hope of getting him as the light failed, got me into trouble more times than I care to remember. I was destined to experience a unique relation-ship with this fish, and I hooked him twice more from the scour below the stone buttress before he moved his lie. On the last occasion he raced to the bottom of the pool as he had done previously, only this time he didn't stop. As he hit the sill, the great fish jumped throwing the hook. As the hook lost its grip in that bony jaw, he crashed back into the water and dropped back over the shallow apron into the large mill pool below.

I thought that would be the last I would see of him, and yet early in the following season fishing the white water below the sill of the old mill weir, we met again and the outcome was just the same. He never returned to his new lie and for some time he eluded me. Never one to give in easily, I continued to try different pools in the vain hope of making contact again. My fish just vanished, I could not locate him no matter how hard I tried. This time it looked as if the game was up.

The River Evenlode suffers from a fast run off, and colours badly after heavy rain. You have to catch the river as it rises, or as it fines down. At the top of the flood the water is the colour of cocoa, and is basically a waste of time. Catch it on a rising or falling level, and you are in with a great chance of fish. Hope of finding my trout had all but gone, then fishing on a rising river following overnight rain I hooked him for the final time in a run below the old mill pool. As my bait trundled below an overhanging willow, it checked and then checked again, instinctively I tightened and felt the weight of a heavy fish. When I hooked the fish I did not know it was Houdini. He remained deep, boring away with strong powerful runs. At no time did the fish surface until the end. I knew it was a heavy fish, but my suspicions were that it was a pike. They often take a worm in coloured water, and on the type of tackle I was using would put up a very strong fight. The longer the battle continued, the greater my suspicion became. After a prolonged fight, my fish surfaced and rolled on his side. When I saw the fish surface I was totally choked – it was the big trout.

There was no mistaking this fish, and after so many lost encounters it looked as if I was eventually to win my prize. The old battler was on his side beaten, and all that was required now would be a steady draw over the waiting landing net. Bad luck, it seemed, haunted me with this fish. Fate sometimes isn't so kind. This time there was still one last cruel trick to play, and fate took the side of the fish. My friend who was with me at the time of all things tangled the net. The more he tried to unravel the tangled mesh, the worse it seemed to get. Frustrated he threw the net down, and announced that he would land the fish by hand. On seeing the panic on my friend's face, I was uncertain about this manoeuvre, but there was no alternative. Exasperated and fraught with anxiety, I conceded. Uneasily I drew the fish within reach of my friend, who then grabbed the trout by the tail and then the head. Just for a moment it looked as if the plan was going to work, but one final twist from the exhausted fish and the great trout slipped from my friend's grasp. As the fish fell, the line parted. For a brief moment, the fish lay on its side in the margin unattached. Overwhelmed with shock I hesitated, then the full horror of the situation struck me, and I leapt forward to grab the trout. There was a certain inevitability about the outcome. Thrusting my hands forward, I just managed to touch the tail of the great fish with the tips of my fingers as he slowly righted himself, and slowly, oh so slowly, slipped away into the murk. That was the last I ever saw of him.

Perhaps it was fitting that he should escape. At the time I didn't think so, and such was my anger over the loss, it nearly cost the friendship of one of my best school friends. Had I landed the fish I would most certainly have killed him, and if I had landed him the first time I would never have experienced all the other encounters with him. With the passing of time I still have a strong recollection of that fish. Would the memory be as strong I wonder if the outcome had been different after the first encounter.

Even at that young impressionable age, that fish taught me that brown trout are greedy voracious predators which are very vulnerable in the confines of a river. The same logic applies to lake systems, once located even in a big lough they are just as susceptible to being caught. Even big brown trout (the worldly wise and crafty ones) which have previously been hooked and lost, are not infallible. Although difficult to deceive at times, sooner or later their instinctive greedy behaviour will get the better of them. I believe that it is possible to drive them away from certain areas by continually disturbing them; this is what happened with Houdini. But even though he moved I still managed to catch up with him, and induce him to take a bait. What we do as anglers can cause fish to react in a certain way. If they are exposed to a negative experience enough times, they will learn to avoid it. This isn't a thought process, but a reaction which occurs without logical reasoning. For example the fish in my aquarium will rise to the surface and commence a feeding response, every time I switch off the pump, irrespective of whether there is food on the surface or not. The stimulus (turning the pump off) is a strong one, with the fish associating turning off the pump with being fed. Pavlov's dogs responded in a similar manner. The same reinforcement also applies to a bad experience. If we disturb fish in a certain area enough times, especially if they are hooked and lost, they will react by avoiding that area. Again this is learnt behaviour from repeated exposure to an unpleasant experience. It doesn't matter how big the water is, this is a simple logic which applies to all fish. Our wild systems are very fragile environments. Never underestimate what we do as anglers to change the reactions of fish within these systems, even if they are large waters.

Although none of my family fly fished, or any of my friends for that matter, I became interested in fly fishing. In fact I knew of no one who had ever cast a fly before, and yet taking such a keen interest in brown trout it felt only right that I should try a method that was so strongly linked to the fish. It was just a question of time before I would cast an artificial fly. In 1963 I began in a modest way to learn the art of fly fishing. With basic tackle, an old 9½ ft greenheart fly rod, and a Milwards level line I started to practise casting a line. It would be another year before I actually caught a trout on a fly. For the time being however I felt it essential to be able to cast a line. Those early practice sessions on the lawn and in the field behind our house, were painful to say the least. The line didn't match the rod, but worse still the rod was heavy. My young hands were not used to the weight of such a rod, and the flexing required to work the line. I knew the principle of casting a line, but without tuition or someone to advise me, it took longer than I had anticipated to learn to cast a reasonable line. Being determined to learn, I persevered. Blisters would form on the palm of my hand, swell up and burst. This was a frustrating handicap, as it was necessary to rest my flailing attempts until the blisters had healed. However, the timing required to cast a line eventually came, but it came at a cost and I had the calluses on my hand to prove it. My reward for such endeavour was that I could cast a straight line, and I could also cast to the area I was aiming for. Not a great distance granted, but it was certainly good enough for me to catch a fish.

By the time I had mastered the basic principle of casting a fly-line, it was well into August. August was too late in the season for the trout of the Evenlode, but there were dace and chub to be caught. My school summer holiday was coming to an end, and I spent the last days of that holiday in 1963 fishing for chub and dace with the fly. The dace were lightening fast when they took the fly, and great fun to pursue because you knew you were always going to have plenty of offers. Timing the strike was the difficult part as they were quick, unlike the chub which were far more leisurely when they rose. I used to fish for the chub with size 10 dry Alders or palmer dressings. The Alder was my favourite fly. Sunny autumn days were ideal, with late afternoon and evening the best times. Chub are shoal fish, the bigger ones tending to be more solitary. So once located there was always the chance of taking several fish if you did not spook them. They were a good substitute, and provided a means of learning the basics of fly fishing, and yet deep inside I yearned to catch a brown trout on the fly. This was going to have to wait for another season.

At the beginning of the following season in April 1964, I located a nice trout holding in a shallow run above a large stone. The run was just below a bridge, and the bridge gave a good vantage point. Standing above the fish I could observe his movement as he held position in the flow. Occasionally he would drift to one side or another to intercept some water-borne object, sub-surface food carried by the current. The weather was cold and dry and I never saw him rise. Leaning over the parapet of the bridge a north-easterly wind blew upstream into my face. It was too cold for fly, and the Evenlode wasn't the best river for fly hatches. I was confident that I could have taken him on bait, but just to catch him was no longer reward enough, I had to catch him on the fly. He wasn't rising, nymph fishing was then unknown to me, and even if I had known of the nymph I don't believe I would have fished it. Dry fly was what I knew, and that is how I wanted to catch my first trout on the fly. If he wasn't rising I would have to wait. There was a risk attached to this, someone else may find him. If they did then he would certainly see the bait. I was prepared to take this risk, as the need to catch a trout on the fly was now greater than the need to catch the fish.

I discreetly coveted that fish, hoping that no other angler would find him. He hardly ever moved his position; occasionally he would drop down behind the stone, but only for short periods. Towards the end of the month the weather turned warmer. The change in the weather coincided with a weekend, and I decided on a soft morning that I would go to the old bridge to check on the fish. As I stared down to the now familiar haunt, I noticed that for the first time that season there were some large olives on the water. Not many, but these were the first flies of note that I had seen. A newly emerged fly sat upon the water, and with wings proudly erect it sailed down over the lie. As the olive came into the fish's window, the trout lifted and took in the fly. There was nothing remarkable in this simple action, and yet it was so profound, it had a far-reaching effect on me. I backed off. This time I had carried a rod with me and feverishly made it up. My hands were shaking with excitement, as I threaded the line through the rings of the rod. With the line threaded I thought about which fly I should tie on. My choice was limited – it would have to be one of five patterns: an Alder, Red Tag, Tups, March Brown or a Greenwells as these were the only flies other than some nondescript palmers I had. My knowledge about natural flies was also limited. I knew that the flies which were hatching and the fly which the trout had taken were olives, but that is as far as my knowledge stretched. Knowing what I know now, out of that selection I would have tied on a Greenwells, but I didn't have the knowledge and chose a March Brown instead. It was the speckled grey partridge hackle at the shoulder that attracted me to this fly. With the rod made up, I made my way around the side of the bridge and down the bank below the fish. I dropped down to the water's edge, hardly daring to breathe as I made my approach, and once in position below where the trout was holding crouched down and studied my target.

Leaning forward, I could see my fish holding position above the large stone. The current came down smoothly until it reached the obstruction, and then it broke off with the greater flow coming down my side of the stone. It wasn't a long cast, which was just as well. My first attempt dropped well short, as I was suffering from nerves as well as poor technique. I let the fly drift down below the fish before lifting off to try and cover him again. The second attempt was still short of the correct line, and as I did not want to scare the fish, I let the fly drift down again as before, before lifting off. As the fly drifted down with the flow, the trout sailed out to meet it. He then backed down for several feet with his nose just short of the artificial, before tilting his head and sucking in the fly. Upon tightening, there was a swirl in the water and that lovely feeling of weight. He shook his head several times and then ran. Leaping to my feet, the rod throbbed, and the line cut through the water as I played my fish out. Although he wasn't a big trout, he was a very important fish. So not wishing to put too much pressure on the hook hold, I played him out with soft hands. Eventually he came in on his side, and lifting the waiting net with my prize inside I was overwhelmed with a wonderful feeling of elation. He may not have been the biggest, weighing about 1¼ lbs, but he was my first trout on a fly. The joy of the moment was indescribable – I was on my way.

The River Evenlode was never a good fly fishing river. One had to cover a lot of ground to fish the shallow trout holding runs, which were, depending on which reach I fished, a considerable distance apart. The water would colour easily and fly hatches were poor. Bait fishing was the more productive method, but the joy of fly fishing was greater, and the river did give me a few fish to the fly. I did have one red letter day when to my father's amazement the fly easily out-fished the bait. He thought I was wasting my time, when I chose to fish the fly in some shallow well-weeded water. Fishing the narrow runs between the weedbeds with a Red Tag, I caught six trout in the space of a couple of hours' fishing. This was an exceptional bag of trout for the Evenlode, and the bait fishers had had no luck in the low clear conditions. It was a day for the fly, and the only day that I took more than one fish using the method. The chub and dace fishing was far more consistent. One thing I do remember at the end of each day, was the toll that that heavy greenheart rod and a line which was too light to work the rod properly were having on my hands – the blisters were almost unbearable.

The water craft acquired in those formative early years, taught me much that I could apply to more unfamiliar waters. It helped my understanding of location, and determining a fish's movements under certain conditions on systems far bigger than my boyhood Thames tributary. Some may find it questionable, that the knowledge gained fishing a small river could prove so useful to an angler when fishing a large lake, but it does. If we are naturally observant, fishing smaller rivers makes one more aware of how fish behave under certain condi-tions, because in a lot of situations we can observe what is happening at close quarters. We can see the distances some fish will travel to find food, how the fish position themselves in a pool or how the fish move in relation to the season. An understanding of the factors which affect fish and their movement within a river system, can, if we are open-minded, be applied in much the same way to a larger water.

Those early days gave me a wonderful insight into the book of angling water

*Watercraft learnt on the meandering lilliput world of a Thames tributary would serve
me well later in my fishing life*

craft. I could not have had a better playing field than that little river, on which
to learn so much about the ways of fish. I spent endless happy hours roaming
its banks in search of fish, and will always remember with affection those youthful
days, and a time which gave me so much. How could I ever forget the autumn
evenings when, after a fine day as the sun went down, the temperature dropped
and an ephemeral cloud slowly rose above the river as it smoked, the mist
billowing out over the banks, to smother adjacent meadows with a rolling
blanket of moisture-laden air. As I ponder, memories come flooding back of the
bitter winter days fishing for chub or pike, when hands and feet ached with cold,
and the hoar frost in the arctic conditions hung from every surrounding tree
and hedgerow: a raw January day of snow laden easterly wind, a wind so cold

that it penetrated every layer of clothing I was wearing, and yet against all expectations the big roach, fish which filled your hand with the depth of their silvery sides came on to feed in the bottom meadow; the barn owls which would systematically quarter the fields adjacent to the railway embankment, or the view from the river, of the friendly roof tops of village houses showing above the railway embankment, the smoke from the chimneys spiralling lazily upwards. Civilisation was never far away, and as I fished I would hear the distinctive sound of the church clock, as it chimed on the hour. The sound of the bell brought a realism of time, to my timeless escape by the river.

2 A Rise out of the Blue

My fly rods lay idle in the corner of the study for long periods during the heawave summer of 1990. Day after day of unbroken sunshine scorched England's green and pleasant land, driving the trout to seek the comfort of cooler, deeper water. Surface fishing on the reservoirs became nothing more than a pipe dream. To achieve any success meant searching the depths with deep-water tactics, using fast-sinking lines. Fishing the sunk line during the early part of the season is fine, but the novelty wears a bit thin under a cloudless sky in midsummer with the temperature in the mid 80s. In hot weather it is difficult to raise one's enthusiasm for such a tactic, especially when it is at a time of the year when we should be enjoying the best of our surface sport.

The familiar weather pattern had set in. Day followed day of hot, bright sunny conditions. Totally unsuitable conditions for surface fishing for trout on a large still water, one would have thought. But then in fishing one just never knows what may turn up. There is always the chance of the unexpected, as fish are such contrary creatures. On just such a summer's afternoon, with the familiar weather pattern well and truly set, a phone call from a good friend, Vaughan Lewis, threw the text book to the four winds and proved what unpredictable creatures trout are. Even though the conditions appeared hopeless, Vaughan, the eternal optimist, called in to Oxfordshire's Farmoor Reservoir to assess the prospects. A sensible person would have questioned Vaughan's actions. The conditions were more suitable for tench or carp; it certainly wasn't the type of afternoon one would have chosen to visit a reservoir in search of top water sport with a fly rod. My friend knew this, but he still went and, much to his surprise, he found trout were moving on the surface. Having discovered the fish were moving, he then rang me. I suggested that perhaps he had been out in the sun too long and was hallucinating, but Vaughan insisted that there was a rise of fish and that they were moving well.

It was early evening when I drove into the car park. The heat was still unbearable and it felt uncomfortably warm. After applying the UV blocker to my face and arms I grabbed my waistcoat and the rod from the car. Then with serious doubts about my sanity, I set off scaling the reservoir embankment and went in search of my friend. A glassy calm stretched out before me, and what breeze there was wasn't sufficient to raise even the lightest of pin-ripple upon the surface. Wafts of warm air lifted all around me, so that it felt as if I was in a heated oven. When the air temperature hits the 80s I begin to wilt. The heat was such that it seemed to be sucking the oxygen from the air I was breathing, sapping me of my energy, and making me feel lethargic. I couldn't help feeling that an ice cold beer and a cool shady spot might be a better proposition. The conditions appeared to be impossible. Nothing I thought would move in this.

Fish of the English reservoirs – a beautiful 5lb rainbow

Then a good fish bulged about forty yards out, followed by another much closer in. I couldn't believe it! The air temperature suddenly seemed to be 10 degrees cooler. Vaughan was right after all.

Walking the reservoir peri- meter to where my friend was fishing, the feeding pattern of trout bulging was repeated numerous times. If I hadn't seen what was happening myself, I would have found it difficult to believe. Trout were rising in what would be considered the worst possible weather conditions: hot, unbroken sun and very little wind. Vaughan wore a smug grin as I dropped over the wall and enquired how he was faring. 'Two,' came the reply. 'Should have had a few more but lost a number of trout or missed the takes completely.' Just as he was speaking, his line shot forward, and as Vaughan lifted his rod the trout jumped twice and threw the hook. Vaughan shook his head: 'That has been happening quite a lot.' Just a bad run of luck, he'll come good in the end, I thought.

The sight of the flat oily surface of the reservoir broken by bulging trout was just the stimulus I needed, and even though it was hot I felt invigorated by the sight of the rising fish. For an angler who loves top water fishing, the sight before me was manna sent from heaven. But what were the fish taking? Vaughan had taken his fish on sedge patterns with some orange in the dressing. He had assumed because of the time of year and the conditions prevailing, that the trout were feeding on the sedge pupae. This didn't seem an unreasonable assumption, so I followed suit and tied a Ginger Sedge on the top dropper, Sedge Pupa on the middle dropper and a Hare's Ear on the point (all size 12). For my leader I chose 5lb pale green Maxima. I gave the line a good stretch and rubbed my leader down with a mixture of fuller's earth and detergent, to help the leader cut through the surface film of the water. Everything was performed as quickly as possible to hasten my first cast. In a mood of excited anticipation I cast out my line. Having made my first cast I watched the nylon leader slowly being drowned by the sinking flies. Inch by inch the sinking nylon, breaking through the surface film, crept towards the tip of my fly-line. Suddenly what was remaining of my leader shot forward. Instinctively raising the rod I was into my first trout of the evening. Rainbow trout are great fighters. They have much better fighting qualities than brown trout and this fish was no exception. After a lively fight I banked my first trout of the session, a fish around 2lbs.

This was to be the first of many trout which would be brought to hand for release that evening, and several more trout quickly followed that first fish. After three or four trout I became intrigued. Considering the conditions, the rise was incredible. With a cricket score of trout possible, my need to know what was the cause for this activity became the greater need. My enquiring mind required an answer so that I could at least apply some logic to what was happening. Could sedges be responsible for the intense activity we were experiencing, and, if so, where were the emerging flies? There was the occasional cinnamon sedge winging its way shorewards, but not in sufficient numbers to induce such a frenzy of activity. The absence of swallows and martins suggested that there were no flies of any species coming off or, indeed, that there was a significant hatch imminent. And it would have to have been a significant hatch, because whatever was the cause of such frenzied feeding behaviour must be present in huge numbers. Water snails or daphnia were now under suspicion. There was only one way to determine the answer, and after administering the last rites to a well-mended 2½-pounder I used the marrow spoon. The content of the trout's stomach would hopefully reveal the solution to my problem. On removing the marrow spoon from the fish's gut my enquiry for an answer was revealed. It was crammed with a crustacean, but it wasn't daphnia. In truth the day was too bright for daphnia to be so high up in the water, but this was the crustacean I expected to find as I couldn't think of any other possible explanation for the movement of fish other than fry, and there were no signs of fry to be seen. To my amazement the answer to this little conundrum was hog louse – *Asellus*, the trout was stuffed with them.

I have caught many fish both early and late in the season which have been feeding heavily on *Asellus*. These trout are usually taken when fishing deep nymph tactics, so they are caught whilst feeding close to or on the bed of the lake. Early season fish are especially prone to bottom feeding and prey heavily on *Asellus*. This is perfectly normal behaviour. The fish prey on an abundant food item, and feed on it where they expect to find the prey i.e. on the bottom of the lake or close to it. However, this was my first experience of trout rising to *Asellus* near the surface over deep water. What made this event even more unique was that even though the conditions were utterly unfavourable for surface-feeding, the trout responded to the stimulus of food in the upper layers.

They moved up from the comfort of deeper, cooler water and gorged themselves silly while the glut of food was on. The sheer numbers of water-lice in the upper layers that day must have been immense to induce the type of frenzied feeding we witnessed. We have no idea what could have caused the explosion in numbers. Perhaps they migrate in the same way as snails, using the surface 'drift' to move them from one area to another. Alternatively, incredible numbers of *Asellus* could have been flushed into the reservoir from the network of pipes that link the paired Farmoor reservoirs, one and two. These pipes are rarely used but, because of the extreme weather conditions, were brought into use that summer.

Certainly that evening on Farmoor was a unique experience for me, and it proved how opportunistic fish are when an abundant food becomes readily available. Not only was it unique, but it also exposed a misconception that some anglers seem to hold about trout feeding in the sun. The misconception is based on the fact that trout do not have eye-lids, and because they have no eye-lids they cannot protect their eyes from bright light. Therefore, as the trout cannot protect their eyes from bright light it is assumed that they do not like feeding near the surface in the sun. I do not hold with this theory, and never have done. Why the trout had been selectively singled out as having no eye-lids I do not know. As far as I'm aware, most species of fish and most certainly all of our freshwater fish have eyes which are essentially lid-less. Some of the bony fishes may have a translucent membrane, the conjunctiva, but this would be the limit of their eye protection. So if the theory about trout avoiding the surface in bright sunlight because they have no eye-lids is correct, then surely this would apply to all fish. The fact that they have no eye-lids isn't a characteristic unique to trout only, and it isn't the reason why they avoid the upper layers or the surface of the water in bright sunshine.

A lot of coarse fish will feed and bask in the sun – carp in particular love basking near the surface on warm sunny days. Shoals of tench, roach, bream or chub can be observed with their dorsal fins breaking the surface of the water in hot, flat, calm conditions. They love the sun on their backs. The only difference between coarse fish and trout is their physiology, with coarse fish more tolerant of warm water. So they revel in the sun, and the trout tend to hide away from it. But if food is present on the surface, trout will rise to feed in hot, bright weather. I have fished to some prolific rises of fish in bright sunshine, when the trout have been feeding on a fall of flying ants or drifting bloodworm for instance. In the hot summer of 1976 fishing under a blazing sun, we caught trout which had been feeding avidly on a fall of ladybirds, and that was a hot summer. Every summer I now catch brown which are feeding on *Caenis*, and the best conditions are bright sun with little or no wind. These are conditions which some anglers would say are impossible, and yet the fish only go down when the food supply runs out. The same conditions prevailed in 1990 when we fished Farmoor and the trout were moving to *Asellus*. Trout are opportunistic feeding animals; if the food is present they will feed on it even if it is sunny overhead.

It is for these reasons I believe the trout stay down in the water during bright weather. It has nothing to do with the fact that they have no eye-lids and dislike the sun. A third factor relates to their vulnerability. Like all prey species, trout feel more exposed in bright light. Therefore they will avoid the surface where they feel more exposed to danger. This is an instinctive reaction but I feel it is one that would be over-ridden by the need for food. Comfort and food are the two main factors, and if food is present at or near the surface in bright sunny conditions, trout will rise to it provided the surface water layer temperature isn't too warm.

Trout are poor risers in bright sunshine for several reasons, and none of these reasons have anything to do with the fallacy that they have no eye-lids. The two main factors which are responsible for a lack of surface activity in hot bright weather are: 1) They are cold water fish so they seek out deeper cooler water for comfort; and 2) In the British Isles and Ireland the food prey on which trout feed do not generally appear to like the heat or bright sunshine. Most species of aquatic flies do not hatch in hot sunny weather and even *Daphnia* will drop down in the water column if the conditions are bright.

It is for these reasons I believe the trout stay down in the water during bright weather. It has nothing to do with the fact that they have no eye-lids and dislike the sun. A third factor relates to their vulnerability. Like all prey species, trout feel more exposed in bright light. Therefore they will avoid the surface where they feel more exposed to danger. This is an instinctive reaction but I feel it is one that would be over-ridden by the need for food. Comfort and food are the two main factors, and if food is present at or near the surface in bright sunny conditions, trout will rise to it provided the surface water layer temperature isn't too warm.

Trout are certainly more difficult to tempt in bright light, but this doesn't mean that they have stopped feeding or that they are skulking away in some deep hole out of our reach. They become more difficult, because any flaw in our water craft or presentation to deceive them is easily exposed in the bright light. In good light the trout see things more clearly, in the same way as we do. Therefore any false movement by the angler is more likely to be seen by the fish, and if there is any flaw in the presentation, the fly will in most instances be ignored. There are always exceptions, but do not bank on too many dumb fish being around to take a poorly presented fly. Bright light and poor fishing technique do not marry well together. I do not like fishing under a bright sun beaming down from a cloudless sky, but if the trout are feeding they can be caught. If you want to catch trout in bright conditions, avoid scaring the fish and work on your presentation.

Trout are very fond of crustacea. Methods and flies for *Daphnia* – or shrimp feeding trout, have received a lot of media attention and, therefore, the majority of game fishermen now know how to tackle fish preoccupied with feeding on either of these organisms. *Asellus*, however, is less well known to many anglers. Perhaps anglers do not like the term water-louse and therefore choose to ignore it as a food organism. And yet when it is abundant trout prey heavily on this small crustacean. At certain times of the season trout show a preference for *Asellus* as a prey organism. Early season brownies can be crammed full of them and yet anglers are still unaware of the importance of the water-louse as a food item. I cannot help feeling that the term 'they are shrimping' i.e. feeding on water-shrimp, sounds more comfortable to a good many fishermen and so they use this term for any trout they may catch which has been bottom-feeding. Many of the trout which have been assumed to be shrimp feeding fish, will, I hazard to guess, have been feeding on *Asellus*. To say 'they are lousing' doesn't roll off the tongue quite as sweetly. Maybe we just do not like to admit that a trout will feed on a low life such as a louse. It's that or the anglers are unin-formed, and do not recognise the difference between a shrimp and a louse. Either way it is an important food organism of the fish, and they love it.

Fortunately we do not need to be concerned about special tactics when fishing for trout feeding on *Asellus*, as the fish do not appear to become so preoccupied that they ignore other food items. This means that we do not have to be overly concerned about specific patterns of artificial flies, or close imitation. Early season trout in particular are quite catholic in their taste and will prey on any type of food organism in their zone. What we find is that the most abundant food organisms are the ones that show up most in the stomach content of trout we catch i.e. the fish take those food organisms which are most freely available. If I'm going to target early season fish feeding on *Asellus*, I prefer to fish nymphs

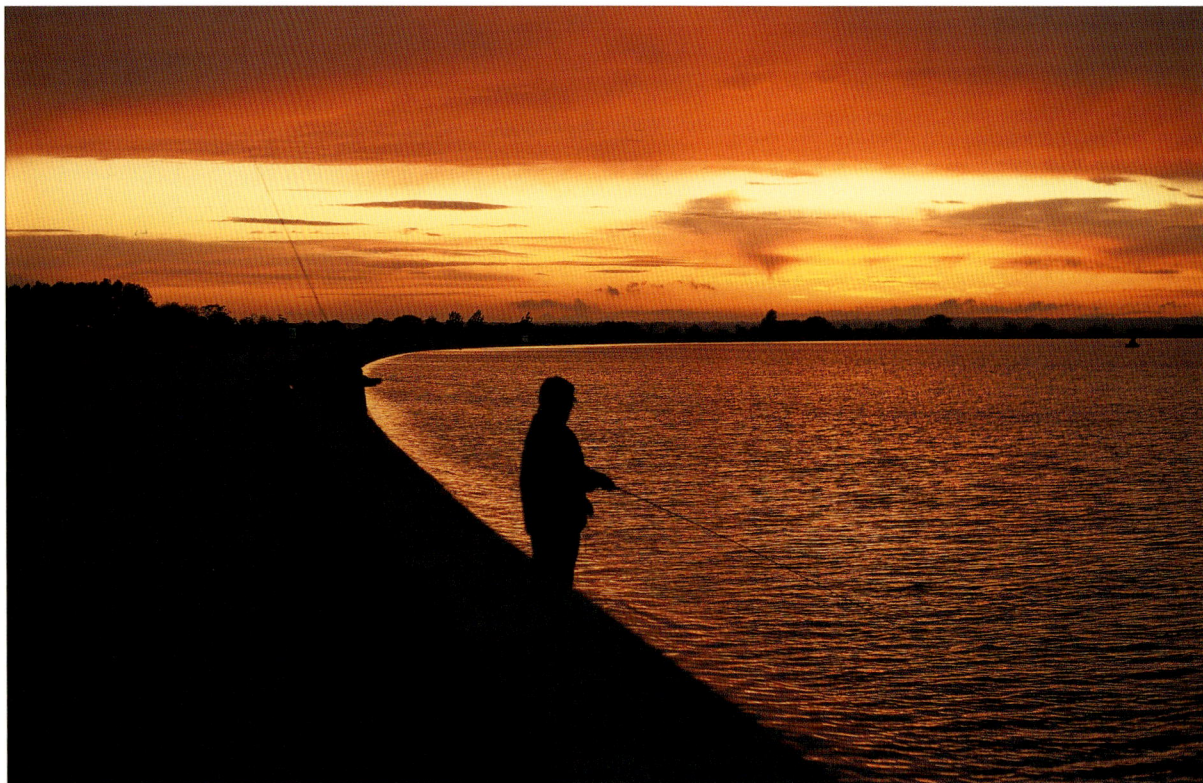

The sun going down after a hot day on Farmoor reservoir

or small imitative flies on a floating or intermediate line with a slow, steady figure of eight retrieve. A floating line, with a well-leaded point fly on a long leader to act as an anchor stabilising the presentation of the rest of the team, can be very effective. A dropper four feet from the anchor fly does the damage, and takes a lot of fish as it rises just off the bottom. Trout tend to stay deep early in the season. To catch these fish we have to go down for them, either with leaded flies or sinking lines. Most general nymph patterns will catch fish, but top of my list would be a scraggy Hare's Ear nymph with a little olive seal's fur in the dressing or a Ginger Sedge Pupa, both in size 12. Flies with some ginger or hare's fur with a little olive fur mixed in, or a light brown body fur work well as my day on Farmoor proved, when the Sedge Pupa or the Hare's Ear were real killers.

As water-lice are detritus feeders, living most of their life on or close to the bottom feeding on decaying matter, surface-feeding fish, such as trout, roaming the upper layers, rarely find them in their feeding zones. So what happened on Farmoor in 1990 was very unusual. I caught those trout fishing over water that was about fifteen feet deep, and yet none of the fish which I caught that evening were any deeper than four to five feet down. In fact many of the trout took close to the surface as the flies were sinking. As the trout were taking on the drop, I realised that the fish were high in the water. There was no need for a weighted pattern of fly, and I kept my flies high in the water by commencing my retrieve early, i.e. I did not let them sink too far down in the water column. Some of the takes were savage and they really zipped off with the line. These aggressive pulls from the fish could easily smash the leader if you were caught unprepared. If one watched the fly-line it was possible to see the take before you felt it. A gentle lift of the rod would then set the hook and avoid it being broken through an over-zealous strike.

If I were purposely fishing for wild trout feeding on *Asellus*, I would fish with a more conventional approach and put my flies into the zone where I would expect to find the trout feeding. I have taken wild browns from the loughs of Western Ireland and the lochs of north-west Scotland that have been full of water-lice. A March Brown or a Hare's Ear fished on a floating or inter-mediate line over rocky shallow water would bring the trout up off the bottom to take the fly with a bang. One pattern with a tail of bronze mallard and red game mixed, a rib of oval gold tinsel, a body mix of hare's fur and olive seal's fur with a red game hackle palmered over the body and a shoulder hackle of a few brown mallard fibres proved to be a real killer. Early season on Lough Corrib this fly proved its worth time and time again. There was a time when I fished this pattern on both droppers and a Hare's Ear nymph on the point, for trout which were feeding avidly on *Asellus*. Such was my confidence in it I could have fished it in all three positions.

Fish which are grubbing about among the stones will still rise to take a variety of flies that pass through their field of vision, indicative of a trout's willingness to take other food items when feeding on *Asellus*. It's that opportunist behaviour of the hunter to any form of prey organism which enters its zone. These fish are not obsessed with one type of food item. Indeed, I remember an occasion on an Irish lough when wild brownies freely took a size 12 Black

Pennell, fished on the point, and all the fish taken were crammed full of water-lice. I cannot think of a more unlikely fly to represent a water-louse than a Black Pennell and it is more than likely that they took it for a midge, confirming their non-preoccupied feeding. Fish feeding confidently take the fly well and will willingly accept a good presentation of a suggestive or imitative pattern, even when they are eating a particular food type. There is none of the frustration of fishing for selective, preoccupied feeders which demand a close imitation fished in a particular way.

A proliferation of *Asellus* on our visit to Farmoor provided us with confidently feeding fish, making the choice of fly pattern less important. A close copy wasn't critical for success and we enjoyed superb sport on a day when we would have been grateful for just one rise. This event has allowed me to highlight a few misconceptions held by anglers and perhaps the importance of a small detritus-feeding, bottom-dwelling crustacean in the trout's food chain.

3 Gay Gammarus

I have a friend, a very good friend whom I have now known for twenty-seven years. When I first met him, I was working for Thames Water as a technician in the scientific services laboratories in Witney, Oxfordshire. In 1982 we received a phone call from a young fisheries officer who was then working for the Thames Conservancy. They needed the services of some lab equipment, and he asked politely if he could come in and do some tests. As I was interested in fishing and the tests were on some small chub samples, I was given the task of looking after this young man. When he arrived at the laboratory, he introduced himself to me. His name was Vaughan Lewis, and he was polite and very mannerly. How a person changes, when you get to know them better! Vaughan came into the labs on a number of occasions to make follow-up tests, and we got to know one another more. He grew more confident, and as the confidence grew the politeness which I now have to constantly remind him of disappeared, but in the process we struck up a friendship, which has lasted over the intervening years until now at least – whether he will speak to me after this I do not know. We both liked fishing, and although Vaughan's taste in music would be different to mine, we did share a lot of interests which were in common with one another. It was only a matter of time before we would fish together.

When I first fished with Vaughan, we fished mainly for coarse fish. On those early forays he came with some excess baggage in the form of a terrier named Gem. She was a constant companion, and always into mischief. One of her favourite tricks was pilfering the lunch. If you wandered away from the rucksack, which used to happen quite often when we were after pike, there was no guarantee that the sandwiches would be intact on return. I'm convinced it was part of her training, as it always seemed to be my bag which she pilfered. One day fishing below Duxford weir, she ate all my sandwiches. Vaughan felt so guilty about his dog's misdemeanour, he shared his lunch with me. We had half rations, while the dog lay on her back with a rather rotund belly. Where she put it all I do not know; for a little dog Gem had some appetite. This dog was always getting into scrapes. A good example of her tenacity for mischief was a freezing January day on Blenheim Lake. We were fishing from a boat over a margin of ice, when a moorhen flushed from some nearby cover. This was too much for our little canine friend, and in a trice Gem was over the side. In her exuberance to chase the moorhen she slid forward on the ice, and went in. The margin of ice between the boat and her position was too wide for us to reach out and pull her in, and she couldn't get back to the boat. We spent a few anxious moments breaking the ice with the oars so that the dog could come back in. Eventually we freed enough ice to allow her to come close enough for Vaughan to reach out and grab one very cold dog by the scruff of the neck. Gem looked miserable as she sat shivering in the boat. Feeling sorry for his dog, Vaughan wrapped his coat around Gem to warm her up, and for once it wasn't me who suffered as a result of his dog's escapades As we fished on, Vaughan shivered while I felt comfortably smug and warm.

As we fished more together, Vaughan took a greater interest in still water trout fishing. He constantly reminds me of some poor advice which I gave to him when he first started. I didn't want him to feel conscious about his casting, so to help Vaughan relax and enjoy himself, I suggested that casting was a minor detail and nothing to be too concerned about. This was a mistake, and I realise it now because at first he was handicapped by the distance he could throw a line. I misguidedly thought that if we were fishing from a boat, he would have plenty of opportunities. He did have opportunities of taking some fish, but they were limited because of the distance he could cover effectively. Vaughan remedied this disadvantage in his own time, and with a lot of practice and a correctly balanced rod and line he put this right. If I were asked now by someone who hadn't fly fished before to take them still water flyfishing, I would without hesitation say to get some casting tuition first. Because, if you can't cast a reasonable line, you are severely handicapped when out on the water fishing, and on a fishing trip you do not want to be wasting valuable time learning to cast. Avoid the frustration, learn to cast before you fly fish; one follows the other and in that order.

We fly fished the reservoirs in England, and for wild fish in Wales, Scotland and Ireland. I enjoyed the wild fishing most, especially in some of the remoter areas which we visited. Even though the fishing was at times tough, we still took a lot of pleasure from being in such beautiful places. Wild stunning country and unusual natural sights were as much part of our trips to the wilder areas, as catching fish. We did catch our fair share of fish however, but if we were to measure our returns against a day spent on the English waters, most anglers would probably have been disappointed. Vaughan took some notable bags of fish, and it would be difficult to single out a particular day as being special. And yet if I had to choose a moment of a day which I recall more than any other, it would be the end of a fishing day spent on Lough Corrib. I wasn't fishing with him on this particular day. At the end of the session when we came in, Vaughan and Andy Thomas, another member of our party of anglers, were already back at the house. They came down to the boat to greet us, Vaughan beaming with a glass of whiskey in his hand. From his expression I knew he had had a good day, and it materialised that he had taken a wild brown of over 5lbs. He was genuinely delighted with that trout, the beaming expression on his face told me that. It was his first wild brown over that weight, a lovely looking fish, that he now has set up as a memento of the occasion.

There was a time when my friend just like his dog – and I would like to add that he peaked in Gem's era – showed an aptitude for falling in. I was amazed by his consistency for getting wet. I would swear that if someone wanted to find water at the driest place on earth at that time, Vaughan would have found it. In fact he was turning it into a bit of an art form. His best performance in front of a crowd was a double twist from a rock on the Ballycurrin shore on the Corrib. A small party had gathered on the Ballycurrin shore for lunch. It was mid-May, and there were mayflies hatching quite close to the shore. It was only a question of time before a fish would rise, and one duly came along. The sight of the trout rising was too much for my friend, and so he strode down to the water's edge, rod in hand. His attitude was such, that is was the epitome of someone about to do some piscatorial damage. However he wasn't content to just fish from the shore, he wanted the advantage of a large rock which was jutting out from the shore. Having gained his vantage point, he looked back and grinning from ear to ear he then proceeded to strip off line and began casting. As he made his forward delivery, his weight shifted and he lost his balance. His arms went up, there was shout of 'Oh no' and then he plunged headlong into the water. This was no simple ducking, it was a full immersion, but he was out in a trice and commendably he came out still holding his rod. Water fell from Vaughan's clothing as he tramped back up the shore towards us. None of could hold ourselves; we all applauded and cheered when he emerged from that mishap. After such a fine display and a superb entry, we named the rock after the diver Brian Phelps. Whenever Vaughan and I walk the dogs along that particular stretch of shoreline, we still pause by the rock and have a laugh about that day.

There was another fall which was equally spectacular, only this time there was no crowd present, just me. It was mid-December, and the weather had turned cold. An anti-cyclone was centred over Europe and the UK was feeling the effect. We were experiencing hard overnight frosts, and windless days with the temperatures only making a few degrees. Hoar frost was hanging from the

Hungerford bridge on the Kennet

boughs of trees, and the hawthorn hedges looked as if they had had a dusting of snow. A hazy mist hung over the Kennet valley. It was one of those days when any noise sounded muffled and distant. The river gurgled and meandered through the town of Hungerford which in the misty conditions Hungerford looked like a town from the Dickens' period. All the shops and houses were well decorated for Christmas. There was hardly a living soul about and surprisingly for a Saturday very little traffic.

We had come to the Kennet to fish for grayling, and although it was cold, we were confident of catching a few fish. The banks of the river were rock hard with frost, and the grass crunched under foot as we walked to the bottom of the beat we were going to fish. At the lower end of the beat we made up our rods. We were travelling light with just one small shoulder bag each. Our intentions were to work our way back upstream towards the bridge, and fish every likely looking swim on the way. I set up a nymph outfit. On the point I tied a well-weighted nymph. This would act as an anchor for the dropper, a small nymph which was tied about two feet above the point fly. The anchor fly on the point can be deadly if the grayling want a fly grubbing about on the bottom. So it isn't just a sacrificial nymph, it is an effective pattern in its own right. In the conditions which were prevailing, I couldn't help feeling that the point fly was the fly which was going to do the damage.

When we fished it there were good numbers of grayling in that part of the Kennet, although I don't know if there still are as I haven't fished it now for fifteen years or more. Grayling are shoal fish: locate one and more likely there will be a number of fish present in the area. Sometimes there can be prodigious numbers of grayling tightly packed into a small pocket of water. Our approach was to search them out in the hope of locating one of the bigger shoals. We worked our way upstream, covering all the likely places, but the fishing was uncharacteristically slow. The mist surrounded us with an opaque shroud. Visibility was possibly several hundred metres or more, but a haze hung over the river and it was cold, barely above freezing. We had covered part of the lower stretch when we came to an old wooden foot bridge. It was no more than two planks wide, but it had a hand rail to one side. The bridge was ancient, and the hand rail decidedly rickety. My friend has an affinity for water, and he loves being beside it, on it, or even over it and he particularly likes being in it. At the

Vaughan standing on the rebuilt bridge, winter 2010

sight of the bridge Vaughan suggested that perhaps we should move over to the opposite bank. This was a cover, for in truth he just wanted to walk across the bridge. I followed him, and as we came to the mid-way point he decided to look over the side on which the hand rail was fixed. There was a nice brown sat just below one of the centre bridge piles, and Vaughan pointed the fish out to me. He lent forward for a better view of the fish, whilst at the same time putting his hand on the rail. As he lent forward the hand rail gave way, the whole thing just seemed to split in his hand. Now Vaughan's entry into the Corrib was classic – it had a bit of style. There was no style attached to this entry into the Kennet – arms were spread, legs were left flailing, wooden debris collapsed all

40

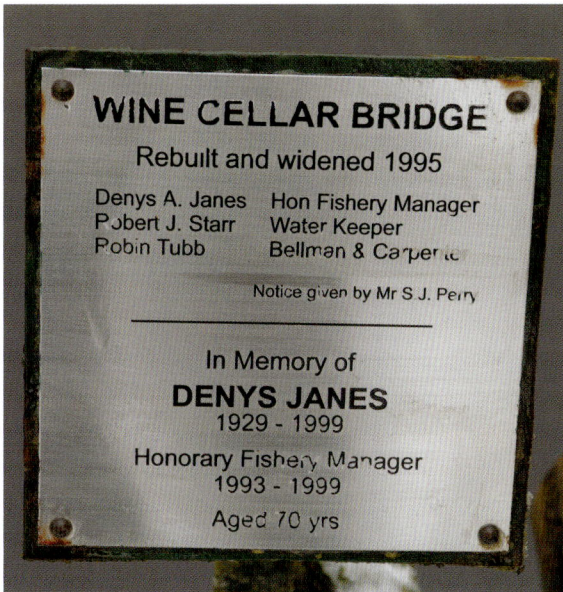

Plaque depicting when bridge was rebuilt and widened after Vaughan's incident

around him. There was a long drawn out shout of expletives, and he hit the water like a hippo jumping into the Zambezi. He lay there momentarily spread-eagled in the water, fully immersed on what was one of the coldest days of that winter. For a moment I was full of shock, but as he regained his feet and stood up, the shock lifted. He looked up at me shouting unmentionables; the water was up to his waist and it must have been freezing. As the shock of seeing him fall in lifted, I couldn't help feeling an uncontrollable fit of laughter welling up inside. I tried to control it, and show some sympathy. It was impossible however, and the mirth just had to come out, and I burst in to unending fits of laughter. Vaughan grabbed his hat and rod, and stomped out of the river. Unsympathetic about his plight, I just couldn't stop myself from laughing, the scene was just too comic.

That should have been the end of our day, as Vaughan's clothing was soaked, and the air temperature was barely above freezing, but he was determined to carry on. We walked back to the car. I followed a discreet distance behind, as I was almost choking to hold back intermittent fits of laughter which kept welling up inside. It was difficult to control, and my friend did not look too amused. Back at the car we rummaged round for some dry clothing. I had a spare sweater, Vaughan had some over-trousers and an old jacket which the dogs used to sleep on. He may have looked more like a farmer's scarecrow, but this didn't faze Vaughan: we were going to fish. In need of some sustenance we fortified ourselves with some food and something hot to drink, before moving on to the upper section above the bridge.

Upstream of the bridge there was a pool. It was on a bend and below a fast, shallow run. The pool was stacked out with grayling, and every time the point fly came through that shoal of fish the line would jag. Just a little hesitation and a forward dip of the fly-line, would result in a grayling shaking its head and putting its flank to the current. As soon as they put their flank to the current they dropped downstream, and it was easy to draw them away from the shoal. We took it in turns with my rod, and picked those fish off systematically one after another. I do not remember how many we caught, but for a while it was quite frenetic. They really had a liking for my shrimp pattern on the point.

Vaughan forgot about his earlier comedy show, and lost his angst to the fishing. Grayling are good fun, and even in the coldest of conditions, just like the chub, they will always oblige and provide sport. Once we had exhausted the fish in the pool, I gave Vaughan a copy of the shrimp pattern which was proving attractive to the grayling and we split up. We roamed the banks of the Kennet on that misty afternoon and took fish, both grayling and a few out of season brown trout from a number of different swims. The fishing wasn't difficult, and the sport could be brisk at times. If you could see the fish, so much the better, but even in the pools where you could not see them it was just a matter of searching them out with the nymph. Once you located them, it was amazing how many grayling could be packed into such a tight area, and how many of the fish could be plucked from the shoal before they split up or went off the take.

About an hour before darkness fell, the mist grew denser and in the failing light a few fish began to move to the surface. The temperature was dropping, it must have been close to freezing at that point and yet a few tiny midges came off and the fish responded to them. I broke down my nymph rig and set up with a really light leader and a size 18 black midge pattern. It was a simple fly, with a few tail whisks, a dark grey herl body ribbed with black silk, and several turns of black cock hackle. For the last hour I cast to rising fish until I lost them to light, and could no longer see my fly. In that hour I covered no more than a fifty yard stretch of water, and yet there was always a rise to cast to. It was just a matter of creeping stealthily into position, and presenting the fly so that it drifted down over the area where a fish had moved. As the fly floated down, a head would lift up and with the gentlest of sips the fly disappeared. A soft down-

A fish of the winter months – a graying being returned

stream lift of the rod was all that was required to set the hook. Once you felt the weight of the fish, you eased off to cushion the strike and avoid a break. It was then just a question of playing the fish out on the light line. As I brought them to hand, my fingers were numbed by both the coldness of the water and the air temperature which was even colder.

The conditions made it impossible to dry your hands after returning a fish, and by the time I had finished my fingers ached with the cold. Frost was spreading its mantle over the ground, the grass glistened with newly formed ice crystals, and as I returned to the car I was joined by my friend. He too had caught plenty

43

of fish, but he had caught his on the nymph. My hands were tingling, and I thought about his ducking earlier in the day. He couldn't have picked a colder day to have fallen in, and yet if he was cold he didn't mention it, but he did ask about the nymph. I told him that it was a fly on which I had caught plenty of grayling from the Test. After trying a number of different coloured shrimp patterns for several seasons, I discovered that the fish had a distinct liking for a pink-coloured pattern. Orange was good, amber, red, brown or black were less effective. Why they should show a preference for the pink shrimp I do not know, but they definitely found it more attractive than the other colours. It is simple to tie on a size 12 or 14 grub hook weighted with lead wire. The body is made up with dubbed pink fur, and a red game hackle is wound over the body. Then a shell back of polythene strip is tied in over the length of the body and the whole is ribbed with gold wire. Vaughan found the grayling's preference for a colour interesting, and he then asked if the fly had a name. I answered 'Yes, but in these times of political correctness I may have to change the name.' 'And what do you call it?' he questioned. 'A Gay Gammarus,' I replied.

4 Sea Fog

I enjoy walking in remote mountain and moorland areas, and if I happen to have a fly rod with me this adds to the experience. In the years between 1970 and 1990 I walked in to some fairly remote locations on my own. Walking alone in such areas doesn't come without its hazards. There is always the risk when walking in such areas that an accident could happen, or that for some reason we may become cut off, we just hope that it never happens to us.

It was mid-June, and Cathy and I were camping close to the Old Man of Storr at Staffin on the Isle of Skye. When Cathy and I first met, and during the early years of our marriage, camping out provided the means to visit some lovely areas within our shores. The two of us both had a love for wild places, and we wanted to visit the remoter areas of our country. As income was tight at that time, camping offered an opportunity to go to the places we wanted to see and experience for ourselves. We had been to Scotland before, but not so far north as we intended to go on this holiday. Like many of the roads travelling to the north at that time (early 1970s), the A9 was not the road that it is now and the journey took considerably longer.

We had spent a week in Scotland travelling up through the central highlands stopping off at various places en route. We then travelled on to Skye for three days. Cathy was now looking through a tourist guide scanning the pages hoping for some inspiration of where to go next on our sojourn north. She had a habit of finding little gems in literary guides. If there was a snippet of useful information tucked away within the pages of a reference book, Cathy would find it. I was thoughtfully viewing the surrounding environs. Stretching away below me was a moorland landscape punctuated by two lochs. The wind-scoured moor was dissected by a single track road, which ran alongside the two lochs in which the fish were rising, and I was tempted to throw a line, but I refrained. Even in this desolate area, the loch felt just a little too public so close to the road and I contented myself to just watch. A boat with two anglers aboard was out, but

Mark Powell lost in a land of mountain loch and moor

they did not seem to be having much luck. From our vantage point we could look over to mainland Scotland, to Torridon and the far north-west. A cap of cloud hung over the highest peaks, with the mountains below brooding, immune to feeling of any kind. I love mountain and moorland areas, I always have, and from my vantage point the mountains looked distant, and out of reach. It was a landscape of sea, mountain and sky, where the only malleable element was the sky. The colour of the sky could change the mood of both the mountains and the sea. Perpetually changing, a subtle change of reflected light and the scene and mood are transformed. Mood is about atmosphere and feeling, a state of mind in which we see something at a particular time. One can never hold onto it, for the mood changes with the light and with time. And try as we might, we cannot transfer this feeling or the mood of the scene to the harsh medium of camera film. A good artist may do it justice but the camera never will.

On our way up through Scotland we had camped in Glen Affric, an area of the UK which experiences night frost for most of the year. Following this we travelled west, and then north up through Glencoe, the site of the infamous massacre, where the MacDonald clan were massacred at the behest of the Scottish Parliament in 1692. Glencoe is a stunningly beautiful place but it is a site which leaves one with a melancholic feeling. An aura of sadness pervades the place even now. After this interlude we moved on to Fort William and Ben Nevis. Unlike Glencoe, one felt enraptured by the scene of the snow-capped peak of Ben Nevis. Every corrie, relief and detail could quite easily be picked out as the sun was reflected back off Britain's highest mountain which stands at 4,406ft. We spent the night in Fort William and then drove on westwards through Glenfinnan at the head of Loch Shiel and then onto the startlingly beautiful shell sand strands of Arisaig. We camped for two nights on the machair at Arisaig, enjoying the most wonderful sunsets and waking in the mornings to find countless rabbits all around us. On the first morning I woke early with a start, as something had bumped into the tent. I looked out and immediately saw the culprits. Rabbits in a playful mood had in their revelry inadvertently bumped into the tent. It was like a scene from *Watership Down*. Late in the evenings the rabbits would still play, but as the light faded there was less frivolity and they would get down to the serious business of eating. We sat outside the tent, talking, or watching the light slowly fade away and inhaled the fresh salty air until night finally crept in. As the light faded we watched the gentle surf break on the beach, and as the waves receded they left an oily skin, a swirl of mercurial water on the sand which would slowly fade away before the next wave arrived to repeat the process. The slow rhythm of the waves and the illumination over the western sky was idyllic. Time now had no meaning, for under nature's illumination we could talk and read for as long as we wished, and in June in the far north of Scotland, the twilights seem as if they could go on forever.

While we were camping at Arisaig we drove over to look at Loch Morar, which was only a short distance away and on an impulse we decided to fish it. I persuaded Cathy to come out with me. We went into the village and bought some provisions for a picnic, and then went in search of a boat for hire. We hired the boat from a farm house which was close to the north shore of the loch. Loch Morar is the deepest loch in Scotland, and reputedly, like Loch Ness, has a monster. Myth and legend it would seem know no boundaries in Celtic folklore.

The boat was a rather old, decrepit-looking vessel, with two sets of oars, left over from the bygone days when two men at the oars were required to take an angler out fishing. We were not intending to go out for that long, and without an outboard engine I had no inclination of going too far. In fact I had no intention of doing any serious fishing. Basically I just wanted to go out for the experience of being there and perhaps to cast a fly upon its waters. As it turned out I never did fish Loch Morar. I thought as I was rowing out, Cathy could trail a fly behind the boat until we got to an area where I could also fish, drifting with the wind. There was a peninsula which jutted out for some distance just up from where the boat was moored, and behind the peninsula was a bay that I thought may offer a chance of a fish on the drift. As we came around the peninsula Cathy hooked a fish, and she became quite excited but unfortunately the trout came adrift. On seeing how excited she became when the fish took, I thought I would continue rowing until she hooked another one. We did not have to wait long, until another trout hit one of the flies, but this fish, like the previous one, came adrift. I could not believe how our luck was running; I so wanted her to catch a fish so I continued rowing. In all Cathy lost four trout of differing sizes, before a really nice brownie of about 1½lbs took. I was surprised by the size of the fish that was leaping at the end of the line, and looking back it was probably a sea trout, but I did not know this at the time. The gods must have taken pity on us because Cathy landed this one. It was the biggest trout of the five she had hooked and it had stayed on. I was so relieved when the fish was boated and Cathy wore an expression of pure delight. The trout was superbly conditioned, and upon seeing the condition of the fish I killed it. It was as fat as butter and appeared to be a young fish. We ate the trout for supper that evening. Its flesh, red from rich feeding, made a delicious meal, eaten under an azure sky and to the sound of the surf breaking on the beach.

After catching the trout I decided to take a break from the rowing, and we adjourned for a break. I pulled the boat up on to a small beach of fine gravel. Behind the beach was a gentle slope of grass, as short and fine as any well-manicured lawn. We ate our picnic on the fringe between the lawn and the heather, and after we had feasted I slumped back into the heather. The sun was warm on my face, and I was beginning to feel sleepy, the exertion of all the rowing catching up with me. I did not wake for at least an hour or more, and when I woke I saw Cathy standing looking out across the loch. She looked a little pensive, and on seeing me awake came over and said 'Dennis, there is a big wave out on the loch'. I looked out across the water. There was indeed a good swell running, and the tops of the waves were creaming as they broke. There wasn't a cloud in the sky, and yet the wind had freshened. It was one of the coastal winds which pick up as the temperature rises. What was a nice gentle wave when we came out had now become a rolling mass of broken water. Looking at the waves, I thought it best that we head back in. Up until now Cathy had enjoyed being out in the boat, but I knew she wasn't going to enjoy what was coming.

The worst section was no more than about 200 yards. It was the section just off the peninsula. Once we were around the point it would be easy to make the mooring. As we hit the point where the wave was greatest, Cathy dropped down off the thwart board and sat on the bottom boards, from where she did not move. The bow of the boat lifted and then pounded into the wall of the wave, and then dropped into the trough behind. The sequence repeated many times. We were making slow progress around the point, but at least we were making progress. I just kept rowing, digging the oars in and pulling as hard as I could. And then… crack! My right arm felt as if the resistance of wave and water had disappeared completely. The oar had broken. For a moment I was sickened by what had happened. We were about two-thirds of the way around the point, and almost through the worst of the water. But without an oar we were done. I would have to drop back and pull the boat up and leave it. And then I saw the extra set of oars on the boards and in an instant grabbed one of the spare oars with such a feeling of relief. We made the mooring, pulled the boat up and silently packed the gear away. As we got into the car, Cathy sighed and said 'Never again.' She never did come boat-fishing again after that day, or fishing at all for that matter. We were never in any danger, but for someone who is not used to going out in boats, it must have been quite frightening. She would come out in a boat to look for wild flowers on an island or to go and see something of interest, but fishing? That was a no-no. As I reflect I can't help thinking how different things might have been had the wind not freshened, as she had enjoyed being out on the water up until that point.

After Arisaig we moved on to Skye, crossed the Sound of Sleat by ferry from Mallaig, and spent three days touring the island. The Cuillin mountains were wonderful, but Cathy found the sharp-edged rocks of the Cuillins too demanding to walk. We then travelled the coast road and camped under the Old Man of Storr. This is where we found ourselves on our third evening. Skye was an interesting island with a varied topography, but the island did not appeal to us sufficiently to make us want to stay. It was a stop-over on our journey to the north of Scotland; as yet we hadn't discovered our final destination where we thought we would spend the remainder of our holiday. We thought we would move on the next day, but where would we go? I couldn't help feeling the mountains in the far north looked far more interesting. Then Cathy came up with her little gem. 'I have it,' she said, and then began reciting from the guide book; 'A wilderness of mountain and moor, wonderful beaches and beautiful scenery, if you like mountain climbing, walking and fishing this place has it all, enjoy.' 'You can't believe all that you read in a guide book, where is it?' I asked. 'Assynt,' said Cathy. 'I've never heard of it,' I replied. 'And neither have I but that doesn't mean we shouldn't go,' said Cathy.

We caught the ferry to Kyle of Lochalsh the next morning, and travelled north through Torridon, the distant mountainous region that I had seen from our campsite under the Old Man of Storr on Skye. Torridon was beautiful, and though we were tempted to stay for a few days the information in the guide book lured us on. We passed the once hallowed sea trout waters of Loch Maree, a fishery now denuded of its famous runs of fish. It is hard to believe that there was a time when one waited for a rod to drop out, to gain access to this renowned fishery. The sea trout runs have now failed for more than twenty years, and with them the anglers have disappeared too. We pressed on, our journey taking us down the north side of Loch Broom and then on to Ullapool where we spent the night. Little did I know then that I would pass through Ullapool many times in the future on my sojourns to the north of Scotland, or spend the night close to the port as a stop-over for the ferry to the Western Isles. Such was my familiarity with the journey I knew that by road in a car I could make Ullapool in just over ten hours from my home south of Oxford – a

Walking out into the wilds of Assynt

distance of 640 miles. After spending the night in Ullapool, we continued on our journey north to our final destination.

It had taken a day of driving since leaving Skye to get to Ullapool. We were in no hurry; the journey had taken us through some stunning country and we stopped off many times en route. What we had seen had enthralled us, the holiday having been a wonderful journey through some of the most beautiful areas in Scotland. With four days remaining we intended to make the most of our time. It was decided that we would camp somewhere close to the sea, and then do as little driving as possible until our return journey home. After stocking up with enough provisions to last several days, we headed out on the last leg of our journey to an unknown site by the sea, close to an area called Assynt. We hadn't seen it, we had no idea if we would like it, but it was as far north as the two of us intended to go on this holiday.

On a fine morning in mid-June, we drove out of Ullapool and through Strath Kanaird heading towards Inchnadamph and Assynt. Some places just draw you in when you first see them; there is a magnetism which captivates your attention. Driving through Strath Kanaird a lunar landscape of mountain and moorland opened up before us. We travelled that road entranced, caught in a web of seduction. Our minds lost to images of wild grandeur. There was no escape. To the west Ben More Coigach, Stac Polly, ahead were Cul Beag and Cul Mor, further on Canisp and Suilven, Ben More Assynt and finally the five high conical points of the Quinag ridge stood out against the sky line. The tarmac passed below the wheels of the car and the colours and the scene constantly changed, but as one vista rolled into the next we were seduced by all that followed. We were addicted to Assynt from the moment we first saw those unique mountains. None of the hills are of a great height. There is only one Munro in the area. However, the lack of height did not detract from the wild beauty of a stunning mountain landscape. Ancient volcanic forces formed this landscape, and it is said that some of the mountains in the highlands of Scotland were once higher than the Himalayas are today. Tectonic plates have moved, sea levels have risen, and time and the weather have all had their effect. Natural forces formed and sculpted what we see today, a legacy to the wonderful architectonic brilliance of nature. Man didn't form this Eden, it is the product of wild uncontrollable natural forces. And amidst the mountains and moorland were countless lochs and lochans. Indeed a man could walk and fish to his heart's content.

We found our campsite at the end of a single track road which led to the sea. It was an idyllic spot. After pitching the tent we spent the rest of the day walking, and just taking in the vista around us. Suilven is the most impressive mountain: at 2,309 feet it isn't the highest in the area, an honour that lies with Ben More Assynt, but Suilven dominates some impressive-looking neighbouring mountains. When viewed from the south or north you can see the full length of this distinctive-looking hill, with the two high points at the western and eastern ends. It slowly dips between the two high points and looks as if a giant has sat on it, but when Suilven is viewed from the east or in particular the west one can see how narrow the mountain is. It looks like a huge column rising from the ground. The name Suilven means the 'Pillar'; it is a rather apt name for such a distinctive-looking hill.

Vaughan Lewis enjoys piscatorial delight with the hallmark of Assynt as a back drop –
Suilven

The following day we were out walking again. We flushed greenshanks from the shoreline of lochans and saw both red throated and black throated divers. The divers have a distinctive call which, like that of the wading birds, really carries. On a windless evening when all is silent, and in the far north-west of Scotland the silence is absolute, the haunting call of these birds resonates off the sides of the hills. It is the most soulful sound. As well as the evocative wailing call, they also cackle, especially when in flight. Because of this cackle, and the way they sometimes tumble around each other in an ungainly flight, they are referred to as loons. On the higher ground we saw countless red deer, and above a crag working the thermals a pair of golden eagles, their primaries spread to catch the rising air to give the birds the lift they were seeking. We watched the two eagles soaring, getting more and more lift from the thermal currents, and then wheeling away into the distance whereupon they were lost from view. In upland areas like Assynt you are never going to see an endless stream of different species of birds, or animals or flora, as this is such a harsh climate in which to live. The flora and fauna which do live in such areas, have adapted to some pretty testing conditions which limits the diversity of species. What you will see if you are observant will be interesting, and even if they are not classified as rare you will certainly see a number of species that you will not see in your native area. One species which did surprise me this far north was a reptile, and our only venomous snake, the adder. We saw one sunning itself beside a jumble of rocks, and I have since seen a few of these reptiles on subsequent trips. Once, in fact, we saw two coiled up beside each other on a footpath beside the River Kirkaig, and as they were reluctant to move, we walked around them. The adder sunning itself beside the jumble of rocks wasn't a one-off sighting.

That evening after we had eaten, Cathy decided she would go to look for flora along the seashore. In my younger years I had no strong interest in plants, but Cathy sowed this seed and my interest in flowering plants grew. I was much keener about observing birds, a subject about which Cathy knew very little, so this allowed us to exchange our knowledge. I would like to think that we both benefited from the information exchanged about each other's interest. On this evening looking for flowers along the sea shore wasn't pulling quite as hard as my desire to go fishing. Cathy's search for flora gave me an opportunity which I couldn't pass up to steal a few hours and go fishing. I looked at the map. There were endless lochs from which to choose. I did not want to go too far from the campsite, so I chose a loch which entailed a short drive and then about a thirty minute walk. There were plenty of lochs adjacent to the road, but I wanted to fish a water which was more secluded.

I parked the car by the edge of a single track road, and then took up my rucksack and fly rod. As I turned to walk out, I met an old man walking the road with his dog. He was well into his seventies, walking with the aid of a stick and a Border collie for a companion. As we passed we exchanged pleasantries, and on seeing the rod bag the old man asked me if I was going out fishing. I told him yes, and then showed him the loch on the map I intended to fish. There was no special reason for going to this particular loch I told him, and I wasn't expecting to catch fish of any size. He was smiling with a knowing expression, his eyes clear and his complexion the colour of someone who had spent a lot of time in the sun and exposed to the wind. With a quizzical look, he said I had mentioned small fish, and that I wasn't expecting to catch a trout of any size. There was a glint in his eyes, the look of someone who has some information you may wish to know. 'Do you want to catch a trout of any size?' he asked me. This took me by surprise, but I replied 'Yes.' He then went on to tell me that he had fished the area all his life, but was now unable to go because of his legs. Most of the lochs held small trout he advised, but if I was interested in catching a decent fish he suggested two particular lochs which would be worth a look. I couldn't believe my luck, he was so kind. When we parted he wished me luck, and then asked 'Have you got a compass?' I smiled and then nodded. 'Good,' said the old man.

The nearest loch entailed a short drive to a peat track where I would park the car, and then a walk out. His advice was to walk the track until I came to a loch, and to then follow the north shore to the head of the loch, at which point I would strike out in a north-easterly direction for about fifteen minutes. He said the loch I was looking for was small, shaped a bit like a boomerang and full of reeds. It could be dour he advised, but if there were trout rising I was in with a good chance. These words were milling around inside my head as I walked out. I followed the peat track until it swung off to the south as it struck the western edge of the loch. Here, I left the peat track and walked the northern shore of the loch. When I came to the head of the loch I took a quick look at the map to be sure of my bearings, and then struck off in a north-easterly direction. The terrain had become one of small heather clad hills and rock, and within the folds in the hills were lochs. I was not walking on high ground and it wasn't strenuous, but sometimes it was easier to skirt around the side of the hill rather than going up and over it. It would be easy to become lost in this undulating country. I followed the instructions and found the loch, just as I had been instructed, nestling in a fold in the hills. Shaped more like a stretched kidney than a boomerang, it was no more than four or five acres and full of common rush. There was an open area of about half an acre of water which was clear of reeds. Otherwise it was mostly overgrown with reeds with small gaps in between. It was around eight in the evening as I walked down to the shore. The

loch looked more suited to tench than trout, and I wasn't feeling overly confident while setting up my rod by the water's edge. I was just wondering how on
earth one would approach such an overgrown piece of water when I heard the
suck of a trout taking in a fly from the surface film. Moments later the fish rose
again. It was rising to small dark sedge flies which were emerging by creeping
up the stems of the reeds. My timing could not have been better and as I looked
over a wider area, I could see that there were a significant number of these flies
coming off. As I scanned the water, I could not only hear but also see several
other trout moving to the small sedges as they were emerging. This was incredible.
What a stroke of luck I thought.

I was fishing with a 9¼ ft split cane rod, and my approach to still water dry-
fly fishing was much cruder then than it is now. There were no specialised dry-
fly patterns, but I knew what I had to do. I needed to fish a static fly. It would
have been impossible to have fished nymphs or wet flies in amongst the reeds.
In fact any method which would have required line to be retrieved would have
been flawed. The situation demanded a method where the fly could be cast in
and left static. There would be no fish-scaring disturbance caused by fly or line
wake, or by the fly catching on the reeds. To avoid becoming hung up in the
reeds, I would restrict my casts, and therefore only cast to a target. And if I
needed to lift off to make another cast, I would either lift the fly off above reeds
if it was sitting in a channel, or very slowly retrieve the fly until it was in a
position where I could lift off without catching a reed stem. I selected a well-
hackled Wickham size 12 from my box, and tied it to the point of my leader.
To make the fly float, I applied a smear of muscilin grease to the hackle of the
fly, and then went in search of a target.

The trout were moving through the reeds in a leisurely manner, sucking in
flies. They were in no hurry. They just slowly swam through the reeds picking
off the flies as they rose to the surface to hatch. The reeds were not closely
clumped together, but they did hamper the presentation. I had to choose an
ambush point where I could present the fly without becoming hung up on the
curved stems of the reeds. There were lots of open channels within the reed
beds, and it was along these channels that I aimed to put my fly. As soon as one
of the trout looked as if it was going to move towards an open channel, I would
try to cut it off with my fly. That was the plan.

I crept along the shoreline keeping as low as I could, as a fish moved towards one of the channels. Once in position and from a crouched stance I began casting. It wasn't a long cast, and the slow easy action of the cane rod made accuracy easier to achieve. The fly dropped into the channel just as my fish came along, gulping in flies one after another. It seemed perfectly reasonable to assume that the trout would take my artificial as it was greedily feeding amongst the reeds, and the fish did with a gulp. As I tightened there was a boil on the surface and the trout zipped off. With all the reeds around, I expected these obstacles to give me a problem when playing the fish, but with a single fly there was no dropper to become caught on the reed stems. The line just brushed through the reeds, and the only anxious moments came when the fish made an acute change of direction. Then the line would briefly catch on the reed stem creating an angle between me and the fish, but as soon as the line lifted off the reeds, direct contact with the fish was resumed. There were no long runs, and I couldn't help feeling that the reeds in some way hampered the trout, but I was relieved when I brought the fish to hand. It was not huge trout, but it was much bigger than I expected from this part of Scotland.

After many holidays in this part of Scotland I now know that the majority of lochs hold small undernourished trout. There are a few lochs which hold fish of the size I caught that evening, and there are fewer lochs still, that hold hefty trout. These lochs can take some finding, unless you are lucky enough (as I was) to meet someone who is willing to share this information. The information is hard won; it requires a lot of walking, and a lot of fishing on different lochs to establish which ones hold the better trout. It is understandable therefore that those anglers who have won this knowledge do not want to disclose the where-abouts of such gems. Four trout rose to my flies that evening, and I caught all four. They weighed between 1¾lbs and 2½lbs. They were quite dark in coloura-tion and in excellent condition: short, stumpy, well-fed fish with large fins. I do not remember seeing any huge fish moving, as the trout I had seen rising all appeared to be of a similar size.

I have since caught a bag of wild browns of that size on numerous occasions in Ireland, and sadly I do not remember them all. And yet that evening was special. I was young and it was the best bag of wild brown trout I had caught at that point in my life. I killed two of the fish and returned the others. I looked

Small and feisty – a typical Assynt brown

at the brace of wild trout lying in the heather, my split cane rod beside them, and felt that glow that only success can bring. The rise lasted for just over an hour, for the duration of the hatch of fly, and as soon as the sedges stopped hatching the trout went down. I didn't move another fish after that. It was a beautiful evening, the sun shone and cuckoos called all around me. There must have been three or four different cuckoos calling from the patches of scrub birch, willow and rowans which grew no taller than a man in the sheltered hollows. I was surrounded by outcrops of rock, and hills of mixed grasses and heather. It was a windswept landscape of open moor, and in the distance, looking eastwards, the five conical peaks of Quinag punctured the skyline. I was alone in the wild, and felt as close to nature as one could be.

The following day the weather held, and encouraged by my success I was keen to see if I could repeat my feat of the previous evening. Again it had been another gorgeous day, warm and sunny with a little cloud and light winds. Now the cloud had dispersed to leave an azure sky that stretched away to the horizon. Perfect conditions for sedges, I thought. As the rise occurred fairly early, and the fish didn't seem to be interested once the fly hatch had finished, I told Cathy that I wouldn't be late back. We had been out walking for most of the day, and Cathy said she would relax and read a book in the sun. We could then have a late supper when I returned. I bundled the rucksack and my fly rod into the car, and drove off to the peat track where I had parked the car the previous evening. When I arrived there was another car parked beside the track, where a woman was sitting beside the car reading a newspaper, and two young children were playing beside her. We exchanged greetings and complimented the weather. She also remarked that she was just beginning to be bothered by midges and may have to move into the car. The dreaded midges I thought, and made a wish for the wind to hold. I said goodbye, hoping that she would not be pestered by the infamous pests of the Scottish peatlands, and walked out along the track.

It was easy walking, and I made good time. In fifteen minutes I was at the head of the loch and struck off north-eastwards as I had done the night before. I had almost reached my new-found gem when I had the strangest encounter. Breasting the hill before dropping down in to folds where my loch was hidden, I saw a man shouting. He was waving his arms and hailing me to stop. I froze, not knowing what to think. Occasionally you may meet someone on a mountain, but this was one of the remotest areas in Scotland. One never meets anyone out on the moorland. Although a good distance off, the man made his way towards me, and I stood my ground. As he approached I could see that he was sweating profusely, and wore the expression of someone who was concerned. He was in his mid-thirties wearing a light blue t-shirt, jeans and trainers. When he reached me he apologised for shouting, but it turned out that he was lost. He said he had left his wife and children by a track, and just taken a short walk from the track, but had walked further than he originally intended and become totally lost. He had been out for several hours, and didn't know which way to go. I sympathised with his predicament, but thought it demonstrated the need for a map and compass in terrain such as this, where it can be so easy to become lost. He was old enough to know better, and had no map, compass or all-weather clothing. To help him I showed him the whereabouts of his position on the map, and then pointed out some high ground to the south-west and where the loch was in relation to that high ground. I also explained to him that as it was seven thirty in the evening, the sun was well in the west. My instructions were that he was to walk towards the high ground and that if he should happen to drop into a hollow and lose sight of the high ground he should check that he was still heading towards the high point when he came out of the hollow. The loch was no more than fifteen minutes walk away, and upon reaching the loch he should then head west along the loch shore towards the sun, as that would take him to the peat track and his family. I offered to go with him, but he said that he felt assured and that he would now be okay. We parted, and he thanked me for the directions. I watched him walk off until I lost him from sight to the contours of the hills. He was heading in the right direction.

I then turned to the north-east to complete the walk towards my goal. On turning I looked out towards the north-west and the open sea beyond. Far away in the distance I could see a grey band. It looked as if it was low cloud on the distant horizon, but it appeared closer than it should be. I couldn't work it out. I sensed that it didn't look right but I could not make out what it was, and I gave it no further thought. My loch was drawing me on. Sitting on the west shore with the sun behind me, the sun was now below the contour of the hill that sheltered my loch, but to the east all was still illuminated by its light. I patiently sat in the shadow of the hill with the rod at my side, and waited for the flies to hatch, and the fish to rise. The midges were becoming a nuisance as the wind was dropping, and I hoped that it wouldn't fall off completely. It had been about half an hour since my strange encounter, and I thought that the lost soul should be with his family by now. My thoughts were broken when the first flies began to hatch, and it wasn't long before the first trout put in an appearance. The fish was moving about sixty yards from where I was sitting, and I moved down confident of making his acquaintance.

As I neared the point where the fish had risen, another bizarre thing happened on this evening of strange events. The light levels suddenly became subdued, all the open ground to the east which had been brightly illuminated by direct sun light, was now rapidly falling into gloom. It was as if an eclipse of the sun had just occurred. With the falling light levels the temperature also plummeted, the flies stopped hatching and my trout went down. This happened within minutes. It was as though someone had flicked a switch. When the trout stopped rising I didn't know what to think, but I thought they would come back on. It would just be a matter of time and sitting it out. A chill breeze from the north-west caught the side of my face, and after the warmth of the day it made me shiver. I turned to the direction from which the chill wind had emanated. A few wisps of mist were floating down the side of the hill, and it was eerily silent. All sound seemed to be muffled. There was not a bird calling. Still I thought about the fishing, but I was also overcome by an uneasiness which I couldn't explain. The gloom deepened and my unease grew, and as the wisps of mist floated in around me I felt a sudden impulse to leave. Why I felt the impulse to leave I do not know, but for once I did the right thing. Fishing has an awfully strong pull. I would go in any weather and go to extreme lengths to fish, but this time my will to stay capitulated. Without knowing why, I hurriedly packed away my rod, slung my pack to my shoulder and began making the hill towards the south-west. Striding out I felt compelled to look back over my shoulder; it was as if I sensed there was something behind me, and what I saw is hard to describe. Over the top of the hill, a silent malevolent wall of fog was approaching. Rolling down the side of the hill like an avalanche of snow, it blanketed everything in its path from view. It was coming quite fast, and I was never going to out-walk it. Within minutes this hideous wall of mist would be upon me. Everything that one could see to the south would be obscured from view. My landmarks would be cut off to my sight by an impenetrable wall of fog. I had to act quickly, and the old man's words came back to me 'Have you got a compass?' I took out the compass and took a bearing off the high point below which the loch I needed to reach was positioned. I knew that if I could make it to the loch the rest would be easy. I had my bearing and started walking, never wanting to look back as this would only serve as a reminder that in but a small amount of time the fog would come in around me, and the world as I saw it would disappear.

It came like a hammer blow, but there was no sudden feeling of pain, a wall of mist just crept in around me and the distant horizon disappeared. Cocooned in a shroud of mist, nothing existed beyond my dome of vision. The loch was only fifteen minutes' walk away, about a mile of open moorland, but when visibility is no more than fifteen to twenty yards, that mile can seem awfully distant. My life was never in danger, as I was well equipped with protective clothing and food and drink. Even with this comforting thought, I didn't want to spend the night out on the moor if I could help it. However if I couldn't find a familiar landmark by nightfall, I would have to think about sitting it out. The fifteen minutes came and went, and I hadn't made the loch. Doubt began to creep into my mind nagging away at any positive mode of thought I could muster. It was taking longer than it should. This was due to my pace slowing, as I was regularly checking the compass to make sure of the direction I was walking. The regular checks and the lack of visibility were slowing me down, and I didn't allow for it. It may have taken no more than a few minutes extra, but negative thoughts were taking over. Perhaps my line needed correcting? Perhaps I should walk more towards the west? The minutes raced by but they seeming like an eternity. I paused to check my compass again by an outcrop of rock. There were some nettles growing beside the rock, their leaves now bearing a silver mantel of tiny droplets of moisture. They looked almost like Christmas decorations. It was silent, all sound seemed to be muffled, suppressed by the blanket of fog. As I stood to check my direction, a sound came to me, through the silence a faint but recognizable sound, the sound water makes when it is lapping onto rocks. Although barely distinguishable the sound drew me forward, with hope rising my pace quickened. Frantically staring toward the direction from which the sound was emanating, I walked on for another forty to fifty yards straining to see further into the mist. Trying to stretch the boundaries of my eyesight more than the light would allow, the loch just suddenly appeared a short distance ahead of me and I was overwhelmed with relief. There wasn't anything mystical about it. It was where it had been for the last 10,000 years or more, but when doubt creeps in all logic is sometimes lost. Such things do not move in the dark, they just move in the mind. The only logical thought process in the last few minutes had been the reading on my compass and it had brought me to where I was now standing beside the loch. Walking across the moor in that fog was the worst twenty to twenty-five minutes I have ever spent out on a moor alone, but once back into a comfort zone all my anxiety was eclipsed by the sight of the loch shore. I walked westwards down the shoreline, comfortable in my mind that in a short time I would make it to the car, and then back to Cathy.

When I arrived back at the camp Cathy was busy cooking. She looked up, smiled, and said that she knew I would not be late back when the fog came in.

This made me think about my predicament and my initial indecision about whether to sit it out or not. I couldn't help feeling that Cathy knew me better than I knew myself. I told her my story, and she was pleased that I had made my decision to move when I did. We couldn't help wondering however about the chap who was lost out on the moor. I did notice that his car parked beside the peat track had gone when I returned to my vehicle, so I assumed that all was okay. It had been an enigmatic experience, a series of mystical events that merged into an evening I could never forget. The supper was also to be a surprise. Camping in remote areas doesn't lend itself to a culinary experience. In the far north-west of Scotland one doesn't raise one's expectations, but Cathy surprised me with her ingenuity. While I had been out fishing, doing a rather poor impersonation of an alpha-male hunter-gatherer she had also been out hunting and gathering. She had managed to conjure up a fresh crab, followed by fresh haddock courtesy of some local lads who had been out sea-fishing, along with fresh home-grown vegetables from a local crofter who liked gardening. In the time I had been out on the moor, Cathy had been busy acquiring and preparing this booty. It wasn't late, probably no later than nine. The sun was still relatively high in the western sky, but because of the fog it was no longer visible to us. It had already set to our world. And as we sat in the grey light on the machair just up from the beach, wearing heavy sweaters to ward off the chill, we listened to the sound of a sea we couldn't see, ate our food, and drank wine as the mist swirled all around us. It was magical.

5 Wild Fish in Wild Places

The year is 1992. An account of this July holiday, a week's fishing on the Uig and Hamanavay fishery in West Lewis on the Hebrides, was published the same year in *Trout and Salmon*.

I lay on the beach at the head of the loch. It was the final day of our Hebridean holiday and conditions were far from ideal, with warm, unbroken sunshine and little or no wind – hopeless for the loch-fisher. The weather was most certainly against us, and with little prospect of a fish, we had decided to adjourn for an early lunch. Rods were lying idle, propped against the prow of the boat, with the dropper flies hanging limp and lifeless. The lightest of breezes passed through and caught the hackles of the bob fly, momentarily giving life to the fly as it lifted on its nylon tether. We had enjoyed a marvellous week's fishing, and a sea trout on this our last day, would be a fine way to conclude our holiday. The subtle hint of wind lifted our hopes, but our spirits faded and sagged as the bob fly fell and the breeze dropped away, leaving the surface of the loch unbroken. Lunch was taken at a leisurely pace. Two golden eagles soared overhead, working the thermals to gain height. Wings outstretched and the fingers of their primaries spread, they effortlessly circled above us. The birds commanded our full attention until eventually they were lost from sight in the gathering haze. As the eagles drifted out of sight, and with our lunch completed, our thoughts returned to the quest in hand.

We ventured out for the inevitable last fling. There was a ferry to catch, and we had no more than a few hours of fishing time before we would have to leave. The clock was against us otherwise we could have waited for the evening, always a good time for sea trout. If we wanted a fish, there was no choice, we would have to take one in the conditions which were prevailing. With the sun beaming down I put up an intermediate line, and to the point of my leader I tied a trusty Silver Invicta, and on the droppers a Wickham and a Butcher. We crept down the northern shore of Roanasgail, our movement aided by the oars of our boatman, Richard Davies. The loch was as flat as a mirror, and I thought our quest an impossible cause, and yet against all the odds I caught two good sea trout of around 2lbs. They both took the Silver Invicta. I had my fish; they brought a conclusion to a memorable week of fishing in the Hebrides.

There are few truly wild places left in the UK where we can enjoy fishing for the migratory species as generations of anglers have before us, and where little has changed, only the fish and the anglers now pursuing those fish. However, it is still possible to find wild unspoilt fisheries which haven't suffered at the hand of man, and some of the remote fishings of the Hebrides provide such an opportunity. Here we find no well-manicured banks leading down to the fishing, or even a hut in which to take lunch, or shelter. Our only shelter will come from the lee of a peat bank or rock set amongst heather and bog myrtle on a remote moorland.

For those who have enjoyed the writings of anglers such as Hamish Stuart, Charles McClaren, Kingsmill Moore and, in particular, Sidney Spencer, wild places still exist where we can ply our trade from traditional clinker-built boats, and use techniques similar to those of which they wrote so evocatively. We now live in a different age, and they wrote of fishing, especially wild fishing which was relevant to their time, but the loch-style methods for migratory fish have not radically changed. We are now better equipped, rods are far superior to those of our ancestors, as are the fly-lines, and yet short lining, pulling a team of three flies through the surface of the water is still as effective as when these great men fished.

The salmon and sea trout fisheries in the Hebrides are made up of small spate rivers connecting a loch or series of lochs. These little rivers are highly dependent on rain to get the fish in. Very few systems enjoy a spring run of salmon (North Uist and Grimersta being the exception), so the salmon are mainly small summer fish backed up by prolific runs of sea trout which begin to move along the coast during June and will run with the first floods that usually occur around mid-July. Once the fish decide to run, they normally race through the small rivers, seeking sanctuary in the lochs, and there they remain until they ascend the head-waters and make for the redds. A journey full of risk, and one which following the act of propagation will end for many of them, especially the salmon, on the spawning grounds. The rivers offer a chance of sport during a flood, but the fishing is limited, and once the water runs off, which it will very quickly, what fish remain will seek out the few deeper pools. So, following any appreciable fall of rain, the chances are that a loch on a migratory system will hold a stock of fish. And this is the beauty of loch-fishing for salmon and sea trout, as once the stock is in we can be confident of drifting over some fish throughout the rest of the season. Unlike a river we will not need more rain to bring fish in: we just need some wind and cloud cover to provide good conditions for sport.

We do not require specialised tackle; the rods and lines used for traditional trout fishing are perfectly suitable for the migratory species, as we are not expecting really large fish, although there are the occasional exceptions. Always travel light. This not only restricts the clutter in the boat but also keeps the weight down if a long walk to the loch is necessary. The one item I consider essential for anyone going afloat, particularly in remote areas, is a life-jacket. Uig and Hamanavay is a remote fishing, and Hebridean weather can be ferocious.

In 1992 the reports from many areas along the west coast were good, most systems enjoying improved runs of salmon and sea trout. Although May and June were dry, the rains of July and August made up for the earlier lack of precipitation. This coincided with our annual sojourn in the Hebrides, so hopes were high as we made our way north-west to the isles. We were not to be disappointed, when, on arrival, our host greeted us with the news that the main run was in and that all the lochs contained a good stock of fish. He was confi-dent, given favourable conditions, that we would enjoy good sport. Our rota for the week was planned so that we would fish the final day on Loch Roanasgail. Roanasgail was the closest loch to the track leading into Hamanavay. With good access, little time would be wasted travelling to and from the loch. This would allow a reasonable day's fishing before having to leave to catch the ferry. Heart-ened by the good news we set off for Dibadale, our first beat of the week.

Loch Dibadale is flanked by a 600ft bluff along its western shoreline which provides a dramatic backdrop and a highly effective wind-break. A long finger of water probing into the mountains, it is a most impressive loch to fish. Surrounded by high hills on three sides with the only open ground to the south, the loch required a wind with some south in it to provide good fishing condi-tions. With the weather our luck ran out. The light winds of the morning were

Richard Davies making a final check of the boat before a day afloat on Dibadale

not propitious to good sport. We were fishless at lunchtime but, as the wind freshened in the afternoon, four nice sea trout took a liking to our flies. All were fresh run, the biggest, a cracking fish of 4½ lbs that took a size 10 Hairy Mary, proved to be our best for the week. It was the last fish of the day, and it hit the fly with a real wallop as we came over an offshore shallow.

The following day we were on Loch na Craobhaig (pronounced Cruvag), the most prolific loch on the estate. Sidney Spencer wrote of a day on this loch in his book *Salmon and Sea Trout in Wild Places*. It is featured in the chapter 'The Point – A Hebridean Day'. I remember looking for the entry of that day in the estate log book, and I believe it was July 1967. That chapter was and still remains one of my favourite pieces of reading. With a wealth of rocky points, fish-holding shallows and an excellent stock of fish that run a short, tumultuous

A well laden boat on Loch na Craobhaig

river from the sea, Loch na Craobhaig offers some superb fly-water. Lying in open moorland, a wind from any quarter will produce a good fishing wave, though a westerly is thought to be best. Again we were plagued by indifferent weather as we pushed the boat out on a light pin-ripple. Richard, our boatman, suggested we try the windward shore to take advantage of what little breeze there was, but except for a few half-hearted rises the morning passed by without result. Two of the fish which rose to Vaughan's, my boat partner, Blue Zulu on the bob were most certainly salmon, but in the light wind they were not inclined to take. Short-rising was a problem we were to encounter again later in the week, when fish after fish would move to the bob fly without taking.

Around midday the weather improved – a repeat of the day before, and like the previous day we were fishless at lunchtime. During lunch I made up a new leader with a size 12 Silver Thunder Stoat on the tail, size 12 Teal Blue and Silver on the middle dropper, and a size 10 Kate McClaren on the top dropper. The new team proved a real winner. In a freshening wind conditions were much improved, and a rapid succession of sea trout fell to the charms of Kate. Vaughan, quipped that he could take a hint and he also got into the action after changing his flies. Sport was fast and furious as we caught no less than 26 finnock and sea trout ranging from 12oz to 2½lbs over the next two hours. It was superlative sport as sea trout, one after the other, exploded on the dancing bob-fly. One fish of about 1¾lbs was so intent on taking the fly that it grabbed it fully six inches above the water after following it all the way to the boat. We could have added to our tally as the 'take' was still on, but we decided instead to move and try for a salmon. We went back to the area where Vaughan had risen two fish earlier in the day, and were rewarded when he came up trumps with a fresh run fish of nearly 6lbs. A great day!

Our come-uppance came on the Wednesday, a real howler sweeping in from the west curtailing any hope of going out in a boat for the day. We were confined to bank fishing and Vaughan elected to fish the river down. I left my rod in its case, and followed with the net, but the fish had obviously pushed on through to the loch so he never required my services. The wind screamed up the glen, and accelerated as it was compressed, like being in a wind tunnel between the mountains on either side of the loch. I remember watching the water spouts spinning, lifting great sheets of water in their fury, and dragging the hydrological load for hundreds of yards up the loch until, energy spent, the load fell back into the maelstrom of breaking waves with an explosion of spray. A boat would have been blown to pieces in that storm, so there was some comfort to be sought from not being out there.

The storm blew itself out, and on the Thursday we were again on Loch Dibadale, but the weather had reverted to almost windless, so we were justifiably pleased when we came off with seven good sea trout to 2½lbs. It was a tough day of light fickle wind or flat calm. All the fish took a size 10 double fished on the point. A longish cast and a steady draw of the line was the requisite to success. The fish would come after the first two or three pulls after letting the fly settle. If you did not get a take in the first few pulls, then basically you were not going to get a take at all. Realising this I lifted a long line, and retrieved only a short length of the cast before re-casting. Every day is different, and we have to adjust to the moods of the fish.

There was little change in the weather for our penultimate day on Loch na Craobhaig. Graham Sinclair, the factor of the estate, elected to act as our boatman for the day. However, conditions during the morning – light changeable wind – were far from easy and by lunchtime we were blank. The weather was far from kind during our visit to the Hebrides, and this day was again no exception. On no day did we enjoy perfect conditions for the duration of a session. On several of the days the wind picked up over lunch. Whether it was due to a sea influence being so close to the coast I do not know, but it was uncanny how the wind picked up in the early afternoon. And so it was on this day, as lady luck played her final card as cloud and wind built from the west. By the time we pushed the boat off the gravel beach after lunch, cloud cover was almost complete and a steady wind began to blow from the west.

Vaughan was the first to break the blank with a sea trout of around 1¾ lbs and I followed with one of a similar size a few minutes later. The light was perfect, although we could have done with a bit more wind, especially for a salmon. I had yet to catch one on this trip, and I was sorely tempted even though the wind was lighter than I would have liked. The temptation proved too great, so I made up a new leader, with salmon in mind – a size 8 Hairy Mary double on the point and a size 8 Claret Bumble on the dropper.

The change of flies proved an instant success, and a good sea trout fell to the Bumble. Following this, a salmon rolled on the Bumble, back and shoulders breaking through a trough in the wave, and missed the fly. After missing the fly I quickly cast in the hope of drawing the fish up again, but he sulked and didn't stir. We then fished over some blank ground with no further offers until we passed a rocky reef, where sea trout came thick and fast. Although I thought the flies were too big for the sea trout, they thought differently taking a liking to their charms. The sport was fast and furious as the fish came crashing after the flies on every other cast. During the frenetic activity another two salmon moved to the Bumble, but neither took the fly. Later the drift took us on to a shallow rocky shoreline where I was subjected to a period of intense excitement and utter frustration as salmon repeatedly rose to the Bumble – and came short.

They rolled on the fly, bumped it with their noses, and rushed at it like reservoir rainbows, following for several yards before finishing with a half-hearted ineffectual rise. Head and shoulders would break through the surface, disappearing with that tantalising wag of the tail, leaving me utterly bewildered. I was at my wit's end to find an answer. Fishing a smaller Bumble or changing the point fly made no difference; altering the speed of retrieve met with similar treatment from the fish. They seemed obsessed with the Bumble on my dropper, but not enough to commit the fatal act. While I was enduring this frustration, my boat partner uncannily could not rise a thing even though we were fishing the same water with similar flies. For whatever reason they were coming to me, but I could not persuade them to take.

As Graham pulled off the lie for the third time I tied a size 10 Stoat's Tail double on the point. This time down the salmon refused to move until we were beyond the last of the known lies. In water no more than two feet deep, close to a rock which was protruding above the surface I raised a fish to the tail fly and everything went solid as the tip of its tail disappeared. There was no obvious follow, just a slow deliberate roll. That salmon had us in a tight spot, with boulders littered all around. It was a graveyard for a loose fly, and at any moment I expected the dropper to become hung up on one of the snags. My luck held and after countless changes of direction we managed to pull out of that rocky nightmare with the fish following, and lead the salmon into open water. Fishing with a trout rod and a No 6 line I was outgunned by the fish; he felt heavy and no matter how much pressure I tried to apply the fish was dictating terms, but once out in open water I could relax and finish the battle. There was a huge sigh of relief from rod and boatman when Vaughan finally sunk the net under the fish and heaved him aboard. We were expecting a fish of between 5lbs and 8lbs, so you can imagine our surprise when we looked down on a salmon of 16lbs. Our host later informed us that it was a record for the estate.

The Stoat's Tail had brought me luck but it wasn't the solution, as more salmon continued to come short. At least the frustration was easier to accept with a fish in the boat. R. A. Chrystal in his book *Angling at Loch Boisdale*, refers to Grimersta salmon coming short at 60 degrees F and I suspect that a warm water temperature was responsible for our experience, too. Vaughan and I later experienced the same sort of behaviour on Loch Arienas on the Morvern peninsula, when salmon repeatedly came short but would not take. This behaviour was repeated over the course of several days, and we had ample opportunities to change flies, but no matter what we tried they were all basically treated with the same contempt from the fish. The salmon would boil below the flies, roll on them and even follow for some distance without actually taking. Occasionally we could induce one to take. However, even after such a triumph we knew that we hadn't discovered the answer. It will remain an enigma, one of those unsolved mysteries to which we as yet have no definable answer.

The migratory fishing on the Hebrides is unique. Numerous moorland lochs fed by little rivers – mere threads of water swollen by summer rain – they are the lifeline to the sea up which the silver fish stream in off the tide. These systems provide some of the most consistent sport with salmon and sea trout for the visiting game-fisher, who can always feel confident that he is in with a chance of a fish. Here in a treeless, windswept landscape of peat and rock we can still cast a fly to wild fish in wild places.

6 Flanker and Lemming

We fished Uig and Hamanavay for a number of seasons, and for several of those visits a young college student by the name of Richard Davies was our boatman. In his student years Richard spent his summer vacation working on the estate. He had a passion for rugby and because of Vaughan's stature, around 6ft and weighing 13½ stone, Richard decided to call Vaughan, 'Flanker'. The name stuck, and when Richard left Uig and Hamanavay and went on to the Uig fishery as a guide, Vaughan and I received an invite from Malcolm Green, the owner of the fishery, to fish the tidal water in Uig Bay. It was a generous offer, one we could not refuse.

We fished Hamanavay during the day, and then went on to the Uig fishery for a brief evening session. I had never caught a salmon in salt water before, and Richard assured me that they fight better in salt than in fresh water. He said I would have a job to hold them on a tight line, as they tended to go ballistic once hooked. The best time was apparently on a falling tide; however Richard stated that he personally had caught well on the flow. As we could only fish the

Uig Bay

73

evening, we were not going to enjoy the luxury of choosing suitable sea conditions; Quite the opposite in fact, as the time of our visit would not only coincide with failing light, but also with a rising tide. This we were informed was the worst condition for taking a fish from the sea. Vaughan and I were pragmatic about the conditions, the state of the tide did not deter us as we were enthusiastic about fishing the salt water bay of Uig for a salmon. At least if the light held up we would see plenty of fish, even if we could not catch them.

As you drive through Glen Valtos and on to Timsgarry, a panoramic view of Uig Bay opens up as you crest the hill above Timsgarry. At low tide and in the right light, the view of the strand stretching out to where it meets the breaking surf of the Atlantic is quite stunning. The bay is flanked on either side to the south and the north by small rivers, and the river which concerned us flowed in on the north side of the bay. Salmon collect in this tidal stretch of the river waiting for rain, or for a high spring tide to lift the levels which will then give them access over the falls to Loch Stacsavat above. The water level has to be at a crucial height for the salmon to run the falls. If it is too high or too low they cannot pass them to gain access to the loch. When the fish enter the system they wait for the right conditions of water height before running the falls. Ideally if you intend to fish the tidal water, a dry spell after the salmon have entered the system is desirable as this will hold the fish back. Also sunny bright conditions, weather which one associates with dry spells, increases visibility and makes seeing the salmon much easier. Actually seeing the target is of huge benefit to the angler fishing in the salt water environs of Uig Bay.

We may have been out of luck with the tide, however where the weather was concerned she did bless us with good fortune. A shoal of fish had entered the system, and the falls were impassable as the water was too low. This meant if the weather remained dry we would have fish to cover at least. All we had to do was find them. We parked the car at the end of the track at Crowlista. As we climbed out of the car you could smell the salt-laden air, and hear the sound of the breakers surging onto the strand just around the point of the headland. The tide was making, and the bay was filling with flood water as we walked through an old gate and across some well-cropped turf. Richard led us down to a narrow path which ran between the edge of a low cliff, and a wire fence. The path wasn't very wide, and there was a sheer drop of about ten to fifteen feet onto the rocks

Playing a salmon in salt water in Uig Bay

below. We cautiously walked along the narrow section of the path until it opened up, and then we descended down to the bay.

The higher ground offered a good vantage point from which to spot the fish, and Richard made full use of the height as he stood above us scanning the bay for a sign of the salmon approaching. When swimming in with the tide, they did not hold in one place, or take up a lie. Instead they swam around in a tight shoal like a school of mackerel. Vaughan and I were lower down at the water edge, so we could not see the fish until they were nearly upon us, but Richard from his vantage point could give us plenty of warning when the fish moved in. We waded out to the edge of the bladderwrack which was waving to and fro in the tide and waited. I was fishing with a 10ft 7 weight rod, and an intermediate line to which I attached a size 14 Silver Stoat treble to a 10ft leader of 10lb B.S. It was just a matter of waiting until the fish came within casting range. I held the fly, and the loose fly-line in large loops in my hand. Small fish, either pouting or pollack, were working the edge of the weed beds. They would dash out from the cover of the bladderwrack and intercept a morsel as it was swept past their hidey-hole in the weed. Crabs crept across the bottom, and ephemeral shrimps darted in amongst the weed. I could see gannets plunging further out towards the main push of water entering the bay. On folded wings they fell like daggers into the sea. The plumage of their feathers glowed snow-white, almost iridescent against the dark curtain of the sky. This was an alien environment, and one I wasn't used to. It felt surreal to be fishing for a salmon in such surroundings.

I waited and watched as the bay filled with water. It is amazing when the tide starts running, how quickly a large area can be flooded. We had been waiting possibly twenty minutes or more, and the bay was well flooded with water when the cry went up, 'Fish'. Richard had spotted the shoal of salmon approaching from the seaward side. Vaughan was on my right and nearest the sea, so he would have first crack at the fish. Low down they were difficult to see, but as the fish came closer I could make out the grey horde approaching Vaughan from the seaward side. There must have been over 100 fish in that shoal, and they crept ever closer. Richard was shouting instructions to Vaughan, and then he was casting. The fish kept on coming, snaking up what was the now flooded river channel. Vaughan cast and swung his fly through the grey horde, but nothing happened and then he cast again with the same result. Salmon one after another were now going past him and coming on to me. I let go of the fly and began to lengthen line.

The front runners of the shoal were about forty yards below me, and cruising about three feet below the surface. My line went out and I swung the fly round just short of the leading fish. My next cast would bring my fly through the approaching salmon. As it swung through the leading group I saw one of the party shake its head, and at the same time I felt the thump, thump of a taking fish as it backed away with my fly. For a moment it was deadlock, and then there was an explosive swirl on the surface and a bright silver fish of about 5½ lbs propelled itself across the water. I prepared myself for the fireworks, but in truth on a 7 weight rod and a 10lbs leader I soon had the fish on a short line. Richard came down with the net chastising me for not letting the fish run, but I felt more comfortable with the salmon under the rod and we soon had him in the net. My first salmon from the sea, covered in sea-lice and a bar of silver. It could not have gone better. I was delighted, and Richard shook my hand to congrat-

76

ulate me whilst at the same time mumbling something about an extreme bend in the rod and being too hard on the fish. We fished on for possibly another hour. The salmon came past again, before we lost them as they moved further up the system with the tide. However neither of us could tempt another one.

Our host was delighted that we had taken a fish on a rising tide, and kindly invited both Vaughan and me to have another crack at the fish. Uig was having a good season, and on our arrival Richard informed us he thought that the total for salmon caught on the system stood at ninety-eight. If this was correct they needed two more for the 100. We were full of anticipation as we walked down toward the bay. Again we minded our way along the narrow path between the cliff edge and the fence. There wasn't a lot of room. Once down by the water's edge we took up positions as we had the night before, with Vaughan on my right. He would have first crack at the fish as they came in. We waited for the cry to go up, and it wasn't long before Richard called out 'Fish'. I could see the grey horde on the seaward side of Vaughan, creeping up what was now the flooded river channel. Like a grey shadow, they just kept coming. There must have been around 150 fish or more in the shoal. Vaughan was casting, and the fish just kept on coming. They were opposite him and soon they would come into range for me to have a crack at them, but before I could make a cast, Vaughan's rod went up to the words 'Fish on'. The salmon lunged across the surface of the channel, and running out a long line charged across the flooded sand on the other side of the channel. It ran Vaughan well into his backing, before he could bring the fish in and play it out on a shorter line. The fish was everywhere and fought like the very devil, but eventually Richard slipped the net under a bright 6lbs salmon, and the customary cheer went up as he waded ashore with the fish. It was also Vaughan's first salmon from the sea, and he was chuffed with his prize.

After we had settled down, we got back to the serious business of fishing, but the commotion of playing a lively fish had split the group of salmon. They were nowhere to be seen. Across the bay to the east, Suainaval and the mountains to the south provide a wonderful backdrop to Uig Bay. When the bay is flooded and the sun is shining the water can at times look a turquoise blue – it almost looks like a tropical lagoon. It is a very picturesque place to catch a salmon. Isn't this the beauty of fishing in wild places, to have such wonderful surroundings in which to pursue our passion? Time was moving on and the light was fading, when Richard called out that there was a small group of salmon approaching. I couldn't see the fish at first; Vaughan was casting and yet I still couldn't make them out. Dropping the fly into the water, I lengthened line. The light wasn't ideal for seeing in, and as they approached I could just pick out the small group of salmon, maybe fifteen to twenty fish, as they passed Vaughan and came on to me. They were hugging the edge of the weed, slowly cruising up the channel. I knew that this would probably be my only chance, as the light was fading, and it was vital to be able to see the salmon to put the fly to them. I let the fly swim round just above the fish. Moving the rod tip to keep it in line with the fly-line, and to slow the passage of the fly over the fish, I swung my fly over the leaders of the pod of salmon. The light was not good enough to see the take. All I could see was the grey shadow creeping across the sand, but I felt the thump, thump and the steady draw on the line. The rod hooped over, there was a boil on the surface and a fish broke away from the group shaking its head. At first it felt like a dead weight, and then my fish ran across in front of me. When it was opposite to where I was standing, I put more pressure on the salmon and it came in on a short line and I played him out. There were no acrobatics or line screeching runs, just dogged resistance until Richard put the net under the fish and carried him ashore. It was a carbon copy of Vaughan's salmon, fresh off the tide with sea-lice attached.

We both had a salmon, and fishing doesn't come any better than that when the spoils are equally shared with a friend. More than contented with a fish apiece, we called it a day and trudged back towards the car. The sun had already gone down, and the night was filtering in as we came to the narrow path between the fence and the cliff edge. Richard was carrying my fish and Vaughan was carrying his. They were walking just ahead of me, each of them with a fresh salmon hanging from their hands. The perfect end to a fine evening's fishing, I studied the salmon hanging limply, and even in the poor light they appeared bright and silver, their tails just clearing the ground, and then they vanished. They were no longer in my vision and I was hurtling through the air and onto the rocks below the low cliff. The rocks came up fast with a crunch. How I didn't smash my rod I do not know, and how I escaped with no more than a badly bruised knee I do not know. I remember the jarring thud as I hit the

Salmon swimming over sand; note the sea lice along the back especially towards the adipose fin

rocks, and the pain in my knee, but nothing was broken. Richard and Vaughan came rushing down to assist; they were obviously concerned as they wasted no time coming to my aid. I was lucky, and came out of that fall with nothing more than some damaged pride and the badly bruised knee; it could have been so much worse.

Back at the lodge we were greeted by our host. When hearing about the fall he enquired as to whether I would need the services of a doctor, but I assured him that I was fine. He did however offer some medicinal whiskey. Half-way through the second glass he enquired about our fishing. We had forgotten about the two salmon. It transpired that my fish was the 100th for the season, and it was another excuse for another top up of the glass. That evening as we made our way back to Richard's house, and he was obviously feeling in a cheeky mood he said. 'I know what I'm going to call you two from now on'. There was a subtle pause before he delivered the punch line: 'Flanker and Lemming'.

79

7 Latchicos in Iceland

'You will never guess which latchico has won the bid for our guided days in the auction,' said Larry. Ah, the Wild Trout Trust auction, I'd forgotten about that 'Who?' 'Come on have a guess.' 'I wouldn't have a clue, put me out of my misery.' There was a brief pause for effect: 'Jeremy Herrrrrmannnn, and what's more he wants to come for the *Caenis*.' 'That's interesting, what do you think?' 'I don't know.' 'he's probably fishing for information.' 'I guess he is, we will have to play this carefully,' announced Larry. After some deliberation Larry suggested that I take Jeremy for the first day, and in his words I was to 'suss the latchico out' and that he would do the second. Latchico, that was the second time I had heard that word in as many minutes. It was part of Larry's vocabulary and as he uses it so often I thought I would look up the meaning. You will not find it in the English dictionary, so I 'Googled' latchico. In the *Urban Dictionary of Slang* it is depicted as – 'A fellow that is bad and is inclined to get worse, or someone who is in a state of decline and not getting better.' And another definition, apparently a Co. Cork expression, stated it is another way of calling someone a ----ing eejit. My friend has another word 'Amadán', an Irish word which basically has the same meaning. He knows a lot of eejits.

The two days which Jeremy had booked, were days which both Larry and I had donated to the Wild Trout Trust auction. It never ceases to amaze me how much anglers will bid for lots which are auctioned by the charity. Bidders willingly make bids well above the going rate, and Jeremy was no exception. He could have easily booked two days with Larry, for much less than he paid for the two lots. The auction is an important fund-raising event for the Trust, and both those who make the donation and those who bid, make a worthwhile contribution to the Trust funds. To a charity which is dedicated to protecting and restoring wild trout habitat by promoting hands-on, practical and effective projects, this is a worthwhile contribution.

It was an early morning in mid-June, when I met Jeremy on the shore of Lough Corrib. The weather was perfect, warm with a light north-easterly wind. I thought it essential that he should catch fish, and so I took him to an area where there was a good head of trout. There was a good hatch of fly and under the prevailing conditions the trout, numerous trout duly obliged and rose for four hours or more. Jeremy was impressed, as, in all the years that he had been coming to the Corrib, he considered that there was nothing new to be discovered. Thinking he had seen it all, the *Caenis* was a total revelation and one that excited him greatly. Although he now doesn't fish competitions, he has won most of the major events, including a world championship which was held in Ireland on Lough Corrib and Mask. After watching him fish it was easy to see why he had been so successful. I have taken a number of anglers out to fish the *Caenis* rise, and very few of them get to grips with it straight away. The majority require time to make the adjustment in fishing to what looks like an easy target. With quick precise casting, Jeremy required no apprenticeship, he was in tune with the fish from the off. I do not remember exactly how many trout he caught that morning but I believe it was around eight fish, the biggest scaling about 2½ lbs.

Larry rang me later that day to enquire how the morning had gone. I said that Jeremy was good, very good and that he had taken a nice bag of trout. There were no big trout in the bag, but in fairness I didn't take him to an area where I thought he would catch a big fish. Larry asked me what I thought, and I suggested that perhaps he should give Jeremy a crack at one of the bigger trout, as you never know if he is successful he could become a future paying client. My friend took this on board, and the next morning he took Jeremy to a bay which held better than average fish. They came off that morning with a best fish of 4¾ lbs, and since then Jeremy has become a paying client for Larry. He recognised that my friend has a great talent as a boatman. But more than that, he also said that he had spoken to several anglers whom he knew around the Corrib, anglers who had fished the lough for a good many years. These knowledgeable anglers had told him that they considered the *Caenis* was a load of hype, and that if it was as good as we were making out they would know about it. Something told him to ignore the dissuaders. And after the two mornings, he said that it was such a unique experience, that he was glad he had ignored the negative comments and booked the two days. Since then Jeremy has gone on to take some impressive bags in the *Caenis*, and because Larry and I introduced him to this hatch, he respected it, and kindly invited us to join a party of anglers to fish for brown trout in Iceland.

In July we flew over to England to meet up with Jeremy's head gamekeeper, Alan Edwards, at Heathrow. We had never met Alan but there was no mistaking our man who was waiting in the departure area. He is mad keen on sea-fishing, and who else we reasoned would be going to Iceland to stay beside a river renowned for its salmon and brown trout fishing with a pack of sea rods. Alan proved to be quite a character, with an infectious enthusiasm for his sport. After flying out to Keflavik (Reykjavik) airport we then caught an internal flight to Akureyri. Unlike Reykjavic which was flat and dreary, Akureyri, nicknamed 'the capital of North Iceland', was scenically very pretty. Situated at the head of Eyjafjoraur fjord and surrounded by mountains, the highest being Sulur 1,213 metres (3,980ft) it is sheltered from strong winds. It is an important port and fisheries centre, with a good natural harbour and although no more than sixty miles from the Arctic Circle Akureyri enjoys a relatively warm climate.

After arrival at Akureyri we then had to wait for several hours for the rest of the party to fly in. And as we had time to kill and a hired four-wheel drive at our disposal, Alan thought that it would be a good idea to try a spot of sea-fishing. He had done his homework and knew that the port offered some excellent shore-fishing. A short drive found us beside the harbour wall where a group of school children were standing in a line, casting out small lures. They were standing in a gap between two moored fishing boats, space was limited and it was one of the few spaces available. Our intrepid sea angler wasted no time in setting up a rod and joining in the throng of adolescent fishers. Larry and I were in stitches watching this full-grown man fishing with a crèche of children. A little girl standing beside him caught a small codling, and a boy a few rods further along the line brought in another of the same size. We cheered when the children caught fish; Alan didn't mind and he caught fish too. Soon the two hours passed, and we left to meet the incoming private flight at the airport and the rest of the party of anglers.

Introductions were made and three vehicles loaded up with all the assembled personnel, luggage and provisions. Ori Vigfursin had arrived and he was to guide us out to the fishing, to the 'trout' lodge on the upper river Laxa I Adaldal. Our journey took about one-and-a-half hours and we passed through country that was not dissimilar to that of some parts of Scotland, but without that softness of a more mature landscape. The waterfalls were stunning, and the topography was a mix of seascape, a few scattered farms on worked land, mountain and moorland. Our route wound its way through broad open vistas under an azure sky, and it didn't seem that long before our little convoy of vehicles were pulling into the Laxa I Adaldal or Big Laxa river valley. A wilderness of moorland and distant mountain peaks, the terrain was suggestive of Arctic tundra. The river flows out of Myvatn lake (midge lake) renowned for its bird life, beautiful natural rock formations, and hot springs, which is situated at the northern part of Iceland and which was created as a result of volcanic activity and glacial action. The river is divided into two sections: the Myvatnssveit upper section and the Laxardular lower section which finishes just above a power station. Below the power station salmon are the main quarry until the river spills itself to the tide.

On arrival at the accommodation we all evacuated and unloaded the 4x4s in a trice. Anticipation was high, as we had heard so much about this river and you could sense an air of eagerness amongst the other rods. All the other rods except for one American angler, had fished the river before and were therefore familiar with the beats. Jeremy decided that, as Larry and I hadn't fished the river before, the local guide Bjarni should accompany us along with the American visitor. It was suggested that he should take the three of us to one of the top pools. Apparently the pool we were to fish was quite a long one, and could easily accommodate three rods.

As Larry and I set up our rods we tried to glean some information from the other anglers who had fished the river before. Several of the fishermen were well-known international competition anglers. There were two brown bowl winners present so we were rubbing shoulders with some very good anglers. What was apparent, was that although our questions were answered we were provided with scant information, and we were basically left to our own devices. The word was, that a dry fly was the method, and that any colour so long as it was black would do. Larry and I were surprised by the lack of useful information, but as everyone seemed ultra keen to be off, we just put it down to their over-zealous spirit to be out on the river.

For most of my dry-fly fishing on rivers I use a 9ft rather soft action 5 weight rod. The action would be middle to tip and if it were compared with the popular American blanks, it would rate as a 4 weight. I have fished with it on the chalk streams of southern England, the rain-fed rivers of the north of the country, rivers in Ireland, the hill lochs of Scotland and the Blue Ribbon trout streams of North America. It was a lovely little rod, made up from a blank produced by Steve Harrison. This rod was my preferred choice for fishing dry fly on rivers, and as we were fishing dry fly I set up with one of my favourite pieces of carbon fibre, matched to a 5 weight floating line with a tapered leader and a tippet of 3lb 0.128mm. To this I tied a size 14 black F Fly. We then, my friend and I, accompanied the American angler with Bjarni to the designated pool.

Home pool beside the lodge is a big wide impoundment, and as we drove up to our beat we passed several of the rods all ready out on the water fishing. As Arctic terns wheeled and hawked over the river, one of the anglers at the head of the pool was playing a fish. Larry nodded in approval, and we thought this was a good sign, but even better was the sight of numbers of fish rising. The rises were scattered throughout the pool, although some areas appeared to hold a greater concentration of fish. We drove on and lost the river to the contours of the land. As we motored up the valley the river broke up into a braided section and then rejoined to form a single channel. In the sections where we could see the river it appeared to be quite fast and shallow with a number of flatter pools. The pool which we were to fish was just above where a braided section came together. It was a long, flat pool headed by a run of rapids that extended for quite some distance, and the tail was broken up by two channels which spilled into the braided section of river.

There were trout rising in the tail of the pool, just above where it spilled out into the two channels. The greater flow streamed out towards the opposite, left-hand channel and this is where the bulk of the fish were rising. Bjarni suggested that the American angler should try for these trout. Whether he listened or not to our guide's information we do not know, but after Bjarni had told him where to go he promptly waded out to the middle of the stream, and began casting. Not to the fish mind you, he just cast a long line aimlessly across the water, and lined the rising trout in the process. Staring in disbelief Bjarni groaned, and then turned to us with an incredulous look on his face

Larry MacCarthy playing a fish on Home Pool – Lodge in background

and shrugged. He probably thought he was in for a tough day. With this he suggested that Larry take the nearside channel, and that I should fish inside the American angler. I dropped down into the river and searched for a rising fish. There was nothing moving in front of me, the other rod was opening up and putting out most of his fly-line. He was rooted to the spot and causing quite a lot of disturbance, certainly enough to put the fish down. I thought it best to work my way up the stream and away from him.

The river was deceptively swift and littered with rough jagged rock, which

85

although it wasn't hard was tough enough to puncture my waders, with an abrasive edge it would most certainly cut a line very easily. As well as the rock, much of the river bed was covered in filamentous algae. Flannels of this gelatinous single-celled weed clung to every rock but there was little evidence of any other soft aquatic plants. The size and the strength of the river flow reminded me of the Madison in Montana. I quietly waded up the stream searching for a fish. Where the water broke in small vortices over which was obviously a submerged rock, a trout rose on the crease of the broken water. On seeing the disturbance I instinctively crouched down, a reaction we all do when we approach a rising fish. There was no point in trying to ascertain what the trout was taking for this was obvious. The surface of the river was littered with the small black fly we had heard so much about. They are referred to as smuts or midges. They looked like smuts (*Simulium*) to me, but I couldn't be certain. What I could be certain of is that they were members of the largest order of flies, the flat-winged flies (*Diptera*). There were millions of them, and they basically hatch on most days throughout July. Although they were much smaller than the size 14 FFly I had tied to the end of my leader, I didn't change my pattern. I would treat the first few rises as exploratory, testing to see what I could get away with. Lengthening line I put my fly down to cover the fish, but although it floated over him, he didn't rise. I repeated the cast and up he came. There was a small rise and I tightened. All hell broke loose. The river was shallow and my trout ran and ran. This is when I realised that standard chalkstream tackle was no match for the brown trout of Laxa I Adaldal. This fish broke me, as did the next. I thought the first trout was an exceptional fish, but the second persuaded me that these trout were bigger than your average river wild brownie.

I increased the strength of my leader to 0.152mm, 5lbs line. The next trout to come my way was played out and beaten, but it took longer than I would have liked to beat the fish. The rod was hooped over, bending almost at the butt when I moved to bring the fish to hand. It was then that I realised that Bjarni had come up beside me. He had been watching from a discreet distance, and came to my assistance as soon as he saw the trout was ready for the net. I drew the trout over the frame of the net and Bjarni shook my hand, saying 'Well done your first Laxa trout.' It was a fish around 4lbs and what a way to start. 'Are they all this big?' I enquired. 'Some are bigger', Bjarni replied, and he grinned. He wasn't joking. Jeremy had told me to expect big fish, but what was apparent was that the average weight was bigger than that of any other river I have fished. The trout were not only bigger than your average river fish, but they also had some serious teeth around the outside of their mouths. Some of the larger specimens sported teeth which were capable of snicking a fine line. This coupled with the swift flow, shallow water and the line-breaking snags meant that I was under-gunned with my choice of tackle. If I had been provided with more information at the beginning I would have set out with a 6 weight rod and 7lb 0.203mm leader. This was the standard of tackle most of the other rods were fishing. However Bjarni liked the rod I had been using and told me to stick with it. It meant playing the fish for longer than I would have wished, but I really did have some fun with my trout. After taking a second fish I walked down to see how Larry was doing. He was struggling. So I told him what fly I had been using and the strength of the leader that I was now fishing. And I also suggested that he look for rising fish and not to waste time fishing the water blind. Soon after the change my friend was into fish too.

Our brother-in-arms from the other side of the pond was still rooted to the spot, casting away. To see him out on the river was a bit like watching the casting sequence from the film *A River runs Through It*, only not quite as pretty. Bjarni waded out and tried to help him. Eventually in frustration our guide took the American's rod and hooked a trout for him, at least he could say that he never came off the river skunked. The fish continued to rise, and Larry and I without overstretching ourselves had a good time. My little rod took on some alarming curves, but as I was advised I stuck with it. It was more fun. Bjarni proved a mine of information. A local policeman who had lived in the area all his life, he used to fish the river with his grandfather, and commented that it was only in recent years that anglers had exploited the dry fly potential of the Laxa. From what we had seen it was obvious that the river held a good stock of fish, some of which ran to a good size. What was more amazing was, that it was harder to catch a trout under 2lbs than over it.

That evening when we went back to the lodge for supper, it was plain to see that there was a sense of rivalry amongst some of the other rods. Larry and I had done well, but some of the others had caught possibly twice as many fish as us. I was asked why I did not fish in competitions, and I tactfully answered the question. In truth I have never felt the need to fish competitions, I love fishing too much. And as I do a lot of boat-fishing, I really did not relish the idea of spending the day with someone whom I did not know and may not like. To me the fishing has always come first – doing something which I enjoy. It is pursuing fish in areas that I love which gives me the greatest pleasure, and my challenge comes from trying to catch larger than average brown trout on the fly from Irish loughs. That is all the incentive I need to get me out on the water, that and doing it in the presence of good company, with friends whom I respect and like. If we catch fish we share the information, and there is no hidden agenda or secrets. One of the rods at the table could not believe that I had been so open about the flies which I use in my book *Trout From A Boat*. He thought that there must be some patterns which I held back, and again this struck me as odd, because why write about something if it isn't the way you feel or what you practise.

It was beginning to dawn why there was a lack of information fed to Larry and me. And I couldn't help feeling that this summed up the competitive spirit of the competition scene. It is OK for you to partake, but it wasn't OK for you to catch fish, certainly not more than some at least. Larry has fished competitions, he has represented his country at international level, and now feels that he no longer wishes to be part of it. Thankfully I have never became involved in the competitive circuit, and now I know that window of competing at the highest level has passed me by. I have the knowledge but I no longer have the zeal to perform over long periods of time. My powers of concentration have waned, as has the hunger for a fish at all costs. From what I have seen I do not feel that I have missed out from not partaking in competitions, and I have yet to see this spirit of camaraderie and free exchange of ideas we hear so much about. It seems to me that the information is never shared until after the event.

That first day, the pools took a fair bashing. The following morning we were to fish home pool for the first session. It was noticeable that there were fewer trout rising than the day before. Larry and I caught a reasonable number of trout, but they were not as large as the trout of the previous day. Most of the fish we caught were between 2 and 3lbs. In the afternoon it turned cold, really cold. It was hard to believe that it was July. Icy air swept down the river valley, a reminder of just how close to the Arctic Circle we were. After lunch we fished

Larry returning a nice brown

one of the middle sections. A pool just below where the river branched, offered some encouragement. It was well sheltered and there were trout rising. Bjarni accompanied us, and I caught some fine fish on small dark coloured Klinkhammers. Larry lost a really nice fish in the tail of the pool just above a long series of rapids, which were known as wet fly or spider water rapids. He had a clear view of the trout and judged its weight to be around 5lbs. The fish broke him, on one of the many jagged rocks strewn over the river bed. He was fishing with an olive FFly and after making a long run the fish kited round and caught the leader on a rock in mid-river. Even though it was cold the fly poured off and the fish responded. Bjarni was good fun, and he kept saying with a deep

89

Icelandic accent 'Those fish like your Klinkhammers' as another trout came up and sucked in the fly. He really liked the rod and so I handed it to him. Bjarni did not take long to catch a fish and then he handed it back to me. It really was an enjoyable session.

Towards evening we saw two gyr falcons, larger and more heavily built than the peregrine they soared down the side of hill behind us and then passed overhead before flying out across the valley. Majestic pale-coloured raptors, they are the winged predators of the mountain moorland terrain in these latitudes. The only other raptor we saw during our brief stay were merlin, there being a family of them not far from the lodge. Their young were noisy. They sat on outcrops of rock waiting for the parent birds to bring them food, and as soon as one of the adult birds came into sight the cry went up: kekekekekee. The sound of their calling pierced the air, and could be heard a good distance off. As a parent bird drew closer so the rapidity of the kekekekee increased until the bird alighted next to its offspring. Then the calling ceased with a flurry of wings.

The troops trickled back to the lodge that evening for supper. All were in good humour, and there was much talk of fish caught and even bigger fish lost. And when the tally was taken that evening, the numbers were more evenly spread. Larry caught my eye and winked; he did not have to say a word.

On the third day we fished the morning session downstream of the bridge which spans the river just below the impoundment, known as home pool beside the lodge. The fishing was becoming more challenging. Although we saw trout rising they were not coming so freely as the fish on our previous sessions. We still accounted for a respectable tally however and after fishing for about three hours, we took some time out. Bjarni took us to see a power station which was sited further downstream at the foot of a set of falls. The power station marked the beginning of the salmon water, but you couldn't fish immediately below the outlet from the turbines. Here we could see numerous salmon up to 20lbs holding in the boisterous flow. The turbulence would fluctuate, as the flow was never constant, and as it settled you could see the fish holding station against the current. Occasionally a salmon would creep forward and go on a walkabout around the outfall, before returning to take its position in the ranks of fish stacked up below the fall. In the shelter of the steep-sided ravine we noticed a number of trees. We had seen very few further up the valley, and Bjarni remarked that there were very few trees in Iceland and that they have a saying that behind every tree hides a naked woman. Out on the more open moorland we saw no naked women, but there were numerous golden plover. They would play hide-and-seek walking ahead of us. Once a safe distance ahead, they would bob up on an exposed rock piping a single note of alarm. It was hard to believe that in a few months' time, these very attractive waders would be heading south for the winter. We see huge flocks of wintering birds on the Corrib. Drabber and not so brightly coloured in their winter plumage, they remain until the spring, when once again the golden plover will head north to breed.

Just below the dam at the power station, we spotted a mink hunting the far bank of the river. A busy *Mustelid*, the dark-coloured predator nosed its way amongst the rocks searching for prey. It was then we witnessed the efficiency of the local network. Bjarni, a policeman by profession, on spotting the mink made a quick phone call. Within ten minutes a 4x4 drew up and two men armed with rifles got out. They were on a mink hunt, and the problem was sorted a few minutes after we left. You would not want to be a mink on an Icelandic salmonid river.

For the afternoon and evening session Larry and I had access to a vehicle. Bjarni suggested that we should try some pools well up the river. They were situated within a long run of rapids, but they hadn't been fished. We had an excellent session, catching some notable fish. One which I caught from some pocket water on a small dark coloured Klinkhammer would have nudged 6lbs. It gave me quite a tussle in the fast water, making long runs out across the rapids and then dropping down with the current. I had to work my way out of the river and then run down the bank to get below the fish. Once below him, I could then make him work against the power-sapping bend of the rod and the force of the current. It was quite an achievement to land this particular specimen without a net. Larry took some quick photographs of the fish, and then I returned it back to the river. With time running out we dropped down river to the pools and pocket water we had fished the day before. Fish were rising but they were difficult to spot in the fast water. We finished our evening session on a high. It was noticeable that the fish in the pocket water, although difficult to cover properly because of the flow, were moving quite freely. Accurate casting was a necessity, as it was impossible to allow the fly to travel any appreciable distance without drag. The secret was to cast a short line, mark the fish well and pitch the fly in basically on the trout's nose. As soon as the fly pitched in, it would fish for only the briefest of time. If the trout didn't take before the fly was dragged out of line by the force of the current, you just covered the fish again. They came with bold rises, and there was no mistaking when a trout took.

At supper that evening the day's tally was taken, and we were up with the leading pack. Some of the rods were now struggling. The obvious pools had been fished quite hard, and the trout had responded in typical fashion by keeping their heads down. There was no talk of competitions, the conversation that evening hovered around growth rates of fish and the pros and cons of hatcheries. One of the topics was about the brown trout of the Laxa I Adaldal. We were all surprised by the average size of the fish when there appeared to be scant food available to them. Certainly there were millions of smuts or small midges, but the trout could not possibly grow to the size they do, just feeding on these small organisms for a few months of the season. Lifting rocks and searching amongst the filamentous algae showed very little sign of invertebrate life. It was a conundrum, and one to which no one could offer a satisfactory answer. Myvatn lake offered a possible solution. Perhaps the trout found richer feeding in the lake and then dropped down the river. This was an explanation proffered by one of the group, and one which we all agreed was a plausible explanation. But in truth we could not come up with a definitive answer. The lake was certainly a big advantage to the angler, as it buffered the river from the effect of rapid run off and coloured spate conditions. But whether it was the answer to why the average brown trout were so big we do not know. One day fishery science will no doubt reveal the answer, until then we have the unsolved mystery. For an angler, mystery isn't such a bad thing.

On the last day Jeremy declared the river open. We could basically fish where we pleased provided we did not interfere with another rod. To Larry and me it was obvious that the river had taken a good beating. In two and a half days, the tally was over 200 fish caught. All on dry fly. Such pressure would make the fishing more challenging, and this we found interesting. I believe that we all knew it was going to be a tough day, as the fervour amongst the party to set up the rods and be out on the river, so prevalent before the other sessions, was now missing. Larry and I were in a more positive mood: we had a plan. With no vehicle at our disposal we asked to be dropped off in the middle section of the river. Our intention was to search out fish which had not been covered before. We decided to fish together for an hour or so and then split up. Larry would work upstream and I would go down. My intention was to work the pocket water in what was known as the wet fly or spider rapids. None of the other anglers had fished this stretch. They had concentrated on the obvious flatter pools, but these pools although ideal for dry fly were no longer producing. The pocket water would be more testing, and yet it offered, I felt, the greatest opportunity to put a bag of fish together.

When we parted, both Larry and I had taken two fish apiece. After the last fish, which fell to Larry, all movement in that section of river ceased. The trout had clammed up. It was time to make our move. I wished my friend luck as he trudged upstream to search out a rising fish. Once he was out of sight I turned and walked with the flow. Keeping low so that I did not disturb the water with my silhouette, I came to an area where there was a group of rocks situated about a third of the way across the river breaking the flow. A fish rose, twice in quick succession below this break. Creeping down below the fish, I dropped into the river about thirty yards downstream of where the trout rose. Cautiously working my way up against the strong flow, I waded to a spot from where I could ambush the fish. It wasn't a long cast, and I pitched my fly in. As the fly settled, I noticed another trout move just above the rocks where the water flattened out slightly. My fly had drifted no more than a couple of feet, when a trout sailed up and took it with a bold rise. A gentle sideways sweep of the rod set the hook, and my fish immediately turned racing downstream. I backed off and played the trout out. It was a nice fish of around 3lbs. After returning the trout I went back to where the other trout had moved just above the rocks. It did not come on my first cast or the second, but I did catch it, a bigger fish pushing 4lbs. In the strong flow this one gave me some anxious moments, and ran out a long line. Fortunately it ran upstream as I set the hook, so I was always in a good position. As was always the way when playing the larger fish because quite simply they took more line, filamentous algae wrapped itself around my fly-line. The further a trout ran, so the greater the amount of algae one would accumulate on the line. It was an occupational hazard when playing trout on the Laxa I Adaldal.

Another two trout came my way from the small pockets of water below obstructions to the flow. All the takes were confident rises; the fish would come up and boldly turn on the fly in a trice. They had to, because in the strong flow there was no time for a leisurely inspection. It was either rise and eat, or let a potential meal pass by. As I dropped down the river I came to an area where there was large rock on the inside of the flow just out from the bank. The flow was deflected by the rock and a crease formed running for about ten yards. It was an obvious place for a fish. There was a steep bank just below the crease, so I scrambled down to the water's edge and leant against the bank and watched. Fly had collected in the small eddy below the rock, I could see countless numbers of them caught in the foam which had washed up against the margin. They fed out into the flow in a constant stream, a better trap you could not imagine. It was a well-stocked larder for a good fish.

As I watched, on the edge of the flow a trout came up and fed. This was the easiest fish of the session to cover. There was no awkward current to contend with, all I had to do was make sure that I didn't line him and put the trout down. The trout took second cast. And when I set the hook, the water exploded and the fish ran out across the river towing a long line behind him. He then turned and ran downstream and thankfully kited towards my bank. I gained a lot of line. At one stage I had to remove the algae from the line as it was clogging in the rings. This was an awkward manoeuvre, and while I was removing the weed I was praying the fish wouldn't run. Eventually the trout came in on its side, and it was a good one. At least 5lbs I thought. With the rod bent double, I was just about to bring the trout to hand when I noticed a fly in the corner of its jaw. It wasn't the fly to which the line was attached, it was another fly, this trout had already been hooked and lost. The moment I saw the second fly in the jaws of the fish, there was an almighty crack. My rod shattered just above the butt and then collapsed down the line. Overstressed, it had finally succumbed to the strain of lifting the trout to hand. For a moment I panicked, but my fish was played out. I grabbed the upper section and used the bend of what remained of my beautiful 9ft rod to land the fish. Once the trout was landed, I removed the fly which was unattached as well as my fly, and then returned the fish which saluted me with its tail and in the process covered me with spray.

Author with a 6lb brown

It was a good forty minutes back to the lodge, but we had over three hours of fishing time remaining. So I walked back to the accommodation and picked up another rod, and was just about to walk back to where I had left off when I encountered a stroke of luck. One of the other rods came up with a vehicle, and as he was travelling further upstream he gave me a lift. This saved me at least half an hour of walking, and thus I enjoyed the extra time on the river which provided me with another two fish. The two bonus trout brought my tally to nine. It wasn't my best total, but the trout being more difficult made it the most rewarding session.

95

Some of the other rods were already back at the lodge when I returned. The news wasn't good: there were mumblings that they had struggled to find moving fish. Larry came back in a very upbeat mood with Jeremy. He had caught seven trout, and Jeremy had accounted for sixteen fish. They were quite a chirpy pair. We talked about our day and then I pulled a fly from my sweater, and presented it to Larry with the comment that, 'I do believe this is yours.' It was an olive FFly, size 14. My friend took one look at the fly, and immediately recognised it. Somewhat bemused, he asked the question, where did I find it as he had run out of that particular fly. Then he remembered the trout that he had lost on the second day. 'Was it a good fish?' he asked. 'It was' I replied, '5+ and it cost me one of my favourite rods.' And then I told him the story. He told me to keep the fly as a memento of the trip, and I still have it. What was interesting was that trout had moved at least 400 yards down river from where Larry had lost it. Jeremy was the top rod, but apart from one other angler who had taken two fish the others had nothing to report. Jeremy had done incredibly well. Although he had the advantage of a vehicle and a good knowledge of the river, he still used his head and went looking for fish. Most of the other rods had patronised the predictable spots, and came up with a predictable result. There was no mention of competitions, in fact the ambience was rather subdued. Perhaps it was because it was our last day on the river. However, my friend and I were quite pleased with our day, as Larry said 'When the going got tough, it was rather nice to think that the two latchicos could come up with some fish.'

8 Working a Salmon

Salmon can be the most contrary of fish. I feel certain that the majority of salmon anglers will have experienced at some time or another, a perverse fish, the one that is awkward and refuses to move, or a fish which comes short and does not take the fly. The salmon which refuses to move to a fly is easily written off as a no-hoper, but what of the fish which rises and then misses the fly? Very often the fish which move to our presentations, and then go into a sulk of absolute denial refusing to move, are the salmon we try again. We try them because it is part of salmon fishing folklore. Rest them, and then try them again with the same pattern or a smaller fly. If we cannot entice the fish to move after a short trial we move on. Sometimes they shut up shop completely refusing to be enticed by the sweetest of presentations, but not always. There are situations where after a salmon has gone into a sulk, that I cannot help feeling we are missing out on a fish if we pass them by too easily. They can be enticed to take, it just takes longer, that's all. If we are patient and committed enough to see the objective through, these exasperating fish can be enticed to take a fly provided we do not scare them.

Vaughan Lewis has a theory for the fish that move to the fly but do not take; he believes they are salmon which are on the edge. When he says this he is not referring to salmon which are active and on the fin, or salmon which are fresh in and looking up, i.e. potential takers. What Vaughan is suggesting, is for salmon which are in the transition stage between being dour and a potential taker. They can be stale fish which are once again coming on to taking mood, or they could be fish that have been in for a few weeks and the taking mood is thus falling off. These fish he believes can be enticed to move to a fly, but more often than not they will refuse it. I seem to have more than my fair share of these obstinate fish, especially in lakes, but then I just think salmon are bloody minded. However it is possible to turn the barometer of cussedness to our favour, and then the non-taker can become a taker. To do this requires a greater

Beautiful Lough Inagh. With no current to work the fly, salmon in still water are prone to coming short

degree of cussedness from the angler. The angler has to work the fish in such a way that the salmon is either angered into taking the fly, or the fish is shown temptation so often that he can no longer refuse it. I call this little ruse, working a salmon, an action that some anglers may frown upon, but it is one I feel sure that a lot of salmon anglers, if they are honest, will have at some time or another used themselves.

I was led to believe that salmon could be easily put down, and that if you were to show them a fly too often they would ignore it and go off the take. Now this may apply to some fish, but it does not apply to all salmon. Angling literature is full of accounts of anglers working through a pool of a river, and as they work down the pool they move a salmon. The book will advise if they are on the pool alone, that the fishermen should back off from the fish they have moved and rest it. We have all read accounts of where anglers have pulled off and rested a fish, and while resting the fish they have tied on a smaller fly, and then moved in and caught it, i.e. they have shown the fish a fly more than once. Sometimes tying on a smaller fly works, but not always and they do not always take second time down. Changing the fly can work, but it doesn't necessarily have to be a smaller fly of the same pattern; it could be a different pattern or a larger fly. There are times when covering the fish with the same fly will work, but it could involve more than two casts to evoke a positive take. What this illustrates is that we can show a fly more than once to a salmon, without the fish clamming up completely. And what is more, if we cover them repeatedly without scaring them, they can be worked into a taking mood. So if we think back over the books we have already read, we have already seen accounts of anglers working a salmon, the only difference being perhaps the authors were not so obvious about it.

Without knowing it I stumbled in to working a salmon on a cloudy day in July twenty-five years or more ago. I was boat-fishing for both sea trout and salmon. The conditions were good, overcast with a nice breeze from the west and occasional showers. Three or four sea trout had already come my way, and there was no reason why I shouldn't catch a few more fish before the session was out. The wind was taking me in to a small inlet, where a tiny burn discharged its waters. Because of its compact size, I would only get one crack at this inlet I thought, as I would disturb it with the boat as I drifted in. At the mouth of the inlet there was a small promontory with a large rock embedded into the bank, and around the rock an overhang of heather. As I came down by the mouth of the inlet, I pitched my flies towards the overhanging heather, and my point fly landed in the heather's shadow. First pull there was a boil to the point fly, and a salmon showed itself with a lovely slow roll but did not take the fly. I knew that if I continued drifting in towards the bank I would scare the fish, so I acted quickly, and without disturbing the area, quietly pulled off. The fish had come short, but I had read the book so I rested the fish and dropped in again. This time the fish swirled at the fly but did not show himself, and again I pulled off only this time I considered the situation more carefully. The inlet was no more than twenty-five to thirty yards in width, so one could cover this fish from the far shore I reasoned. With this in mind, I rowed the boat well up away from the inlet and walked down to a position opposite the promontory.

To cover the fish meant casting across the wind, as the wind was left to right, it was ideal for me as a right-handed angler, so it wasn't a difficult cast to make. The action of the wind would form a belly in the line which would make the presentation to the fish more attractive, as the fly would swing through the curve of the belly as it followed the path of the fly-line. Improved presentation wasn't the only positive factor to be gained from fishing from the shore. Providing I didn't bungle the cast, being further away from the fish had its benefit too, as the salmon was less likely to detect my presence. This was an added bonus, and I felt fairly confident as I approached the lie. My point fly, a size 10 Stoat's Tail had been now refused twice. A change of fly would not do any harm I thought, so I changed to a size 12 Hairy Mary. I lengthened line to get the distance, and then pitched my fly in to the lie. Again on the first cast with the new fly, the salmon swirled at the fly, and then dropped away without taking. I repeated the cast several times with the Hairy Mary, but no further offers were forthcoming, so I changed again to a small shrimp pattern, and the same reaction from the fish happened again. First cast the salmon just swirled at the fly but without any conviction, and then went into a sulk. This was becoming frustrating; the fish was obviously interested but not enough to take the fly. I changed the fly again, this time to a size 12 Teal Blue and Silver trout fly. I had great faith in it for sea trout so why not give it a swim for a salmon. Whether it was because of an inspirational choice of fly or the result of repeated casting I do not know, but when the Teal Blue and Silver landed under the shadow of the heather as the other flies had done previously, and I pulled as I had done so many times before, all went solid. On feeling the hook, the fish made a lazy sideways jump and then swam out into the open water. He could not have been more obliging. I played him carefully, conscious of not putting too much pressure on the trout hook. Although I didn't know it, there was little fear of losing this fish unless I did something silly, as he was well hooked in the scissors, and that fly was never coming out. Eventually the rod pressure told and the fish came in on its side. As I rarely carry a net and this day was no exception, I tailed the salmon and laid him out in the heather. He weighed 8½ lbs and on a trout rod – a very welcome prize.

Why after all those refusals did that fish take? Was it a touch of inspiration on the part of the angler and his choice of fly changing to the Teal Blue and Silver, or was the fish simply tempted or annoyed into taking a fly which had entered its zone of vision once too often? I would like to believe it was the former, but I can't help feeling it was the latter, although I did not think this at the time. Either way the salmon had been worked into a condition where it took the fly, and for me this was the most important reaction: it concluded with a positive result.

This was the first time that I recognised the significance of what I had done. Unwittingly I may have coaxed a salmon into taking a fly before that day, but I have no recollection of it. What this experience showed me was that it was possible to repeatedly cast a fly to a salmon without putting the fish down, and it was also evident that you could not only show a fish the fly more than once, but that you could also provoke a positive response from the fish by doing so. This was a significant breakthrough, and from this experience I can now say that I have since caught many salmon which I would have given up on previous to that day. It is interesting how we anglers acquire knowledge from our experiences, and then store it away for some later occasion when a similar situation presents itself. Some anglers seem incapable of acquiring such knowledge. Maybe they are not so observant, but those who do make the breakthrough will use the information to their advantage when the need arises.

There are many instances on both lake and river where I have worked a salmon in to taking a fly. What they all show me is that there are no hard and fast rules in fishing where the outcome can be guaranteed. Fish will always have the last word, and all we can do is work the percentages, and try to work them to our favour. If you find that a certain ruse works, then follow it up when a similar situation presents itself. It is having the confidence to do such things, which helps one to pull off a positive result.

When working a salmon I work on the basis of covering a fish with a fly, and showing that fish the fly only. It is vital that the fish should not detect your presence, or that you line him with your fly-line as either will make the salmon clam up. Also when a fish refuses a fly, it doesn't mean that it will not take that fly, for I have taken a number of salmon on a fly they have already refused by repeatedly covering them with the same pattern.

I have worked salmon on a number of Scottish west-coast spate rivers and loch systems: the River Aline on the Morvern peninsula and on the lochs of South Harris, and Uig and Hamanavay on Lewis. These fish have come after repeatedly showing them the same fly. Why should a fish which isn't feeding, suddenly take a fly it has refused many times before? What is it that makes them take: anger or temptation? I do not believe that we will ever know a definitive answer to that question. What is important is that a fish which has refused a fly, can be induced to take it by repeatedly covering the fish with the same fly. Sometimes the fish may require a little more subtlety from the angler, where a change of pattern or a change to a smaller size of fly will press the right button. It may defy logic but it works. Also changing to a larger fly can sometimes work too. A good example of this happened on the River Erris at Bangor.

It was early April, and I had arranged to fish Lough Carrowmore. The weather gods were not on my side however as we were battered for four days with gale after gale. The lough never settled down, and nobody was going out. I called in to see Seamus Henry, the owner of the West End Bar at Bangor, on the evening of the fourth day. The evening was foul: a sleety rain had been falling for several hours. Gales were forecast for the following day (my last at Bangor) and there was little hope of fishing, let alone of getting a fish. Seamus suggested that the river might be worth a look the following morning. On his recommendation, and with some words of encouragement, I tried the lower pools on the river. The morning was clear and cold with a fierce north-easterly wind, and the hills around Bangor were covered with a dusting of snow. It didn't look too promising, and I was in two minds as to whether I should go: it was a choice between common sense and my angler's yearning for a fish. Common sense lost.

Looking over the bridge I could see the river had lifted a little, a few inches, no more, but enough to give me encouragement. I elected to fish one of the lower pools and I fished down the pool, a step at a time, methodically covering the water. A cold wind hit me, and I was questioning my sanity. Maybe I will try just the one pool, I thought. Step and then cast, more wind, and more negative thoughts began to creep in. Two-thirds of the way down the pool, something quite surreal happened: my fly was coming round in a nice curve when the outline of a fish appeared just below it and made a lovely slow roll. I

Lough Carrowmore

waited for the line to go tight, but it didn't; the fish had missed the fly. I tried the fish again. Nothing. Rest, I thought, and try again. This I did, and again the salmon came up, but it was a repeat of the first rise. No contact. Rest the fish again, and try a smaller fly. This time as I worked down the pool there was swirl in the water. No rise – just a movement to betray his presence. I then tried a bigger fly, with no response. A change of pattern produced the same result. My salmon had gone into a sulk. In the cold water of spring, salmon are usually free-takers, but this boy hadn't even touched the fly, and now he was refusing to move.

Finding a springer is 90 per cent of the game, but unfortunately I seemed to have blown my chance. It was difficult to leave. Try him again, I thought, but this time I put up a sink-tip line and tied on a three-inch Waddington, which is a rather big fly for the water height in question, and for a west of Ireland spate river. I worked my way down to the mark. When I reached the point of my salmon's lie, I didn't know what to think. I made the cast, and the fly fished round just as before. This time, however, there was no visual rise – no movement in the water, just a heavy throbbing sensation at the end of the line. The unthinkable had happened… the fish had taken the big fly. When I landed the salmon, the fly was well back in its mouth. Spring salmon are the loveliest of fish and this one was no exception. At 12lbs it was a bar of silver, with a neat head and deep flanks. Against the odds on a tough day, that salmon had given me something to positively fish for. A truly memorable experience!

12lb spring salmon

From river, lake or the sea, I have taken salmon by working them. Each one is different, in that some fish require a change of pattern of fly, some may require a change of fly size and others just respond after being repeatedly covered by the same fly. Stealth and a dogged determination are key, but the underlying trend is the same – you keep on working the fish.

9 Ireland – First Salmon

When Cathy and I married in 1972 money was tight. We were saving to buy a house, but house prices were creeping up, and we were locked into a race of trying to raise enough capital to put down as a deposit on a property. This meant we were saving just about as hard as we could, so there was little money to spare for luxuries. Any thought of a holiday was out of the question, just a distant dream, or so it seemed. On a Saturday in early July Cathy decided to visit her parents. This would have given me an opportunity to go fishing, but the fishing could not have been great, for I cannot remember where I went or what I caught. As it was July I had probably been tench or carp fishing. Later that evening when I returned home, Cathy was waiting for me with some news. She was always subtle in the way information was presented. Handing me a glass of wine I waited for the news. There was a brief hesitation, before Cathy smiled and looking at me inquisitively asked if I would like to go to Ireland. Before I could say something, Cathy quickly added that I would love the country, and there was plenty of good fishing. I was uncertain. Ireland was basically an unknown to me; the troubled north of the country was constantly in the news, but if the words 'good fishing' were a lure, they were the right ones. I was certainly mouthing the bait! She then went on to tell me how my in-laws had planned to go to Ireland that year, and in response to an advertisement in *The Times* newspaper had booked a house in south-west Cork. It was a large house, and there were plenty of rooms. They had offered a place if we wished to go, and thought that there would not be a problem booking two extra passengers on the ferry. I had never been to Ireland before, and I didn't know what to expect, but Cathy was confident that I would like the country. Her confidence persuaded me, that and the words 'good fishing'.

There were not many weeks to plan for this trip, and I had no idea at the time what to take with me. Other than Cathy I didn't know anyone who had been to Ireland before, so I had no one to look to for advice about what type

Vaughan Lewis searching for a fish on Lough Lehanagh. Inagh one of the many beautiful areas I have fished in Ireland

of fishing tackle I should take with me. With no friends who could proffer advice, I read all that I could about the area we were going to, and the type of fishing that would be available. To be truthful in 1972 there was scant information available. However, I did glean from odd snippets of information in tourist guides, and from a few old fishing magazines that I could find good salmon and sea trout fishing in rivers and loughs, plus bass from the storm beaches and wrasse from the rocky inlets off the coast, all within a reasonable distance of where we were staying. The brown trout fishing was not regarded as highly as the fishing for the migratory fish, as the browns tended to be of a small size. As I had not fished for either salmon or sea trout before, the opportunity to have a crack at these fish seemed too good to miss. Both would be new to me, so to hedge my bets I took fly, bait and spinning tackle with me. There were four of us travelling so I tried to keep the tackle to a basic minimum, and I took two rods: an 11ft through action Avon rod which could double as a spinning and a bait rod, and a 9½ ft fly rod for a 7 weight line. As well as the two rods I also packed a fixed spool reel loaded with 8lb line plus a spare spool containing 10lb line, and a fly-reel containing a 7 weight floating fly-line, a box of assorted wet flies, and a box of spinning lures. These few bits and pieces were easily accommodated in a small Brady bag. Apart from a few loose hooks and weights that was it, except for one other item which I collected a few days before we left.

In the weeks before we left for the ferry, I was feeling both excited by the prospect of going to Ireland and a little apprehensive also. Cathy was full of confidence, as her father was from Co. Cork. She had been over to Ireland on a number of occasions with her parents. She assured me that I had nothing to worry about, and that I would enjoy it. Her confidence reassured me, and it was that more than anything else which convinced me that we had made the right decision in deciding to go. I thought about the fishing, and the prospect of fishing for salmon for the first time.

The weeks quickly slipped by and we were enjoying a nice spell of weather, and I was growing concerned as we only had a few days to go, before we left for our holiday. Three days before we were due to leave the heavens opened. Little things make a difference. Sometimes catching a fish, isn't always about what we do on the day we catch that fish. In 1972 I did a lot of coarse fishing as well as fly fishing. I was used to bait fishing and I knew from what I had read that salmon could be caught on worms. If they could be caught on worms, this would be meat and gravy to me. Wasn't I brought up on bait fishing, and bait fishing even for salmon didn't seem that daunting a prospect. They were fish after all. What I needed was the bait, and as the heavens opened up, that I thought should be no longer a problem.

At that time we lived in the small market town of Witney, in south-west Oxfordshire. In Witney there was an area of playing fields called The Leys and the well-mown grass of The Leys was a great area to collect lobworms on a wet night. This was an activity to which I was well accustomed at the time, and I visited The Leys on a regular basis to collect lobworms for bait to use on my local rivers and lakes for tench, chub and barbel. As it was raining, the conditions were ideal for collecting worms, and I needed bait for my visit to Ireland.

On wet nights the worms come to the surface under the cover of darkness. If you tread softly, as they are sensitive to vibration and if you have a quick hand, you can with the aid of a torch collect a lot of worms in the right conditions. The secret to this exercise was to scan the grass with the torch until a worm was sighted. Once located, one moved the beam so that it wasn't directly shining on the worm, as they also are sensitive to light. If you were prompt moving the light, the worm would remain on the surface. With the worm on the edge of the illumination, you then crept forward until close enough to make a grab for the exposed part of the worm. Once you had made your move, one had to be quick, as the worms are very fast retreating back down their burrows. If they sense the slightest vibration or detect the light source, they retreat in an instant. A stealthy approach, a quick grab, and then a steady pull was the answer. A tug of war would then take place, and if you held the worm and pulled smoothly, very often you would end up with a prize to drop into the bait bucket. If you were over-zealous with the pull, one could end up with part of a worm, and if you held them too lightly one ended up with nothing. Watch a blackbird quartering a lawn searching for worms and you will see what I mean.

On this wet night in late July 1972 I was out collecting worms from the well-mown playing fields of The Leys. It should have been a walk in the park. I had probably been at it for the best part of an hour, and in an hour if you have a strong back on a good night you can collect the best part of 100 worms. My bucket contained a wriggling, writhing mass of *Lumbricus* and I was well into my session. However, I was so involved with my collecting I hadn't noticed a police car pull up on the park road. It would appear that the local constabulary had been watching me for some time, and probably thought that I was some lunatic who required sectioning. For who in their right mind, would want to creep about over the grass shining a torch at the ground on such a wet night. It was late, approaching midnight. My antics hadn't escaped their attention, and to them I must have looked suspicious. Eventually their curiosity got the better of them. Suddenly I was caught in the beams of two torches, and they were moving in my direction. At first I did not know what to do, and blinded by the light I couldn't see that they were police officers. I was 22, and pretty fit. I thought about dropping the bucket and running, but curiosity was getting the better of me too. I turned my torch off and waited. As they approached I could just make out the uniform, and realised that they were police officers. I was glad I didn't run, but what on earth did they want? They came straight up to me, and asked me what I was doing. When I explained to them what I was up to, they looked at me incredulously. One of them even said that he didn't believe me, and I found this irritating. To prove my point I held the bucket up under the nose of the disbelieving officer, and shone the torch on the contents. He almost convulsed. He got the message then, and they both left. What they thought at that time I do not know, but as they had scared every worm in the near vicinity, I did not care. I couldn't imagine them making the same mistake again. I finished collecting the bait, and then left expecting to see a blue flashing light behind me at any time on the drive home. None came, and I had my bait.

Ireland was a mystery to me. However I couldn't have had a better intro-duction to a country I have now grown to love. We were staying in a house just outside the small town of Glengarriff in south-west Cork. The area surrounding where we were staying was lovely; I especially liked the rugged contour of the Bhearra Peninsula. A mixed topography of mountain, moorland and seascape spread out on a moving canvas as we toured around the peninsula. For the first few days we explored the environs local to where we were staying. The weather was fine, and we made the most of it. Then on the third evening it rained, heavy rain. I was bit naïve when it came to salmon fishing, but I knew enough to know that rain was a good sign. The next day we made enquiries at the local post office about the fishing. There was a small river which flowed into the sea at Glengarriff, and we discovered that it held salmon, and that for a small fee we could fish the river. I can't remember if the fee was for a licence or for club membership, but I do remember that it wasn't expensive.

The river was quite short and consisted of a series of slow-moving pools, most of which were not that wide. It wasn't the sort of water I was expecting to fish for a salmon; I had visions of a big powerful river where salmon were leaping through rapids or over falls. The Glengarriff River wasn't quite what I had in mind, but I was assured that it held fish, and in the current conditions was worth a try. After we were married Cathy very rarely came fishing with me. Her main interest was wild flowers. So it came as a bit of a shock when Cathy

Lough Conn. Another of Ireland's gems. A good cast for both trout and salmon

said that she would come with me to lend a bit of moral support. Maybe she sensed something which I didn't, or maybe she just wanted to put me at ease. I had no idea of what to do or where to go. As one of the first pools on the river was vacant, and it was handy beside the road I decided that that was probably as good as anywhere to begin. There was no science attached to this decision, it was just one of convenience.

The Glengarriff River was a small spate river. It reminded me of my local River Windrush in Oxfordshire. It was certainly no wider, but didn't have the length of the Windrush. The watershed drained off the Caha Mountains, and much of the river was thickly wooded. I do not remember it being that long, maybe only five or six miles of fishable water with a limited number of pools.

The top pool was quite a big pot below a waterfall. This was a popular pool, but I never fished it as it always seemed to be occupied. Some of the anglers used to stand at the head of the pool on a buttress of rocks, and there were certainly fish in the pool as I saw a lot of striking going on. However as I wasn't sure about their methods, I left well alone.

Our pool was quite long with a narrow neck. The main run of water ran down the far bank, opposite to the road side of the river. On the near side the water was slack with a large back eddy, before it ran out into the tail of the pool. At the neck the current was fast, but the water wasn't broken. It came in, in a rush, pushed down the far bank and then steadied as it flowed out at the tail. There was also a thick line of alders overhanging the far side. It was a pool with classic features, and with my understanding of fishing small rivers I could see where the fish might lie. I learnt my craft on a small river. This would be bread and butter fishing to me, or so I thought. The only drawback was that I was fishing for a species of fish which I hadn't caught before, but it couldn't be that difficult, I reasoned. After the heavy rain the river was in full spate, and carrying a little colour. Even with my lack of experience I knew that the fly was out, so I decided to start with the worm. I set up the 11ft Avon rod, and attached the reel loaded with 8lb nylon. To the end of the line I tied a size 6 hook, and then pinched on a couple of split shot about two feet above the hook. With this I would cast the bait in at the head of the pool, and work it down the run along the far bank. If there was too much weight on the line I would take one of the shots off, and if there wasn't sufficient I would add weight. It was a simple rig, but I thought it was essential to keep the bait moving. Trout were salmonids after all, and this was the method which worked with them, so why shouldn't it work with a salmon.

My side of the river was fairly clear of trees, so I could drop down with the bait if I wished as it worked down the pool. Before I made my first cast, a salmon leapt on the far side and just above where I was standing. The sight of the fish improved my confidence. At least there were fish in the river. Cathy saw it too, and gave a knowing smile, a smile which suggested that she had seen it all before on previous visits to Ireland. The water was almost flush with the top of the bank, and I could see submerged grasses and bracken fronds waving in the current. Floodwater had overwhelmed them. However soon they would be exposed to the air once again, for on a spate river the flood doesn't last for long. Where the main force of the current came through the neck, there was a small back-eddy on the far bank, a little indentation before the current then ran down the bank under the alders and out towards the tail of the pool. This was the ideal spot I thought to place the bait, and so I cast into the little indentation and then ran it down with the current. It took a bit of fiddling with the weights to get the balance right, but as soon as I had the right amount of weight on I could keep the bait trundling down with the current. If it stuck, I would just raise the rod a little to ease the bait back up and into the flow to keep it moving. My bait was fishing well or so I thought, but no fish other than eels came to appropriate my bait.

Repeatedly I cast to that little spot on the far bank, one cast after another, and ran my worm down with the current. No salmon came, but we did see several fish leap. After a time I began to have doubts about the method, my confidence in the worm was wavering. The water appeared dark and peaty. There was colour, but not too much, and the river was dropping. Perhaps a spinner might be worth a try? This thought was going through my head as I made another cast, and met with yet another blank run. You can only do this so many times, I thought, before you try something else. My patience was wavering, and my faith in the bait was diminishing with every cast. It is sometimes difficult to determine which cast will take the fish, and I had now reached a position where I had to give the spinner a try. Casting the worm into the little indentation as I had done so many times previously, I gave the rod to Cathy to hold whilst I looked for a spinner. My lures were in a small box which was tucked away in my shoulder bag, which lay on the ground behind us. I turned and knelt down to take a spinner from the bag. Just as I opened the bag, literally seconds after casting the worm bait I heard the words, 'Dennis there is something pulling on the rod.' Without looking I dismissed it, thinking it was the pull of the strong flow and suggested this to Cathy. Reaching forward to place my hand in the bag to take out the box of lures the words came again: 'Dennis there really is something pulling on the end of this rod.' I turned around, to see Cathy hanging onto the rod which was nearly bent double, and the determined expression on her face told it all. She was not going to let go of the rod, but she didn't know what to do. All this happened within a few seconds of me casting the bait out to the same little niche which I had covered so many times before. It is an event which is impossible to explain, but Cathy was definitely hooked into a salmon.

I rushed to her side, and checked the tension on the clutch of the reel. It was adjusted to give well below the breaking strain of the main line. If the salmon ran there was no reason why the line should break, and provided Cathy could keep the rod well up there was no reason why she shouldn't land the fish. She was anxious and wanted to give me the rod, but I said no, this was her fish. I just kept my hand under the butt section of the rod a little way above the reel, to prevent the rod from being pulled down in a straight line to the fish. This would hopefully avoid a line breakage. Cathy wound when I gave the instruction to wind; I had never seen her look so determined. The salmon ran, jumped, almost tail walking across the flow, and then dropped down with the current shaking its head, but it stayed on. As the fish tired I tightened the clutch, just a little, but sufficient to put more pressure on the salmon. It came up and I knew it was beaten. I told Cathy to keep the pressure on, and in no way was she to let the fish pull the rod down if it tried to surge off. The net was a few yards behind us. I made a quick rush for it, and was back at her side. All was well and with the net well sunk, I told Cathy to walk steadily backwards away from the water's edge. The rod was well bent, but thankfully everything held and the salmon was drawn over the net. 'Have you got it?' came the softly spoken words from behind me. I turned around and lifted the net. Cathy was beaming. She dropped the rod, and rushed forward to give me a hug. That was the best moment we ever shared together on a fishing trip. I killed the salmon and then held it up; it was about 6½ lbs. 'Do you know what?' I said. 'What?' said Cathy. 'You have caught a salmon before me, and you don't even fish.' There was a brief pause and then Cathy said 'Perhaps it isn't as difficult as you make out.' There was a cheeky expression on her face and I had no answer.

There was no point in continuing with the fishing, as the drama of what had just happened was all too much. A man and his wife came down from a house which overlooked the river to admire the fish, and one of the first things I learnt about Ireland, was that few events happen without someone noticing. The other point I learnt that day was that news travels fast. We left the river and went back to the house. Cathy's parents were delighted. There was fresh salmon for supper, and their daughter had caught the fish. To celebrate we drove in to Glengarriff. There was a bar in Glengarriff, called Ryan's Bar, and that night I discovered just how quickly news can travel. With a little help from her dad, the news spread that Cathy was the girl who had caught a salmon from the river. People – total strangers – came up and bought pints of Guinness for the couple in the bar. Special attention was paid to the girl. Me? I was just the guy with the net.

At that time in Ireland if you wanted to find out about local information, the public bar was the place to go. It didn't seem to matter which night of the week it was, Ryan's Bar was always a hive of activity. That night I soon discovered that although the river was poached, it was a good river for a fish. It would appear that I had underestimated that little stretch of water. The rest of the holiday was one or two nice days and then rain. So the river was constantly coming into spate, and with each little freshet a few salmon would trickle in. I dearly wanted to catch one of these fish, so the next morning I went down to the river again for a few hours. Flushed with success, Cathy decided not to go. In fact she did not fish again for the rest of the holiday. On arrival at the river I discovered that the spate had run off. The water had cleared and it was well down on the previous day. So I crossed over the river and tried a pool above the one we had fished previously from the opposite bank. It was heavily overgrown, and there was no hope of fishing a fly so I stuck with the bait and crept up the bank towards the pool. The light was good, and although the water appeared dark it was deceptively clear, and I could see in. Crouched down and creeping up the bank of the pool I systematically scanned the water ahead of me. When I came towards the head of the pool I couldn't believe my eyes. There, lying about three to four feet down were around fifteen or more salmon. They hung in the current almost motionless. It was like looking at a shoal of chub on the River Evenlode. Suddenly my confidence soared; I was used to this type of sight fishing. Now I was on familiar ground, and what is more knew I was going to catch one of those salmon.

The area over which they were lying was about half the size of a tennis court. They were randomly spread out, but the rest of the pool appeared to be empty. I backed off and set up my rod. This time after tying on the hook I added no weight at all. The flow had dropped, and I wanted to drift the bait through the fish and not below them. Baiting the hook, I just passed the hook through the bait once leaving a lot of free movement for the worm to wriggle and writhe in the water. I then moved forward, and keeping well below the fish I cast the bait in. It fell well upstream of the salmon, as I did not wish to scare them with the entry of the bait. When the bait came through the salmon, I could see that it was below them. The next time I cast well ahead again, but when the bait was a few yards ahead of the fish I raised the rod to lift it in the water. This time the worm came through, basically at eye-ball level. It drifted by several fish, and then one swung out a little and intercepted the bait. I could see the gills flare as it took and the mouth munching on the bait. The fish was upstream of me, the angle of pull was perfect and I was pulling downstream of the fish. All my mentors, and everything which I had read about salmon with a worm, had told me that when worm-fishing you let them take the bait right back. I wasn't used to this, I could see that the salmon had the bait, and yet I had been told to wait. When a chub takes the bait, I wallop it, when a barbel takes the bait, I wallop it, and likewise when a carp takes the bait, I wallop it. I walloped this salmon. You could see it hesitate for just a moment, and then it raced up the pool.

The salmon headed for the top of the pool. It was taking line at a steady rate but by applying some side-strain with the rod I turned it. As soon as it turned, the fish came back towards me, and as it came down the pool I backed off. The salmon kept coming, and I led it towards the tail where there didn't appear to be any fish. In the sluggish tail I played the fish out and landed him. It was my first salmon, and it weighed around 6lbs. Fresh run, a silver bar bearing sea-lice. I was elated.

Whilst playing the fish the rest of the salmon split up, but only briefly. As most of the play took place well away from the main group of fish, the rest of the salmon did not take long to settle back into their previous positions. I repeated the feat three times before they had had enough and shut up shop. The fish were of a similar size, between 5½ and 7lbs, and all fresh run. I killed two of the salmon and returned the third fish. These were to be the only two fish I killed as we had enough fresh salmon for the holiday, and I was given instructions that we did not need any more fish. In the next week and a half I caught eleven salmon from that little river, all by sight-fishing and all them on the upstream worm. I struck them moments after taking the bait and not one of those salmon was deeply hooked; they were all hooked in the scissors, and I do not remember missing many fish. One which I do remember turned towards me as he took the bait, and was therefore facing me as I struck. The bait was just pulled away from the salmon as he mouthed it, and I made no contact with the hook when I lifted the rod to strike, but one very surprised fish turned in a flash and promptly shot away.

What amazed me was the number of salmon which I saw in that little river. I do not know what the river is like now as I have never been back to it. On that holiday however there were salmon in every pool. What it showed me was that Irish rivers at that time were very well stocked with migratory fish. None of the fish which I saw were huge, and I only saw one salmon which I thought would make more than 10lbs. This fish was lying with two smaller salmon, under a raft of rubbish which had collected on the branches of an overhanging alder tree. They were not that far out, so all I had to do was drop the bait in and follow it down with the current until it passed through them. Being so close to the salmon you could see every movement. After three or four passes with the bait, one of the smaller fish just moved to one side and intercepted it. I was more or less standing over the top of the salmon, but a downstream sweep of the rod set the hook. Upon feeling the hook the salmon just shook its head, and then twisted from side to side before running upstream at great speed. The commotion disturbed the other fish, and they just disappeared. After landing the hooked fish, I looked for the bigger salmon but he never returned to his lie and I never saw him again. Most of the salmon which I have caught since that holiday have been caught on the fly and have come from searching the water; in other words I could not see the fish before I caught them. And yet on that holiday, apart from the fish which Cathy caught, I saw every salmon which took the bait. It was unique.

I could not have had a better introduction to Ireland. A modest, understated little river, flowing through a heavily wooded valley with the Caha Mountains as a backdrop beyond. It was idyllic. The people were friendly, and there was always good banter in the local pub. For that first visit I concentrated on the Glengarriff River. I didn't fish the mountain lakes or the lough in the Healy Pass which had been recommended to me on one of our visits to the local pub. Whilst touring Kerry I saw Lough Currane which I fished on a later trip. As

Mark Powell on Currane, one of the first loughs I fished in Ireland

well as Currane I also saw the River Laune, and the Caragh system. A few years later I would fish the Laune with a banker from Kilorglin. We enjoyed some fabulous sessions fishing for sea trout on the tidal stretch, just above the town.

After several holidays in the south of the country we moved further north to Sligo and Donegal and the counties in between. I remember when we camped on the shore of Mulroy Bay in Donegal, and the vast shoal of mullet feeding on bread introduced as waste from a bread factory which was situated on the shore of the bay just outside of Milford. The mullet would come in to feed on the waste bread as it was thrown in at the end of the working day. All one had to do was wade out, and fish just over the edge of the bladderwrack to catch countless mullet. The fishing in Ireland then was raw and hugely untapped. As a consequence if you were flexible with your approach there was always good fishing to be found no matter where you travelled in the country. As a result of that first visit to south-west Cork, I travelled and fished over much of Ireland. And later in 2001 we moved permanently to the country which had captivated the two us for so long, to County Galway and the shores of Lough Corrib. Cathy was right. The fishing was good, and I did like the country. Its moorland, mountain and seascape, and, angler or not, she did catch the first salmon. Looking back, it is so hard to believe that it was all so long ago.

Spring salmon, Carrowmore

10 Tim

We should never make a decision when our minds are clouded by emotion. It interferes with rational thinking and we allow the heart to rule the head. It is said that you do not choose your friends, they choose you. If you are a keen angler you will spend many hours in pursuit of your passion, and if you like company, you will choose your friends wisely. As a boat-fisher I have spent many happy hours within the confines of a boat, sharing that limited space with some of my best friends. Dogs have also shared that space. They are great companions especially if you are fishing alone. Over an eleven year period between 1996 and 2007 one dog in particular was a constant companion. He has featured in many of my photographs and was always at my side and never let me down. His name was Tim.

This story begins with an advert in the classifieds section of what was at the time my local paper, the *Oxford Times*. It was early December 1995, and I was musing through the pages of the local paper. I had scanned the usual topics, the local news, the property section, sport and the local fishing report, none of which registered a note of strong interest. Life in our area of Oxfordshire seemed to be quite normal, everyone appeared to be winding down, preparing for Christmas. The kitchen was warm and cosy, Cathy was baking, the boys (Jonathan and Duncan) were playing and with the range plying heat to my back I read through the classifieds section. My reverie of non-committal perusal was broken when a small advert suddenly struck me, SPRINGER SPANIEL PUPPIES FOR SALE.

There was no pre-planned motive to my looking through the classifieds for a dog. In fact scanning the classifieds had become normal practice when reading the local papers. You just never knew what might turn up! Sometimes I found the classifieds more interesting than the main topics. Looking at this advert, something registered a response from me; the time now seemed right for another dog. It had been six months since our last dog, a lovely looking springer bitch had died, and if you are a dog-loving family it feels there is a little something missing if you do not have a dog around the house. I showed the advert to Cathy, who raised her eyebrows, smiled and said 'Go and have a look.' The boys were unaware of what we were discussing; we hadn't mentioned the word puppy and I thought it best not to tell them until I had checked to see if they were still available. A quick phone call revealed that from a litter of nine, two bitches had already been chosen, which left three bitches and four dogs. My tranquil evening was definitely over, as two of the puppies had already been chosen, and it was near Christmas – puppies would be on people's wanted lists. Decision time was approaching fast. I made an appointment to see the litter that evening.

The owners of the litter lived no more than twenty-five minutes from my home, but on a dark December evening, finding the farm house down the end of a rutted track proved to be more difficult than I expected. When at last I arrived, I was shown through to where the puppies were housed in an outbuilding adjacent to the main house. As they were being weaned from the mother, the dam was screened off from her playful brood. I looked at the mother, a compact black-and-white spaniel with a good head. Her offspring, two black-and-white, the rest liver-and-white were at play, and mum seemed unconcerned. The two that had already been chosen were the two B&W bitches, so this made it less confusing when looking over the remaining puppies. I examined the litter for a positive sign, a signal that might suggest that I should choose one over the others. They were in a playful mood, cavorting, fighting and chewing soft toys. Life was good for a young puppy and full of fun. Little did they know that soon they would be scattered to the four winds, and their lives would never be the same. It was a canine crèche of young spaniels, one tumbling over the other in play, and I had to narrow this down if I were going to choose one. There were two well-marked dogs with a lot of brown that were catching my eye, and as I was watching I inadvertently dropped my hand over the screen in to the play zone. A dog mostly white with a patch of brown towards the hind quarter, and a brown head with a narrow blaze, immediately came up to my hand and started pulling on my fingers. On feeling his needle sharp teeth I lifted my hand. I briefly looked at this friendly puppy, remarking 'My, what sharp teeth you have' and then discounted it, and tried to concentrate on the two well-marked dogs.

Young exuberant spaniels never keep still, and all the rough and tumble made it difficult to concentrate on the two dogs. I suggested to the owner that it would help if he could separate these two. As soon as the selected pair were separated, it was easy to make a decision and I left having chosen a springer spaniel puppy with a lot of brown in his make-up.

It was arranged that I would call back a week later to collect my dog, as by then it should have been fully weaned. I returned home with the news that we were to become the owners of a spaniel puppy. The boys were excited and Cathy gave me a hug. After much debate a name was chosen: it was to be Toby. Items were purchased to make our new family member feel at home, as well as the obvious pieces of doggy kit such as a lead, feeding bowls and food. A week soon passed, and when the appointed time arrived I ventured out to collect the dog.

When I walked in to the outbuilding of the farm house, a different scene to that of the previous week lay before me. Where it had been all activity, snarling yips and yelps, little heads and busy tails of the week before, now all that frisky young life and exuberance had gone. There were only two puppies left. The rest of the litter had been collected, and the compound now looked so different. It no longer had that warm friendly feeling and I felt sorry for the two remaining puppies. I dropped my hands in to the enclosure, to attract the pups' attention. And without any sign of hesitation, who should come up to me but the puppy which was mostly white with the brown head. The same little dog which had come so boldly to me the week before, and just like before he began chewing on my fingers. Toby wasn't so confident without his brothers and sisters around, so I walked in gave him a gentle rub and picked him up. As I went to move out of the compound, I bent down and gave the last remaining puppy a rub. He looked so alone now in such a big area. The little dog hung on to fingers, the cuff of my jacket; he did not want to let go. His legs were spread; he had the tenacity of a terrier. I thought, yes you will make someone a nice pet. 'This is a bold little dog' I remarked to the owner, 'When is he going to be collected?' Then came the pull, the little tug on the heart string. 'He isn't going to be collected' said the owner. 'No one had chosen him, it would appear that potential owners do not like all the white.' I was holding Toby with my right hand, and the other little dog was all the time pulling on my left hand while I was talking to the owner. As it was now close to Christmas and the New Year, the owner said they would advertise the puppy and try to move him on after the festive period. Now I felt sympathy for the little puppy. No one wanted him and I knelt down to give him a final rub before leaving. As I knelt down the puppy was all over me, he ran up my thigh on to my lap, pulling at my jacket and sweater, and rolling over at the same time. 'This little dog is sending a message,' I remarked, and the owner, who was quick to see it and most probably did not want to be stuck with the puppy over Christmas, said 'You can have him for half price.'

When I arrived home Jonathan and Duncan were looking out of the kitchen window, and as soon as I pulled on to the gravel drive they rushed to the front door to hasten my arrival. Two very excited boys watched me walk in to the hallway with a box clutched under my arm, and they then followed me to the kitchen. I opened the box and took out Toby, to lots of 'oohs' and 'aahs'. The two boys and Cathy were all making a big fuss over the new member of our family. Seeing that Toby was the centre of attention, I left the kitchen to close the car door. Jonathan and Duncan were very excited; they were all over Toby when I walked back in to the kitchen. As I walked in Cathy looked up, the expression on her face was priceless. 'Dennis!' On the palm of my hand was the little puppy I could not leave behind. After explaining my little story, there were no objections. It only meant doubling up on the items we had already purchased for Toby, and twice the carnage that young puppies leave behind them. We now had two dogs. Tim had now come in to our lives.

As a hunting dog Tim was about par; I have had a number of dogs which have easily outclassed him in this respect. His one real claim to some form of hunting prowess came on a January day whilst out shooting with Vaughan Lewis. We were hunting some rough ground adjacent to the River Windrush. The river was swollen from recent heavy rain and as we came to a high bank, Tim flushed a cock pheasant from a patch of briars. Vaughan shot the pheasant, but unfortunately the bird pitched in to the opposite bank. Tim looked at me, and then without hesitation leapt from the high bank in to the swollen river and retrieved Vaughan's bird. Vaughan, who was at that time a strong terrier man and never short of a word, was lost in admiration. Then came the words, a little choked in a hushed tone of respect that I will never let Vaughan forget: 'A terrier would never do that.' It was Tim's moment in the hunting field, but then I knew, he would never be king of the rat pile.

Tim got caught up in a number of escapades including walking in to the back of a Securicor van, which came on a daily basis to collect parcels from our factory premises in Burford. The driver would normally have a tea break when he called on Wychwood, as it was his last pick-up before going back to the depot to unload. Tim loved cars or any motorised vehicle. It was a warm day and the back doors of the van were open with just a few parcels on the bed of the van. Tim walked in, settled down behind the parcels, and fell asleep. I was busy with work and unaware that the dog had gone missing until Dave the delivery van driver rang, and said he was at the depot and that Tim was in the back of the van without a delivery tag!

But his greatest adventure, a unique event in Tim's life, one which most certainly few spaniels could lay claim to have experienced, came whilst out walking around the local gravel pits near to Standlake, Oxfordshire, my home village for twenty years. The walk around the local lakes was a favourite romp for Tim, and one area that he liked in particular was where a large bed of Norfolk Reed grew along the margin of one of the flooded pits. Every time we came to this bed of reeds, Tim would leap with gusto into the reeds and thrash through them. One could follow his progress through the reed beds, as the seed heads swayed to the weight of his forward movement. On the evening of Tim's escapade, the sun had already gone down and the wind had died, as dusk was falling. He leapt in to the reeds as usual, and moorhens scattered and sedge warblers chirred their displeasure. Halfway through the reed bed his forward motion suddenly stopped, a moment of hesitation and his movement changed direction. He charged back along the same way he had gone in. He exited the reed bed like a thunderbolt, and ran in under my legs looking sheepishly back at the reeds. I was just about to burst out laughing, when the reeds suddenly started swaying, and swaying quite violently where Tim had come to an abrupt stop. Whatever was the cause of this movement was coming our way and quite fast. Suddenly a head appeared at the edge of the reed bed, and I was taken completely by surprise. It was a head which I recognised, but I could not accept what I was seeing, because it was an animal that did not exist in the wilds of Oxfordshire or in the wilds of Britain for that matter. I do not know who was the most shocked, the creature in the reeds, Tim or me. And when this animal turned and leapt in to the lake with an almighty splash, I do not who was the most relieved – Tim or me? When it resurfaced about 100 yards offshore, the head was unmistakable. It then dived and we never saw the creature again. I knew what I had seen, but the experience seemed surreal, and hard to accept. As soon as we arrived home, I looked our exotic friend up in a reference book. It was an animal I had seen with the boys only a few weeks previously at a zoo. On looking it up, there it was, unmistakably: capybara, the largest rodent in the world.

Our rodent friend had escaped from a local university farm, but the escape had been kept quiet, and no one knew of it until Tim's experience in the reed bed. Roy Westwood who was then editor of *Stillwater Trout Angler* and the *Angler's Mail* found the story interesting, and published the account in the *Mail*. We then had enquiries from the BBC and ITN wishing to know if we would go on a local news broadcast, but I declined – Tim wasn't up to it!

From the moment he came into our lives Tim was a constant companion, rarely leaving my side. It was inevitable that he would come fishing with me, and this was one discipline where he did excel. He may not have been the greatest shooting dog, but as a companion in a boat he had no equal. From the moment he first took to a boat at the age of eight months, he was a committed soul mate. On his first day, a warm Hebridean day, he followed me into the boat without hesitation. With little wind and no cloud the fishing was slow. It took a few hours for Tim to adjust. He got caught up in my line, was under my feet and generally made a nuisance of himself, but given enough time he settled down. With little happening in the way of action, he decided that a sleep in the sun was a good idea. He climbed on to the cuddy of the boat, stretched out and went to sleep. The sun was warm on his back and he was enjoying life. This was bliss until he decided to roll over. He then found out that you cannot do this on the cuddy of a boat without experiencing a shock. As he rolled over, he slipped over the side of the boat. It must have been quite a shock, because this was the one and only time he did this. All future snoozes were close to me, usually on the duck boards at my feet.

Tim spent eleven seasons with me in boats and in all that time he never cost me a fish. We had a few near misses but never was a fish lost to my rod through any fault of his. The only trout that did break free where my dog was the cause for its loss, was to my friend, John Donlon. We were on Lough Mask in the mayfly, and John hooked a lovely trout in an area which held good fish. The

A spring salmon is attracting Tim's attention

trout sounded and with his rod well bent, all seemed to be going fine. Upon seeing John into a fish, Tim left my side and moved to where the action was. Unfortunately there was a lot of loose line on the floor of the boat, and as soon as Tim sat beside John to view the proceedings, the fish decided to run. Of course the line came up tight, as Tim was sitting on the loose coils on the boards of the boat. John desperately tried to free the loose line caught under Tim. It was sickening to watch as I could see what was going to happen. Although he managed to feed some line to the fish, it wasn't enough, so John's rod straightened and the trout broke free. John is not one to get flustered or hot under the collar, but he just looked down at the dog and said 'Timmy what have you

126

done?' Tim just sat unaware of his misdemeanour, looking out over the front of the boat wondering where the action had disappeared to.

When after salmon or sea trout Tim was a friend at my side, an observer, seeing and taking in all that was around him, and if the fishing was slow he was an excuse to take a break and go for a walk. But when after brown trout he was a different dog, and the observer now became game finder. He knew what those little rings breaking the surface of the water meant, and on the good days, the busy days when the action would just keep coming, he would never sleep. He would sit on the middle thwart looking forward for the next rise, the next piece of action, and if the action slowed I would get the quizzical expression, a look that suggested 'Come on master you are getting sloppy!'

They say that dogs have poor eyesight. How poor this is I do not know. What I do know is that my dog would look at a rise even when it was a good distance off. Now whether he could hear that rise and pinpoint it accurately or whether he could also see it I do not know. But if a trout rose, Tim would look to where the fish had risen. There was no question of a mistake! He always looked to the position where the rise had occurred. A dog's senses are so much more finely tuned than ours, and we should always trust those senses. Dogs depend on sight, sound and scent much more than we do. We have lost that edge, as these are factors which are no longer so essential for us to survive.

In the fading light of late evening just as darkness closes in, a key time for a big fish, my eyes become less effective and I depend more on my sense of hearing to mark a rising trout. Nine times out of ten, you will hear them before you see them. At night when you hear that distinctive sound of a trout taking in a fly from the surface film, you look to the area where you believe the sound had come from. Our eyes are not so effective at night, and our sense of pinpointing a position from sound alone is not so highly tuned either, and as a consequence we do not always guess right with our choice of direction. Sometimes it may take two or three or more rises before we can locate a rising trout in the gloom, and this can be valuable time lost especially if the trout is moving away from us. A dog's senses have not been eroded in the same way as ours, and Tim's sense of hearing and of pinpointing the whereabouts of the sound was far more acute than a human's. At night, Tim's eyesight was probably no better than mine, but his sense of hearing proved to be invaluable, his ears became my eyes. I learnt to trust my dog; if I heard a trout rise and couldn't see the position, I looked to him for information. The direction of his gaze would tell me where to look. Upon straining my eyes to the limit and scanning the water over the area where my dog was looking, I would, more often than not, see the tell-tale sign of a rise. If I couldn't see a rise I trusted him enough to keep scanning that same area, and if no other rise was forthcoming I would fish blind. He proved to be right time and time again, and I caught fish that I knew I would never have caught without him. It could be said that Tim had become an indispensable part of the team, a night aid.

When I moved to Ireland we explored much of the vast expanse of Lough Corrib together. Some areas I now know intimately, others not so well, but there isn't much of Lough Corrib or its surrounding environs that we haven't visited at some time or another. If out for a long session, I would always take time out and go ashore to give Tim a break. It was an excuse for me to stretch my legs also, and we would explore different areas of shoreline together. This way I discovered much about the surrounding environs, particularly the birdlife and the flora. There is so much to see and take in. And with my dog at certain times of the year, especially during the spring, the most enchanting season of all, I will go to a particular area of the lough just to see a particular plant in bloom or a species of bird on its breeding site. Around the shoreline and islands of Lough Corrib there is so much to marvel at. It is there for all to see if we look for it, nature's garden at her most wonderful, wild, and beautiful.

He was always a constant shadow, so where I went he followed. This was never a problem, but it did cause me some anxious moments one evening. We had been fishing out of the back of Inishmicatreer. With a strong south-east wind blowing we had plenty of shelter. However the wind was strengthening all the time as the evening wore on and it was blowing a gale when I came off the lough in near darkness. For those who know the area, you will know of the bunny-hole, under the causeway which connects the island to the mainland, and if you know it well you will also be aware of the effect of a gale force south or south-east wind on the south side of that particular stretch of water. It blows straight onto the opening of the bunny-hole and straight across the rocky shallow inlet you have to negotiate to gain open water. Also as you clear the opening one has to kick the boat to the left, eastwards to avoid a large rock just outside the opening. As I came into the bunny-hole I could make very little headway against the wind blowing through it. I did not have sufficient momentum to push on and clear it. So I left the engine running in neutral, jumped out of the boat and pushed the boat through and clear of the rock. Once I had the boat clear and on the right line, I jumped in again and motored out. The wind was pushing hard onto the side of the boat, and negotiating the rocky inlet in near darkness in that wind was no easy matter. Once clear of this hazard, it would just be six or seven minutes of driving into a slappy wave which would spray one with water as the bow of the boat cut through the wall of the wave, before I would reach the home mooring.

As the bow of the boat grounded on the gravel of the home mooring, I was relieved to be out of the turmoil. It felt as if we were in a different world in the lee of the wind under the shelter of the slope and the trees, I jumped out of the boat and without thinking said 'Come on Tim.' And then it dawned the dog wasn't with me! Suddenly I realised that he must have followed me when I jumped out of the boat, and with my attention focused on manoeuvring the boat I hadn't noticed that he was out there with me before I jumped back in again and motored off. It would have been easier to have driven round by car, but that would have taken too long. In that time Tim could have easily risked trying to swim against the sea which was running. There was nothing for it, I couldn't leave him. I would have to go back. The boat surfed the swell which was running, and we flew back. Then I had to negotiate that rocky inlet again, and all I could hear was the roar of the wind and the sound of water breaking on the rocks. The water isn't deep in that inlet. I could easily have waded ashore if the boat had become grounded but in the gale and the dark it would have been difficult to have pulled the boat off. As I cleared the inlet I could just make out the sound of barking above the roar of the wind. Tim was standing on a small point and as soon as he saw me he began barking for all he was worth. I couldn't take the boat in so I called out and he swam out to me. As soon as he came within reach I grasped him by the scruff of the neck and hauled him into the boat. Reunited he gave himself a good shake, spraying me in the process, as if I wasn't wet enough already. His tail never stopped wagging as I ran the gauntlet one final time and journeyed home.

Tim enjoyed the walks, but he loved the fishing too, especially when the trout were coming regularly to the boat and the more a fish splashed or jumped, the more animated Tim would become. But once the trout had been landed, he lost interest. If I brought a fish to hand, he would follow the fish right in. Sometimes he would lean over the gunwale of the boat to get a closer look, and I would raise the fish for him to give it a lick before I released the trout. As soon as the fish had disappeared, he was back on the thwart looking for the next one, and if I brought the fish in to the boat he would look at it as if to say 'I have seen plenty of those,' before taking up his adopted position on the thwart. I think it would be fair to say that Tim has probably seen more wild brown trout over 5lbs than most dogs living today. But my dog's interest didn't only centre on big fish. Like all true angling sportsmen, it was for him about simply being

Tim witnessed many of these beautiful creatures. A Lough Corrib brown

there. If fish were coming to the boat that only added to the pleasure of being there, and not only would he become animated when a trout jumped or splashed, he would also become vocal. He was not only a distinctive landmark in a boat if you could see him. Fishing friends who knew of Tim's vocal trait would say that they knew when I was out even if they could not see the boat. They would comment that they knew if I was catching, and that they could tell by vocal length and the volume of my dog's bark how big the fish were. The intensity of the barking did seem to increase if the fish were bigger and they created more commotion in the water. Fortunately it was only a handful of anglers who made the connection with the barking.

The eleven seasons that Tim spent with me in a boat, spanned a period filled with some superb fly fishing, especially for wild brown trout. A period of exceptional quality, and one filled with never to be repeated days of sport. The fire that fuelled the drive and ambition that motivated me so strongly then, perhaps doesn't now burn so brightly. But I still love to fish, though I've just become more selective about the days I choose to go out. And yet when I look back over that time, some of the conditions that I went out in were nothing short of atrocious. Some of the days produced good fishing, especially if the weather turned for the better, but there were also days when I was beaten off by the conditions. Good settled weather conditions, and good fishing go together, especially when we are hunting a fish that responds to a hatch of fly. We had so many good days fishing together, my dog and I, that it is difficult to select one above the others. To me the best days were those when I caught a bag of bigger than average fish. The big days, days of plenty did not quite have the same meaning. The days when fish came freely to the boat still provided a lot of pleasure, but they did not quite match the days when I caught a good fish, or a smaller catch of better trout. It is a value which is difficult to define, but it is similar to the value I put on wild brown trout over stocked fish. To me the wild fish will always have that edge, even though the stocked fish can provide a lot of fun.

I would put Lough Corrib at the top of my league of wild brown trout fisheries. It is such a huge expanse of water, and one which provides such a variety of different areas to hunt. There are so many fly-rich shallows, close in and well offshore. Small intimate bays with a silty bottom, or much larger bays with a marl bottom all provide food-rich areas for the trout to grow large. Countless islands provide shelter, and even in the worst of conditions the lee of these islands produce a micro climate for adult fly and angler alike. It is an anglers' paradise, particularly for one who enjoys imitative fishing to rising trout. If I had to single out a particular day with Tim as being the most memorable, it would have to be a day on Lough Corrib. And if I were to choose Lough Corrib as the venue, it would only be fitting that I pick the day I caught my biggest fish, even though I know there was a large element of luck involved in the capture of that fish.

Although we do not care to admit it, there is always an element of luck involved when fishing. More perhaps than any other sport, we can reduce the amount of luck by what we do as anglers but you cannot totally isolate it. I know anglers who have had bad experiences with the weather; it doesn't matter how good they are with the rod and line if the conditions conspire against them. There are those who go to meticulous lengths to choose a period at the height of a hatch of fly, such as the duckfly, olives or mayfly. And yet when they arrive at their destination, they find that the hatch has been early or will be late because of unseasonal weather conditions. We need that little extra other than being able to cast a line, and being able to present a fly to a fish. And the same applies to catching bigger than average fish. We need that extra little bit of luck at certain times. We can shorten the odds by choosing areas that hold big fish, or where big fish go to feed, and we can fish these areas at key times such as when we expect a hatch of fly. But even when you have done your field work and chosen correctly, you still require fish to be present, fish which are willing to accept a fly. The day I caught my big fish, I didn't choose an area that held a concentration of better than average trout, or an area where the bigger fish go to feed. I chose an area which trout were moving in to, prior to spawning. Fishing such areas produces a mix of sizes, so my fish could just as easily have been 1lb, as 10lbs.

It was a day in the third week of August 2002. Cathy and the boys were in England visiting friends. The weather had been lovely, settled and warm with a west to south-west wind. This day was a repeat of the previous few days, and although arguably conditions were not ideal for fishing as it was a little too warm, it was such a lovely day I decided to go out on the lough. I put together some food for a break, and loaded the gear in to the car. There was no need to whistle up Tim, as he had already seen the rods being loaded, and was already sitting in the car. We drove down to the mooring, unloaded all the impedimenta one requires for a day afloat, and I tackled up. My last few trips had all been on the upper area of the lough, and I had been catching a few sizeable fish on dry mayfly patterns. The trout I were catching, were not as consistent in size as the trout from lower down the lough. But from the area I was fishing in a catch of four or five fish, one good one would show up. A few days previous I had taken a trout over 6lbs from the same location at the north end of Corrib. The trout I felt were beginning to move into this area prior to spawning. A short but substantial river, which it is known to hold big fish, flows into a bay on this side of the lough. And it was the pull of this river, which I felt was attracting the bigger fish to the area I had chosen to fish.

I tackled up with a Ginger Mayfly on the point, and a Claret Bits and an Orange Bits on the two droppers. Fuel tank connected, and all the gear stowed away on the boat, we pushed out from the mooring and headed northwards. Six or seven minutes of motoring took me across the mouth of a long narrow bay, and through a shallow channel which led to the opening under the cause-way which connected an island with the mainland. Once clear of the causeway, we pushed on northwards for another fifteen minutes. Thankfully the wind was light to moderate in strength, as a big wave can build in this area with a wind from a westerly direction. With fleecy white cumulus cloud overhead, and a warm wind on the side of my face it was good to be out on the water as I headed the boat towards Ben Levy, the distinctive mountain which stands out at the north end of the lough. It isn't particularly high (416 metres) but it is a substantial lump, one of royal stature which is obvious to all who set sail on this part of Lough Corrib. It is a landmark which stands out coveting the lough and all that is below it, the king who sits at the head of the table.

In an area just north of an island, I cut the engine close to two markers that mark one of the boat channels in to the bay. I would be drifting over some shallows, and then out over deeper water. Ahead of me about a mile distant, stood another marker, a distinctive white beacon. I would be making long drifts in this area, along different lines and I wasn't expecting the sport to be too hectic. But this is an area which can throw up the odd good fish, and my recent results gave me some encouragement. With this positive thought in mind I let the boat go with the wind. I would not be working to features or in confined areas. So I could relax and fish the water before the boat, and as the day was fine I was happy to just let the boat go. If a trout should rise within casting range I would cover it, otherwise I would just fish the water blind. I had seen a good mix of fly, mayflies, sedges, a few olives and buzzer, but there was no heavy hatch of any one species, certainly not enough to bring a rise on. Although there didn't appear to be sufficient fly around, and it was August, one of the toughest months on the western loughs, I still felt confident of a fish or two. The day felt just too good for it not to happen.

Tim took up his position on the thwart adjacent to me, looking out expectantly over the open water forward of the boat. The first drift brought no response from the fish, and took the best part of an hour to fish out. I began a different line out from the two markers, and early in this drift a fish came to the top dropper, the Orange Bits. A trout of about 1½ lbs came blind, and took with a confident rise. The strike was easy to time and I played the trout out to the side of the boat, where after a quick admiring glance I released him. Things were looking up – we now had a fish to the boat. Soon after this another came, with a quick splashy rise to the same fly, but I missed him. The nature of the take suggested he was a spooked fish. Something had alarmed the trout in the final moment of the take, perhaps a movement in the boat from either Tim or me, or perhaps the fish had seen the leader. Whatever the reason it was an abortive rise. The rest of the drift was uneventful. The open water beyond the shallows wasn't producing. I tried a different line which covered the edge of the shallows, and this time I didn't allow the boat to drift quite so far out over the open water. However this line was unproductive also. We had been out for nearly three hours, and it felt like a good time to take a break.

In August, the islands and the shoreline around the lough no longer resonate to the sound of birdsong. Whimbrel and the dense flocks of golden plover no longer fill the sky. The gulls who time their return to the lough and their breeding season to coincide with the huge hatches of springtime flies, have now because of the reduced fly hatches left the water for a more bountiful food supply, off the land. Arctic terns still dive and swoop low over the waves, but they are more dependent on the water than the gulls. Fritillary and red admirals now replace the earlier butterflies. They feed on fruit and late flowering plants. Along the marginal edge, purple loosestrife and Himalayan balsam add some late colour, but the woodland canopy is now too dense for the flowering plants that grow on the woodland floor. However, there are other treasures if we look. This is the season for the fungi and fruits. Chanterelle mushrooms, a prize fungus grow under the birch and hazels, whilst hazel nuts and blackberries are ripening among the hedgerows in abundance. If we have an interest in nature, we can always find something of interest along the lough shore, and on this day, a really fine August day, we take extra time out for a second brew of the Kelly Kettle. I'm in no rush.

Back on the water I decided to try a drift from a marker west of the island, and then down along the shore of the island and out over the open water towards the white beacon. Close to the shallow by the first marker, a small fish about ¾ lb took the Claret Bits. It produce some excitement for Tim, as the fish made quite a commotion in the water, but we soon had the trout to the side of the boat and released it. Towards the end of the island another fish came to my Ginger Mayfly on the point. Again the rise came without warning; it took on the blind. A better fish, this one puts in a good bend in the rod and gave a good account of itself before I drew it to the side. A beautiful hen trout of around 2¾lbs, well marked with a striking tail. The light was good and I was almost tempted to take a photograph of the fish, but thought better of it and released the trout none the worse for its experience. That fish made the day and although sport wasn't hectic, the day had still been very enjoyable.

The wind had eased slightly, and the wave had now fallen to a light ripple. We made slow progress down the open water, but well down the drift over deep water, I came onto a pod of three or four trout feeding on small midges. They were behaving almost like daphnia-feeding trout, continually moving at the surface taking in the small flies. I needed to work the oars to pull the boat over to where I could ambush this group of trout. Trout that are feeding together like this are usually confident takers, and once in position I took one of the fish on the Claret Bits. It was a nice looking brown of about 1½ lbs, and as fat as butter. The drift had produced three trout, and I thought that perhaps sport was on the up, but after this we hit the doldrums and apart from one other abortive rise, there was no further action.

It was just after six when I decided to try a drift from the original mark, where we began in the morning. The cloud was breaking, and the evening light was getting brighter. Conditions now were less favourable and I felt that our fishing day was coming to a close, as we hadn't seen or moved a fish for some time. We passed the shallows and were out over the deeper water. In the light ripple I could spot a fish if it rose quite some distance away, but there were no signs of trout moving near the surface. It is funny how sometimes one can have an inner feeling that one is going to catch a fish, even in August, and earlier I had felt confident of a fish, even though this was the dog month of the season. Now that feeling was waning; I didn't believe there was another fish in the day, and thoughts of retiring were creeping in. Sometimes I will make a decision to go without any deliberation, when I can see I'm wasting my time, and some-times depending on how keen I'm feeling, it can take a while to let go. Cathy and the boys were away, and the urge to return home was not quite so strong. I continued with the fishing, even though my confidence was waning, my mind was wandering, when out of the corner of my eye, just on the edge of my vision, an apparition of a large back and dorsal fin caught my attention. It may have been on the periphery of my sight but I knew what I had seen. The fish moved on the right side of the boat, about twenty yards out and was going right to left. I knew from the forward motion of the roll, the direction which the fish was travelling. It was the lazy porpoise-like roll of a big fish, and I thought it was a salmon. I have taken salmon before on dry fly, particularly in nice weather. So without hesitation I lifted off and covered the fish. The fly fell about two yards ahead of where the back had gone down, where it sat on the water for a moment and disappeared. It wasn't the rise of a big fish; there was no sign of a big neb or a great whorl in the water, the fly just simply disappeared, but I knew it was the fish I had seen roll.

When I lifted, everything went tight. There was a brief hesitation and then the fish ran. It took me just to the backing and then went down, the line was strumming through the water and there was a feeling of great weight. The fight was never hectic, just dogged, and the fish stayed well down in the water for ten minutes or more. This battle rumbled on for some time, and I still hadn't seen what was attached to my line. I was still thinking it was a salmon, when slowly my fish lifted in the water. Tim was looking in the water just as I was, as the fish came up to the strain of the rod and made a pass in front of the boat. Until then my adversary had remained out of sight and was a salmon. Until this moment in the fight, I never was too excited or anxious, but my mood changed when the fish came in to view, and the reality dawned. It was a brown, and it was easily the biggest brown I had ever hooked on Lough Corrib.

Suddenly the fish had taken on a different meaning, and I wanted him badly. Tim also sensed this new-found exhilaration, and joined in my duel with a chorus of vocal harmonies, as he could now see something tangible at the end of my line. It is impossible to put in to words how I felt in those anxious minutes before the trout was landed. My mind was filled with a cocktail of emotions. I resented the fish for not coming in quickly. He resisted the pressure for some time, and all I know is I wanted him, I wanted him landed and he wouldn't give in as quickly as I would have liked. I tried to remain positive and not think negative thoughts, but I was anxious. And yet although I may have been anxious, I never changed my way of playing the fish. There was never a moment during that fight that I ceased the constant pressure I put on the rod. I have seen so many trout lost by friends who were afraid to put pressure on a fish during key times of the fight. In a prolonged fight the hook hold can loosen, and if any slack is given to the fish, they have an opportunity to shake free of the hook as the hook just simply drops away from its hold in the jaw. I couldn't say that the fight was enjoyable; certainly as soon as I knew that the fish was a brown, the fight verged on insufferable and yet I was also inebriated with an overwhelming feeling of bliss. Relief only came when the trout slid over the rim of the net. The elation when I lifted the folds in the mesh of the net around the trout, was as great as it could possibly be. I remember dropping the rod, and then grabbing the mesh and supporting the weight with my left hand as well as lifting the net head with my right hand, and hoisting the brown in to the boat. The brown lay on the boards of the boat, and as I parted the mesh I was overcome with joy. I had no human companion to share the moment with. Tim was sitting there on the middle thwart looking unabashed, and I just grabbed him and gave him a big hug, but I know he would have preferred chocolate.

The fish looked big. It was twenty-eight inches long, and I knew it was over 10lbs, it should have weighed more but it weighed 10lb 6ozs. It was an old fish that was just starting to diminish in condition, but I didn't mind its slightly aged

Sunset on Lough Corrib. A good time for a big fish and Tim shared many such moments with me

appearance, as it was my biggest brown from an Irish lough. It is hard to believe that such fish will rise to a fly, but there in the side of its jaw was the Ginger Mayfly that had been responsible for the brown's downfall. I'm certain this fish wasn't feeding, but had just come up for a swim around. Big brownies sometimes do this in nice weather, perhaps they like the sun on their backs. And yet even if that fish wasn't feeding he still took my fly. It is a big fly and when it landed in his window of vision, I feel it was too good an opportunity for him to pass up. This was his downfall. That fish now adorns my study wall, a reminder of that day and a time spent with Tim.

138

Back at the house I was too excited to relax, the adrenaline was still flowing. I felt a need to tell someone about my fish, so I first rang Cathy and the boys to tell them the news and then Vaughan. My mind was racing as I put the phone down. Due to the heady infusion of success I was still running on a high, and couldn't settle. For me the thought of catching a wild brown over 10lbs had remained a dream for so long, I began to think it was a goal which was unattainable. I went to the window and looked out over the lough, where the sun was low in the western sky. It would be about another fifteen to twenty minutes before it would disappear behind the mountains. The wind had dropped and the evening was still pleasantly warm. I selected a bottle of wine, picked up a glass and walked out through the French doors. Tim followed. We walked down the track to the lough shore, and there I sat on a large rock positioned to one side of the mooring, and watched the sun go down behind the mountain of Ben Levy. The mountains in the west were now silhouettes, but Ben Levy dominated the horizon. All the colours of the evening sky were reflected in the calm surface of the lough, and I was in a reflective mood as the great orb sank lower in the sky. I thought of how I had shared the moment with those that meant most to me, and how there was nowhere else in the world I would have rather been at that time, than sitting beside the lough which had given me so much.

On a fine day in late August 2008, I was relaxing in my armchair stroking Tim's forehead. He loved contact, and his eyes closed to the touch of my hand. He was well over twelve years old, his body was failing, but the head still looked good. Racked by arthritis, the ravages of time had taken their toll; his hind leg muscles were wasting away, and his body was that of an old dog. Due to the arthritis he hadn't been in a boat with me for twelve months. Looking at him on that late August day and the way he was losing condition, I felt a sudden compulsion to grab my camera and to take a photograph of Tim. Together we walked down the track towards the lough, as we had done so many times before. Once at the mooring, I stepped into the boat, but Tim couldn't follow so I had to lift him in. I placed him on the centre duck board, and took some photographs of him. As I took the photographs I took a broader look at his face, to see the old spark was missing. The purpose of being in the boat no longer meant anything to him; his gaze was expressionless, the meaning of the boat had gone.

I knew he would never sit in my boat again. When I think back over all those years we had spent in a boat together, he hadn't ever let me down. A constant companion, Tim was not only there to share in my failures, but he was there with me to share the moment of my biggest fish from Corrib, and all those other moments of triumph with me as well. I'm glad that that little dog, mostly white with a brown head, grabbed my finger and asked to be picked, and I'm glad that I made a decision ruled by emotion and not the head.

Tim at the age of 12 years. His body may have been fading but the head was still good

Comment – Vaughan Lewis about Tim

A soft wind nipped the water, ruffling the surface of the bay into a series of gentle peaks and troughs. Under the sintered sky, our boat made slug-like progress. Ahead of us, Dennis and his boat partner....and of course Tim. The plump gloss of his coat apparent as he stood in his usual spot. Front feet firmly planted on the gunwale, with his rear perched on the middle seat, he scanned the water in front. The Colonel: Master and captain.

For the third or fourth time that day, Dennis' rod bent to the insistent pull of a trout. And as it did, Tim tuned up. His howling bark had greeted each and every fish played in his boat for years. And across the still acres of Lough Corrib, the hounds of hell themselves could not have created more noise. A bend forward from Dennis and a glittering splash of spray in front of the boat indicated another successful release. The Colonel's bark subsided.

Time passed. A third boat entered the bay and set up a drift to our right. Two more fish from Dennis' boat were marked in style by Tim, inevitably drawing the newcomers closer. Despite their close attention, they were unsuccessful. A quick spin of the outboard slipped them across the bay to a new drift. The reward for their impatience was the opportunity to enjoy two bravura perform-ances from Tim as more fish were guided to the boat and released. The third one was just too much for them; from across the water, a plaintive cry 'Jaysus, t' fella wit' the spaniel's got another .....'

11 Fingers

We were standing looking out over the bay; the expression on our faces must have looked a bit like children in a Charles Dickens novel with no money in their pockets, looking through the window of a sweet shop. What we saw and desired we could not have. Unlike in a novel there was no benevolent aunt or long lost uncle, a kindly soul to come along and give money to satisfy our craving. The epicentre of our desire required more than a shilling across the palm of our hand. What we needed and desired most was a boat, a boat which was light in weight, one which we could carry to the bay which was now cut off from the main lough. This would give us access to an area of the bay that was lightly fished, and the area around the bay was steeped in history of big fish. 'I know a man!' said Larry.

'Aye, aye I'll sort you out a boat,' said the voice on the other end of the phone line. 'Problem solved,' said Larry as he put the phone down. And we waited, and we waited. Thoughts of the bay drifted to the back of our minds. The buzzer hatch passed, the olives came and went, the mayfly had finished and the sedges were almost over when Larry received the call: 'I have that boat if you're interested.' It was late July. We hadn't seen the craft, but my friend Larry, who is a bit of an Arthur Daly, first enquired 'How much?' There was a pause on the other end of the line. 'One hundred pounds,' was the reply. Larry looked at me and winked 'Done,' he said. 'Oh no,' I thought.

Laurence Barkey the man responsible for the call, and good friend of Larry's had located a boat in deepest Armagh, and he was dealing with a local farmer who owned the boat. Once the deal was done, Laurence arranged to bring the boat down at the weekend, and before he rang off he said 'Oh, there is a trailer as well.' 'Even better!' said Larry. When Laurence arrived with the boat, Larry called me over to have a look. The two Ls were deep in conversation when I arrived at the yard. Two of Laurence's fingers were well bandaged, and this was the topic of their conversation. Larry was laughing, as Laurence retold the saga of what had happened to his hand. It transpired that when Laurence called on the farmer to lift the boat and tow it down to Co. Galway, they found the boat was locked to an old chain. The farmer had lost the key, so he fetched an angle grinder to cut the chain. It must have been a bit like a scene out of the *Texas Chainsaw Massacre*, the farmer coming out with the angle grinder, and then while trying to cut the chain slipping with the grinder cutting two fingers of Laurence's hand to the bone. Apparently there was blood everywhere. Laurence was lucky. He had to have stitches and a tetanus injection, but it could have been far worse – he could have lost his fingers. However if Laurence was looking for sympathy, he wasn't going to find it from Larry, who when he heard the story, burst into laughter. Larry isn't only an Arthur Daly, he is also, like many of his fellow countrymen, quick witted. He punched the air, his face beaming 'We have a name for the boat,' he said. My friend was in good humour. He looked over towards me with a question: 'Well, and what do you think of *Fingers*?' Larry's words were running around inside my head, pulses were racing through my brain, looking for a synapse to bridge a positive thought as a reply. I was searching, but I couldn't find a positive comment that I could make with any sincerity. It was difficult to keep a straight face. I was looking at something which looked like it had come straight out of Steptoe's yard. It was about ten feet long, and quite wide in the beam. Paint was flaking off the inside and the outside of the hull, revealing a number of areas which had already been repaired. 'Will it float?' I asked, as I had severe reservations observing several holes in the bottom of the hull. 'Nothing that couldn't be patched with a bit of fibreglass and some resin,' said Larry, and as it was almost detached from the hull, 'What about the transom?' I asked. 'A bit of resin and some angle brackets will solve that,' said Larry. 'Oh my God,' I thought.

Larry was keen to try the bay before the season was over, and *Fingers* would allow us to do that. If we found that the fishing was good, he suggested we could find a better boat for the following season. Looking at my friend's face, I knew he wasn't joking. We were committed and there was now no turning back. The repairs were made, and plans prepared for the launch, if you could call it that. We were originally going to carry *Fingers* in over land, but we soon discovered that although the boat was only ten feet long, it weighed an absolute ton. Unless we could collar together a team of donkeys, portage was not going to work, so we had to find another way in. In high water it is possible to take a boat into the bay, but the levels were now well down and impassable to normal lake boats. However, *Fingers* was not a normal lake boat; she was short and wide in the beam with a very shallow draw. It would be thus feasible according to Larry to take the boat in by water. This meant negotiating a sluice weir, and a length of shallow rapids before going through a narrow gut into the bay. I had my doubts but it did sound possible. 'Who is going to take it down to the bay?' I asked. 'I'm driving the car,' said Larry. Larry was going to drive the car back down the access road, park it and walk in to meet me at the bottom of the bay.

He said he would drive around and meet me at the far end of the bay, but before he left he waited to make sure I passed over the weir and down through the rapids without a mishap. If his waiting was for my reassurance, the sentiment was lost on me. So that is how I found myself waving goodbye to my friend as I set sail in *Fingers* on her maiden voyage. We had launched the boat on the main lough, so I then had to row around to the overflow where I would take her over the weir, down the rapids and through the narrow gut, before rowing over a mile to the far end of the bay in a craft that more resembled a coracle than a boat. I just let *Fingers* go with the current, trying to keep the head of the boat as straight as I could. We went over the drop of the weir, and her keel, or what was left of it, grounded as we pitched into the white water. Larry had his hands together as if in prayer, but we came out of the white water unscathed and as he waved I disappeared down the rapids. The boat bobbed down the rapids, and then through the narrow gut without mishap. We were in.

I found negotiating the route in was far easier than the row to the far end of the bay. It was over a mile of arduous exercise to say the least. *Fingers* was not built for slicing through the water or going straight; she was the most difficult craft to push through water, and holding a straight line was next to impossible. She behaved a bit like a coracle, spinning and turning to every stroke of the oars. I found a short shallow stroke was the best for keeping the tub moving in the direction I wanted to go. It took a lot of strokes to cover 100 metres, and by the time I had covered that distance, a lot of water had to be bailed out. The journey seemed to take an eternity. An endless sequence followed of rowing like hell, stopping and bailing out, and then rowing like hell again, but eventually the end came into view. Larry said it was a bit like watching a water skater moving down the bay, as the oars were moving like the legs of the insect and the boat just seemed to be going nowhere. I was relieved when we pulled the cockle shell of a boat up, and berthed her in a narrow inlet for protection. The next time out we would have the rods with us, and hopefully all the effort would be worthwhile.

August isn't the best month on the Western loughs, particularly if you wish to hunt rising fish. However, we had no choice. We wanted to fish the bay, and now we had a boat, far away waters were calling. For this first trip, as the wind was light, Larry took an electric outboard. This is a tough month, and had we been out fishing on any other area of the lough we would not have been too confident, but on this evening, our first session on the bay, we were full of expectancy. The wind, or rather what little wind there was, was blowing from the south-west. With this in mind, we decided to go to the far end of the bay and work our way back. This plan, although good in principle, proved to be flawed. It was over a mile to the opposite end of the bay, and in a boat like *Fingers* with her sleek lines and low friction paint, the journey against the wind took a lot out of the battery. We tried a drift across the top end of the bay, but the fish seemed to be keeping their heads down as we neither moved a trout to our flies nor saw a natural rise. As we had drawn a blank, we thought we would try a different line along the far shore and down onto an island. The engine was fine at first but as we neared the far bank, the boat slowed further, if that was possible. It was now moving at a snail's pace. I looked at Larry, and Larry looked at me, and this time I was quick off the mark! 'I'm not rowing,' I said, and Larry burst out laughing. We were going with the wind, so we decided we would just let the boat go until we found some fish, and then take it turns with the oars. About a quarter of the way down the far shore, the wind died. We were left becalmed, there were no fish rising and the sky was clearing to the west. This was not looking good.

Beyond the island the bay widened, and on the side we were on there was an area that had looked promising. We would move to this area, and stake it out until the sun went down, and then with any luck we would see a few fish moving. It made sense and there was some logic to the plan. The only problem was going to be moving *Fingers*. Larry rowed. We patiently waited, and there was not a breath of wind. As the sun sank lower in the sky, a few sedges and some late mayfly spinners fluttered out over the water, but still nothing stirred. The sun had dropped below the horizon before a fish moved. It appeared to be a small fish but at least it was a rise. It was on Larry's side of the boat, and he covered the fish which took a sedge pattern within moments of the fly falling onto the surface. On tightening, a perch of about 12 oz spluttered to the surface of the water. This was the one and only fish we saw move, and it was the only fish we caught that evening. In near darkness we came off the bay of our desires, skunked. 'It was the conditions!' said Larry.

I was beginning to think we had misnamed the boat, and this conviction became even stronger a few days later. The weather turned and it began to rain, heavily, for several days. Then we had a period of strong wind, and then more rain. The lough began to rise, and we did not make it back to the bay before the end of the season. At the end of the season we take all our boats off from their moorings on the three main loughs here in the west of Ireland, and put them into storage. After lifting our boats, we then decided to pull *Fingers* up to safety and tie her down. It would have been impractical to take *Fingers* off we reasoned, due to the inaccessibility of her mooring. We needn't have worried about this consideration, as upon reaching the mooring, the boat was nowhere to be seen. It was gone, and no trace of the boat was to be found. The chain was still attached to a fence post which was now underwater. We could see the chain but the boat had vanished. This we thought was the end of *Fingers* and of our hope of fishing the bay from a boat the following season....

On a day of gale force wind in May the following year, I went to the bay to fish from the shore with Vaughan. We had a good day, but no big fish. Before we walked out I looked at the inlet where *Fingers* had been moored, to see that the chain which was now just above the water was still there, but there were no signs of the boat. We should have called it *Jonah* I thought as I walked away, and the bay and the boat drifted from my mind....

Until, that is, I received an excited phone call from Larry. It was a wild day in late July, and the wind was too strong to go out on the lough. Larry, who was accompanied by two clients from Andorra, decided to fish the bay from the shore for pike. While his clients were fishing, Larry took time out and ventured down to where *Fingers* had been berthed. The water level was now at summer low, and when Larry scanned the area, he saw a boat under the water. It was covered in mud, but there was no mistaking it. It was *Fingers* alright. He called his clients over, and they pulled the boat ashore. Larry finished his phone call saying there were a number of extra holes in the patched-up hull, but other than this damage she was okay. He didn't say how big the holes were, but a lot more fibreglass and some extra resin later, *Fingers* was deemed seaworthy. It was late in the season, just like the previous year, but once again we had a boat on the bay. There was no holding us back this time.

A week passed after the discovery of the boat, but the weather remained inclement: windy, wet, and totally unsuitable for imitative fishing. To further compound our problems, Larry had clients booked for most of the next week and I was travelling to England to meet up with family and friends for eight days. Time was passing, and soon it would be too late in the season. On my return, Larry was free and the weather had taken a turn for the better. I hadn't been fishing for over two weeks, and I was chomping at the bit to go. It was decided that we would have a crack at the bay the day after my return. The day could not have been a better one. It was warm with high broken cloud and a light to moderate south wind. We were in shirt sleeves as we walked down to the mooring. It was around noon and with the prevailing conditions the day really felt promising.

I don't know if I believe in fate. I do however believe that certain events happen because of key decisions we make. If we analyse these decisions we can usually find a creditable answer – sometimes something may occur which verges on the supernatural – but again if we look for reasons to explain what has happened there is usually a logical answer. Sometimes an event may happen through pure coincidence or even that intangible luck factor, whether good or bad. If we are honest with ourselves we can usually explain why most things happen, and they happen because of decisions we make, good or bad. So when I say that I had a feeling that one of us was going to catch a good fish that day, it wasn't a statement based on some supernatural intuition, nor a statement that was just plucked out of the air. I said it because I felt it, and why I felt it was obvious to me. We were going to fish a bay which held big trout, we knew this for a fact, and the weather was perfect. And fish, just like any animal, or even humans for that matter, respond to the weather.

As we tackled up by the boat I was feeling very confident of fish, and I tied up two of my favourite sedge patterns to the copolymer leader. A Fiery Brown sedge on the point, and a Chocolate Drop on the dropper. There were a few natural flies around, but I never expected to see a hatch of fly of any consequence, and I didn't expect to see moving fish. The trout I thought would come on the blind, and the patterns I had tied up were two good flies for bringing up fish. I looked up at the sky. The light was good, the wind was steady, soft and from the south, and everything about this day felt right. I then made my statement to Larry. I thought that one of us would catch a good fish. He, however, said nothing and merely gave me a quizzical look.

As the electric engine had performed so poorly the last time we were out in *Fingers*, Larry decided to bring a small outboard. This engine, just like the boat, was a bit of a patched up old thing, which we knew by the name of Putt Putt. The outer casing may have been that of an old Evinrude, but that was the only part of this two stroke we could account for. Its pedigree may have been doubtful, made up of cannibalised parts from other broken down old engines, but Putt Putt was reliable. She never let us down, and this was just as well, because *Fingers*, who had been submerged for nine months, now had no oars. They must have floated away when she went down. Going out with no oars was a bit of a risk, but the bay wasn't that big, and there was never a risk of getting into problems with the weather. It would have made life difficult had the engine broken down, but that would just mean that we would have to get out and tow the boat back down the shoreline to the mooring, which in *Fingers* would have been easier than rowing anyway. Rods, bags and food stowed, we were ready to set off on our odyssey.

Unlike in the UK, the seasons in Ireland begin on the first of the months of February, May, August and November. Autumn begins on the first of August, and there is a saying here in the west, that the summer ends with the Galway races. The Galway meeting is one of the main events of the horse racing calendar here in Ireland, and very popular with the punters. This meeting had come and gone, and we were now in the autumn of the year, but the day did not seem to me remotely autumnal. There was vibrancy to the day, a feeling reminiscent of early summer, and yet I knew we would see very little by way of a hatch of fly. The fish, if up and looking, would be more opportunistic, and readily willing to accept any good mouthful that might come their way. It would be a question of searching one out. We made our way to the top of the bay, just as we had done the first time we were out in *Fingers*. On the way up I looked around. The east side of the bay was heavily wooded with outcrops of limestone. Along the shoreline on the west side of the bay, great lumps of limestone deposited by the glaciers when the ice receded over 10,000 years ago, lay scattered on the limestone bedrock. A gentle slope sweeps up to an environment of heath and bog. In the spring sandpipers and ringed plover nest along the shoreline, and further back are snipe, redshank, lapwing and curlew. If one were to walk in, the air could be filled with the emotive call of these wading birds. It is such an evocative sound; whenever I hear them I am lost to visions of wild places. The call of the wading birds and the wild go together.

Midway through our journey Larry noticed a boat moored close to an outcrop of rock in the bay. It was one of several boats belonging to eel fishermen who netted the bay for eels. He may have noticed the other boat, but I couldn't help noticing the sealant between the transom and the hull of *Fingers* was breaking down. Thankfully however, the angle brackets were holding. Larry motored over to the boat and looked in. There was a set of oars lying unlocked on the bottom boards. And Larry being Irish and this being Ireland, he thought that it would not be unreasonable to borrow the oars and return them later in the evening when we were coming off the water. In Ireland I have found that many items are borrowed in this way. It is taken as a token of goodwill that the owner of the said item will not mind. But usually these acts of kindness by the owners of such items are carried out unbeknownst to them. We now had a set of oars. One never knows when a set of oars may come in useful after all!

At the top of the bay we began our first drift. Much of the water we covered was dark and featureless. There were no obvious food-rich shallows. A few scattered beds of *Potamogeton* grew here and there, but the bottom where we could see it appeared to be dark and silty. The lack of weed may be due to the fluctuation in water height of the bay, which can rise and fall after heavy rain. In winter the level can rise as much as nine feet or more. This fluctuation may account for the lack of soft bottom weed in some of the shallower areas. The top end produced no response from the fish, and apart from a pod of three or four trout that were smutting on something small it produced nothing of interest. We tried the smutting fish for about twenty minutes, changing to smaller flies and lighter leaders. But they were tricky, and when we did get a chance to cover them they never made a mistake. Eventually they went down, and it became apparent we were wasting our time in this area. We started to work our way down the bay.

Down behind an island where the bay opened up to its widest point there was an outlet on the east side that dropped through a narrow gut into another much smaller bay. And being the intrepid explorers we were, we decided this small bay was worth a cast or two. With a bit of sharp manoeuvring to avoid rocks and the tangle of nets left by the eel fishermen, we dropped in. Much of the water was shallow. It would only take two or three short drifts. As Larry lined the boat up for the first drift, he took the boat close to the shore, in under a buttress of rock, and cut the engine. We were no more than a few feet from the rock, and the disturbance caused by our arrival woke what had been sleeping on the top of this buttress. Without warning the head of the devil himself appeared over the top of the rock, no more than a few feet from where we were sitting. I looked at the evil apparition and into his eyes, the pupils of which were mere slits, dilated slightly, but the animal never flinched. He then voiced his disapproval, and the head of a rather large billy goat disappeared. I was instantly reminded of Larry's encounter with another goat, on the appropriately named Rams Island.

It had been a tough day, and Larry was not in his usual good humour when he went ashore for lunch on Rams. He sat down to eat his food, and remarked that he could smell a goat. No sooner had he made the remark, and taken a mouthful of his sandwich, when something hit him hard full in the back. Larry was sent sprawling, and he is no small man. He rose in a rage, sandwich sent flying, 'I'll kill the ****ing thing!' he exclaimed. Luckily for the goat Larry did not find it, but he vowed to return to Rams and shoot it. Time has passed and the goat is still there. Seeing the goat on the buttress reminded me of this, and when Larry said 'Look at that ****ing thing, I hate them,' I knew why and rocked back in laughter. It was at this precise moment when I rocked backed that we found out just how unstable *Fingers* was. The side of the boat to which I rocked back, dipped to within an inch of going under the water. Larry shouted 'What the ****ing hell are you doing?' I was staring into the abyss of the disaster that was looming. I immediately reacted by moving in the opposite direction, and fortunately for us the boat came back with my movement. We avoided a dunking, but it was a close thing. Expletives were still being uttered in the stern of the boat, and then all went silent. For a moment we just looked at each other without saying a word, and then spontaneously we both burst into laughter. I was thinking of the goat. Larry was just relieved we hadn't gone overboard.

After the incident with the goat we settled down to the fishing. We were covering water about four to five feet deep. There was no sign of a moving fish to be seen, but if there were trout present they would have no difficulty seeing the flies, we reasoned. As the boat came down onto a small weed bed close to the shore, Larry rose a fish to one of his sedge patterns. It was the first rise of the day, on lifting all went tight and the fish immediately tore off to the right across in front of me and carried on going. My friend chuckled as he always does when he is into a fish, and I pulled in my line and grabbed the net. The line was cutting through the water at a fair lick, and I remarked to Larry that it looked like a good fish the way it was running. Larry was hesitant, as he wasn't so sure, and then all went slack. It had thrown the hook.

This wasn't going to be a day of plenty and that was a bitter pill to swallow. We didn't see the fish, so we had no idea of its size, but from the way it was running with the line it looked a good one. For an angler a fish lost is the hardest part of our sport, and a part that we all have to come to terms with at one time or another. No word of consolation can change what has happened. It is gone. We have to move on. There was no cursing or admonishment from Larry. These things happen and he knew it. He just checked the hook to see that all was fine, and we carried on.

We fished out the small bay but no other trout moved to our flies, so we decided to move out to the main body of water. Just as we were about to leave, we heard the sound of an outboard engine kick in. I looked down the bay, and in the distance a good way off I could see two lads in a boat (just like the one we had taken the oars from) leaving their mooring. It was the eel fishermen. They were coming out to check their nets. In disbelief we stared at the bottom of the boat. 'The oars,' said Larry. 'But you said it would be OK to borrow them' I said. 'I know but the situation has now changed,' he said. I looked back. They were coming towards us fast. We headed for the boat moored by the island from which we had taken the oars, and away from the approaching eel fishermen. *Fingers* was not built for speed. I do not know what she was built for, but it wasn't speed, and nor was Putt Putt. The eel fishermen were gaining on us. A bit like the Terminator they kept closing the gap. This was a mismatch. As we approached the moored boat Larry suggested that I surreptitiously throw the oars into it, and he would keep motoring past it and onto an island on the other side. There we could stop and have a bite to eat, creating the ruse that this had been our intention the entire time. I looked back, fearing that the eel fishermen were now close enough that they would see me throw the oars into their moored boat as we passed. We passed the boat, I threw in the oars, and we drove up to the island....

The two eel fishermen stopped at the boat and looked in. One of the lads scratched his head and made a comment to the other, who also looked in and then shook his head as if in disbelief. Larry and I were unloading the food and preparing a brew, but at the same time we were taking quick glances to see how the situation was working out. The boys gave up looking. Whatever they were searching for they could not find it. They then drove up to the island, and as they passed they slowed down. The chap on the engine stood up and called over, in slow broken English, 'Don't throw litter in the boat.' They had obviously seen me throw something into the boat, but they couldn't figure out what it was. They thought it was litter and that is what they were looking for. Not only did they incorrectly assume that we had thrown litter into the boat, but they had also decided to address us in the ridiculous manner in which people address those whom they believe cannot understand their language! Our pursuers were not the outraged avengers we thought they were. Rather they were just following their normal route across the bay. Once again that day Larry and I stared at one another in disbelief, but the humour was building. He started to smile and the smile broadened. I tried to remain serious, but with my companion that was impossible. Moments earlier we had been villains on the run, and now we were litter louts. This was all too much. In a fit of uncontrolled mirth we roared with laughter. The two eel fishers who were not party to the joke motored off in disgust.

The day was still holding up well; intermittent sun with good periods of cloud and the same light to moderate wind from the south. These were conditions which offered so much, and yet we were still to put a fish in our boat! We would fish the widest part of the bay next taking several different lines from the island down, and then drift on down to the bottom end. Although I had changed flies for the smutting trout, I had fished the same two sedge patterns which I had tied on when we tackled up back at the mooring for most of the session, without bringing up a fish. The lack of success however, did not break my confidence in these two flies. It is so important to have confidence in what you are fishing, and these two patterns have caught me so many big browns, that my confidence never wavered. And so it was that I began the second session with the same patterns up. The lack of success wasn't because of poor fly selection, it was about finding a fish. We fished out the first drift and drew a blank. No fish came to our flies and we had seen no fish moving. Apart from the smutting trout earlier in the day, we had not seen a natural rise. Our next line would begin about fifty yards outside of the island and we would drift closer to the opposite shore.

It was early evening and the temperature began to drop, I rolled down the sleeves of my shirt and put on a sweater and then my waistcoat. In my haste to start fishing again I forgot to put on my lifejacket. In a boat this is unforgivable and in *Fingers* it was nothing short of reckless. I fished down that shoreline oblivious to my predicament, concentrating on my two flies. We came to an area where there were some huge rocks standing on the shore. They looked a little like Neolithic monuments, but man hadn't shaped or left these rocks along the shore of the bay. The forces of nature had brought these pieces of limestone to rest where they were now standing. After looking at the stones, and thinking of how long they had rested where they were now standing, and what forces had brought them there, I returned my attention to my flies. And then it happened. The moment I knew would come – a moment which for an angler makes a good day even better. I had never thought it would take so long. My flies went out searching the water as they had done so many times before, that it had almost become automatic. Cast; leave on the water for ten or more seconds; lift off; pause; change the angle; and deliver again searching new water. So many times that day I had repeated the manoeuvre without response, so why should this be any different? My flies sat there on the surface of the water as they had done so many times before, and then this wonderful apparition of a large brown trout appeared below my dropper, the Chocolate Drop. It happened so slowly you could see every detail of the fish. It was pure theatre itself. I live for such moments. The trout materialised from the inky depths, and then paused below the fly, eyeing it with the air of a fish that had seen these things before. It was heavily spotted, you could clearly see the spots and the golden brown flanks, and then with a leisurely push of the tail it came up, opened its jaws, and the fly disappeared. All that was left where my fly had been were a few bubbles on the surface of the water. I could see the fish going down with my fly, its jaws closing as I tightened.

The moment I tightened, the fish went down, leaving a great swirl on the surface. Brown trout rarely fight with any bravado. I couldn't say that the fish leapt in a crescendo of spray, or that it ran on reel-screeching runs. It was a typical brown trout fight, one of pulling hard and boring down under the rod. They remind me a bit of barbel, the way they fight it out on a short line under the rod, straining everything to the limit. That is exactly how this fight went. Eventually my fish came up, and Larry was there with the net. When the brown came into the boat, Larry gave me a gentlemanly hug, and said well done. As we parted the mesh of the net, Larry remarked that I had made a prediction that we would catch a good fish. He does listen to what I say, even though he doesn't always acknowledge it. He then exclaimed it was one of the best looking brown trout he had ever seen. Heavily spotted, perfectly proportioned with a huge well-spotted tail. The fish looked a picture. It weighed 6¼ lbs. He took some quick photographs of me with the fish, and then I returned my prize to the inky depths from which it had so majestically materialised.

It was only when searching for the camera, that I realised my lifejacket had been left on top of the rucksack. I was thankful that *Fingers* had behaved herself following my omission of common sense, and that we had made no rash movements whilst I was playing the fish. After releasing the trout, and returning all the impedimenta back to their rightful places, we fished out the rest of the evening, but no other fish came to the boat. It was as if the day had one fish in it, and that is all the day was going to give. But what a fish. Little did I realise then, that my trout was to be the only trout that we would catch fishing from *Fingers*. In fact after my capture, I was warming to this tub of a boat. She had given us a trophy trout, and there was no reason to believe that in time she wouldn't give us more trophies. But that wasn't to be. Days after our session the heavens opened up and this bay, whose level can fluctuate so much, began to rise.

Fingers *turned out to be a one trout boat but with a fish of over 6lbs I can't complain*

We decided that this time we would take no chances with *Fingers,* and moved her from the original mooring to higher ground at the top end of the bay. We lifted her a good ten feet above the water level, and this, we thought, would keep the boat out of harm's way for the winter. But we were hit by a deluge in November. Houses were flooded and roads were cut off that hadn't been cut off for years. As the waters subsided we decided to go and have a look at the boat, just to make sure that she was okay and above the danger zone. But *Fingers* wasn't where we had left her; in fact she was nowhere to be seen. We

155

have been through this before, we thought, when she went down the previous year. So we put a feeler out to see if someone had found the boat washed up on the shore. News came filtering through that bits of debris from a broken boat had been found over a distance of several miles. Bits had even been washed down and collected on a hatchery screen. We heard that the colour of the debris was blue. Now this in itself was no guarantee that the debris was related to *Fingers*. But later a piece of transom was found, a piece with a metal corner bracket attached. *Fingers* may have lived a charmed life, but there was no coming back from this.

12 Mayfly Sheelin 1993

What makes a particular day or event memorable, a passage in time which opens a window in our mind that never fully closes? If we wish to recover that passage in time, all we have to do is open the window. Many fishermen I am sure have a library of memorable fishing days, as I believe it is in our nature. We observe and we store information so that it may again prove useful one day. But in the store we have particular days or events that stand out. They become classified as most memorable. It's like an archive stored in the brain just waiting to come flooding back through the open window. Some of my most memorable days have been spent in the pursuit of wild browns, days of an exceptional capture or bag of fish. These are the days we savour most and never want to forget. But there are days of another kind that remain just as memorable. There are unforgettable moments which for one reason or another remain embedded in our thoughts, ingrained memories that remain with us for life. And the longevity of these memories may not necessarily be attributed to days littered with success, but they are moments that we as anglers may count ourselves privileged to have experienced. I had such a day in the mayfly of 1993 on Sheelin, a day of mixed fortune.

How you measure the quality of sport experienced whilst out fishing is down to personal preferences. It is difficult to define but to me for a day to become memorable it has to meet certain values. I enjoyed reservoir fishing and I still feel that a grown on rainbow from the richer reservoirs takes some beating for its sporting value, but wild fishing would always have the stronger pull. Wild fish provide a greater sense of fulfilment; they always will. To pursue and capture a wild fish has always meant more no matter what size the quarry, and if an opportunity to fish for wild browns of a high average weight should arise I find this possibly the greatest fly fishing experience of all.

Ireland has a wealth of superb wild brown trout fishing, particularly on the larger loughs of the midland plain and the great lakes of the far west. The

157

magnetism of fishing mayfly on these waters is a tradition that has been handed down through generations of fishermen, and it draws anglers from all over the world. Although the midland loughs can be dour at times particularly when compared with the more productive western fisheries, they do produce some of the finest wild trout in Europe. In May 1993, the word was out that the mayfly was up to coincide with our visit to the Emerald Isle. I had four fabulous days on the Corrib, and we then went on to Sheelin for three days fishing, where, if we were lucky with the conditions we were hoping to fish the spent gnat to a rise of trout before returning to England. Sheelin is renowned for the spent gnat fishing, but timing is all important. Ideal weather conditions and a fall of fly need to coincide to produce a good rise. If such factors do conspire to produce a big fall of gnat, this fly can produce the biggest wild browns to the fly. A gnat rise on Sheelin is an experience never to be forgotten, and although the lough has a reputation for being dour I have to say that because of the size of the trout you see when they are moving it is the most exciting water I have fished in a rise.

We were late leaving the Corrib on our fifth day, and it was just after lunch time that we arrived in Finnea. The daytime fishing had been typically slow, but a few fish had been taken the previous evening, and we were informed that the lough was enjoying the heaviest hatch of mayfly seen for a good many years. As the daytime fishing was slow we were in no hurry to rush out on to the lough, so we relaxed and ate a late lunch before venturing out. Conditions were ideal or so we thought, with a soft south-westerly wind as we ventured out on to the lough in the late afternoon. As we motored up the lough towards Kilnahard, it was evident that there were certainly plenty of fly on the water. We began a series of drifts starting from Crane Island and progressing up the lough to Merry Point, but unfortunately as the evening wore on the wind strengthened and there was no rise. With no obvious fall of fly materialising, and no fish showing I switched from dry fly to wets for the last two hours. In the failing light and increasingly blustery conditions, I took a fine brown of 5lbs14oz on a Ginger Bumble.

The following day the wind had veered through 180 degrees, and we were met by a very keen north-easterly wind as we ventured out from the southern end of the lough. With the wind coming from the north-easterly quarter, we

Thomas Lyneh playing a good fish behind Stony Island

decided to try some drifts off the mouth of the Inny river, Inchicup Island and Curry Point. It was a long haul before we had the shelter of Derry Point, but once we were out of the worst of the wind we made easy progress up to the north end of the lough. On our way up the lough it was evident that even though the conditions were far from promising, there was a good hatch of fly coming off. Wind and wave however were killing off any hope of a rise, so we began with wet flies. The Inny Bay produced no fish, but we did manage a brace of browns between 1½ and 2lbs drifting from Inchicup down to Church Island. As the morning wore on the wind eased, and began to change direction. Conditions were certainly improving, and if anything the intensity of the mayfly hatch had increased. We did not appreciate just how much fly was coming off, until we motored in for lunch.

Over lunch, conditions continued to improve and the wind became softer, veering from an easterly direction through the south, before finally settling into a moderate westerly. With a light cover of cloud and an increase in temperature, the flies poured off. We now began to appreciate the scale of the hatch that was taking place. Looking out to scan the lough for signs of a moving fish, the surface was covered with the upright wings of emerging or hatching fly. Everywhere we looked there were mayfly. The marginal bushes and reeds were covered with resting flies, the surface of the lough supported countless thousands of miniature sail boats, and our clothes looked like we had been exposed to a hatch of *Caenis* that had been feeding on steroids. I have never before or since witnessed a hatch of mayfly like it.

Mayfly laying up in the reed beds waiting for evening when they will take to the wing to dance the flight of the spinners

The abundance of fly was immense even by Sheelin's standards. The atmosphere was overpowering, and we could sense that something special was going to happen. All afternoon the flies continued pouring off, but there was no movement from the fish to the emerging duns, and by early evening when we retired for dinner we had had no further offers. This did not surprise us as Sheelin is a fickle water, and the daytime fishing to emerging duns was always slow even at the best of times. But this day still had a special feeling about it, and we felt confident that if the conditions held we would see some fish moving to the gnat later. We were not taking any chances, and following an early evening meal we were back on the water earlier than usual just in case. Swarms of flies were massing over the marginal trees like great, moving amoebae, flying in tight clusters. Forever changing shape like a large flock of birds, these clouds of dancing insects could be seen above the trees all along the lough margin, but their density seemed to be greater along the Kilnahard shore.

The fresh winds that had been blowing from an easterly quarter for the first half of the day, had caused a big build up of fly on the western shore. Because of this, we elected to fish off the west shore, the same shore that we had fished the previous evening. As we began drifting from Crane Island down towards Kilnahard and Merry Point, the first fall of gnat drifted out from the trees and onto the water. We were none too early, as like snowflakes in the wind, clouds of flies drifted out before us and settled on to the surface of the lough to complete their final objective in life. Like the surface of a lake covered in leaves after an autumn gale, the water before us was simply littered with fly. It was a never-ending carpet of spent and egg-laying adults. When I looked at my artificials lying amongst all those natural flies the situation felt hopeless. How on earth was a trout going to pick out my artificials in what resembled a lottery draw?

There was no chance of taking a fish on the blind. We needed a target. Fishing two dry mayflies and full of anticipation, I was ready to cover any fish that came within range. Even for a notoriously dour water like Sheelin, I could just sense a rise was going to come. The fish could not ignore this amount of fly. The wind was blowing slightly offshore, and this was taking the fly well out. The wind was perfect and the light was good. A gentle wave rolled by taking the countless fly with it. Something surely had to come. Eagerly scanning the water

161

for a rising fish, my first opportunity came early in the drift when I noticed a movement well downwind of me. A fish was up, gulping down mayfly spinners one after the other. I was locked into the fish. Time was suddenly racing. In what seemed only moments the trout came within range and I was casting. The fly needed to be right in front of the trout, otherwise it would be totally ignored. I made several casts before putting the fly where the fish just came on to it without deviation of his course, and the artificial disappeared. It was a good brown of well over 4lbs, and a very good start. Shortly after this another fish of around 3½lbs followed, and my confidence was flying. As the fall of fly intensified, the bigger trout began to move and the next rise I covered produced a solid take. The heavy fish took line, turned and ran in towards the boat, then swung off to my right powering under Bruce's line on a long unstoppable run. This was undoubtedly a very good trout, and as the run slowed the fish leapt showing great silvery flanks. As the trout crashed back in to the water, the line fell slack. I reeled in with that sinking feeling that only a fellow angler could know, after a big fish has been lost.

Bruce caught the next two trout – fish of 3½lbs and 2lbs. The trout were now rising well, and we were both seeing big fish moving in the waves. I was trying to discipline myself to target one of the bigger trout, so probably missed out on a few opportunities before I saw one of the larger boys within range well downwind of me. I thought the first cast straight would take him. However even though the cast was good he ignored my offering, and drifted out to my left. The trout looked enormous, the dorsal fin cleaving through the water as the fish came up and took another fly. Well over two feet long, the fish appeared to be moving in a very leisurely fashion through the water, but he was covering the ground deceptively quickly. My pulse was racing as I covered the fish again, and he rose just beyond my fly pulling out slightly away from me. Head and shoulders appeared through the waves, and the back disappeared with a slow movement from the tail, reminiscent of a salmon. He was now going left and away from me, and a more difficult cast. I covered the area I thought, just beyond where the trout had disappeared. As my fly alighted on the waves his great head came up, and sucked in the fly. There was a great commotion on the surface as I tightened, and I felt the weight of another very heavy fish, as solid as a rock. The tail disappeared and the trout plunged downwards beneath the boat, and hung there in typical brownie fashion. With the rod hooped, a size 10 hook, acres of space and the line tight, I felt confident of landing this fish. He made no long runs but just held station beneath the rod, the line whining to the strain of his heavy weight. My confidence was not justified however, as the weight just vanished from the end of my line, leaving me again with that emptiness that occurs when a great fish has been lost.

The light was now fading fast, and it was no longer possible to see the size of the trout clearly rising at distance. I caught a small fish of around 1½ lbs following the loss of the second big trout, but my thoughts were still with the big trout lost when I quickly unhooked and returned the fish without giving it a second look. This was wrong of course, but at the time I felt annoyed with my run of luck with the bigger ones. Bruce meanwhile was covering a good trout, on his side of the boat. The fish was slowly swimming around, mopping up just about every fly it came on to. You could hear the slurps in the gathering gloom, as it sucked in yet another fly. While covering this fish, Bruce had the misfortune to tangle his line. The resulting tangle was terminal, which meant breaking down his line and tying up a new leader, so he invited me to try for the trout. I covered the area where I thought the fish to be, but could not see the flies in the fast-fading light. The trout rose, we could hear it slurp down a fly but I hesitated with my strike. I did not want to spook the fish if it hadn't taken my fly, so I felt for the trout slowly tightening in to what felt like an increasing immovable weight. The next moment my rod was wrenched down. The reel began to scream. 'Whoopee!' My earlier losses were forgotten, as another heavyweight powered off. With the rod well bent and the reel making a merry tune, I was a happy man but my elation was not to last as once again when well in to the fight my rod straightened, the line fell slack and my fly came back without its prize for the third time that evening.

In his book *Letters To A Salmon Fisher's Sons* A. H. Chaytor says 'Of the pleasure of success in fishing I need say nothing. We all know it; and we have all felt it.... but even success has its limits; the fish is caught, the thing is done. It is our lost fish that I believe stay longest in our memory, and seize upon our thoughts whenever we look back to fishing days... the fish that has beaten us and left us quivering with excitement and vexation, is hooked and lost again in many a year to come.'

One that didn't get away – 8lb 12oz Sheelin brown

Chaytor was talking of salmon, but they are well-chosen words and we can equally equate those words to brown trout. We remember big fish which are lost just as strongly as those we have landed. Why? Because these bigger trout are rare, and this makes them all the more unique, and once hooked they become memorable. And once lost they become history; they only then exist in our mind, for the time has past and you can't change it. The lost fish are the ones that haunt you, particularly if they are big trout; they stay with you for life.

Footnote: It was the loss of these fish, and another big fish in September of that year, that exposed an ongoing problem where dry fly was concerned. A problem I was aware of with reservoir fish, but one that became unacceptable after losing those big wild browns. If I had lost these fish through bad luck or poor fishing technique, I would have no option but to accept it, however none of the fish broke me and I am pretty certain that they were all well hooked. This problem

164

of fish inexplicably coming adrift only seemed to arise with dry fly, and in particular with big brown trout. It was specific to the method, and the problem had to be in the equipment I was using. As I did not experience similar problems fishing wet fly or nymph, the fault had to be something specific to the method. To lose such fish through poor technique is inexcusable, but to lose them through tackle failure is unacceptable. Fly fishing isn't that complex and if we look at the equipment we require for catching fish, we can break it down in to a few basic items – rod, reel, fly-line, leader and fly. If I am not experiencing a similar problem fishing nymph or wet fly, and the only item of tackle that changes for dry fly is the fly, then the problem had to be with the hook. For nymph and wet fly, I use hooks of either standard or heavy wire gauges. The strength of these wire gauges is such, that they were never tested to failure limits whilst fishing, but for the dries where I want the fly to float, I use fine wire hooks. The finer the wire, the more critical the limits of strength become. Therefore a weakness with a fine wire hook is more likely to be exposed, when subjected to stress. Reputedly of good quality or so I thought, the brands of Japanese hooks that I was using at the time although I didn't know it, were slightly undertempered, thus they were not properly hardened and therefore prone to opening or gaping. Where big, hard-mouthed, strong pulling fish were concerned, these hooks were found wanting because of this very reason. A good fine wire hook is difficult to find, but I never intend to repeat similar failures again through poorly tempered, soft fine wire springy hooks that will gape and continue to gape without breaking. A big wild brown is a difficult fish to tempt on a fly. If you can deceive such a fish to take the fly in to its mouth, you have the hard work done. Achieve the deception, and the outcome should be a successful one, but loss through tackle failure in this day and age is simply not acceptable. Irrespective of brand name, diligently check those fine wire hooks before tying that fly, and if you intend to fish for big wild browns with a dry fly, and use the Japanese brands, I would suggest you fish a medium wire hook and avoid the finer wire gauges.

13 Tales of the Unexpected

Fishing isn't an exact science. It helps to have an understanding of the ways of fish, but even after many years of experience we cannot always predict how they will react on a chosen day. As our knowledge broadens we can ascertain to a degree, what hatches of fly will occur at certain periods of the season, and given suitable conditions we can make a fair assumption of how the fish will react to these fly hatches. We then plan our sessions accordingly. During the spring, summer and autumn there will be periods within these seasons when given suitable weather conditions we will have a fair idea of what to expect. However we cannot guarantee that the trout or the hatch of fly will conform to these predictions, for there will always be odd exceptions. That is the way nature works. And nature will always throw up an oddity no matter how hard we plan.

On 1 June 2007 I made a decision to fish the lower Corrib, I was hoping to find some trout moving to *Caenis*. The previous evening had been wet, but the wind fell light overnight and changed to a light south-east to east wind. It was cold and overcast when I ventured out at around 7.30 in the morning. Normally if I were going to fish to a *Caenis* hatch I would be out on the water much earlier in the day, but as the temperature was so low I didn't think that it was worth my while going to the effort of being out for a dawn start. In the prevailing conditions I wasn't expecting a hatch of *Caenis* until 8.30 or later, and until there was a hatch of fly I wasn't expecting to see a rise of fish. Well I was right in one respect, as I didn't see a rise of fish when I went out, but I was wrong with my prediction about the hatch. It never came. Nine-thirty came and went, 10 o'clock passed. Still no sign of fly. It was obviously too cold, and with no fly there was no sign of a rising fish to be seen. The wind remained light; it was almost calm and the air felt heavy with humidity, but there was a distinct chill. I would give it until noon I thought, and if nothing was forthcoming by then, I would call it a day and come off the water.

My love is sight-fishing, and if I'm using dry fly in a light ripple or calm

Lady angler Sue Wherry playing what turned out to be a personal best wild brown –
Lough Corrib

conditions I rarely fish the water blind. I much prefer to hunt the water until some moving fish are located. On this particular morning I had hardly touched the rod; it lay idle across the thwarts of the boat. By 11 I had searched a lot of water, and it appeared lifeless as nothing stirred or broke the surface. Thoughts of heading back in were growing stronger as I pulled into another area and sat and patiently waited whilst scanning the surface for some sign of a moving fish. It is my belief that too many anglers commence fishing as soon as they reach a chosen spot. They do not take time out to observe if there are any fish moving, or if there is any hatch of fly on the water. Irrespective of whether there are positive indications or not, they just start fishing. To me there is something mechanical

167

to this type of approach, and it is one that would not suit me. I like to see some form of positive indication to give me confidence that I have made the right choice. As I searched I noticed an odd lake olive beginning to emerge. Just a trickle of fly, nothing unusual in this I thought. If the conditions are suitable, a few of these ephemerids will emerge on most days throughout the season from April onwards. And the conditions were perfect: overcast with good humidity and cool. If it were late April or early May I would have expected a good hatch of fly, but not in June. The main season for the lake olive was now over, or so I thought.

For the first twenty minutes or so the trickle steadily increased, until by 11.30 it had grown into a full-blown hatch, as heavy as any hatch of lake olives I have ever seen. The black headed gulls were down and feasting, and more importantly the trout were responding to the fly also. My rod may have lain idle for three-and-a-half hours or more, but once I saw the first fish move to the fly, I broke down my *Caenis* cast and put up a Hare's Ear Dry and a Ginger Bits, both size 12. It was a classic olive hatch, and in the low temperature the duns were sticking, ideal for the dry fly fisher. Shortly after 11.30 my rod was bent, and I came off later in the day having caught eleven cracking trout. Most of the fish were between 2lbs and 3½ lbs with the best pushing 5½ lbs. The Ginger Bits accounted for nine of the trout fished on a 0.165mm leader. The fishing and the hatch of fly was more reminiscent of late April, so it was hard to believe that it was June. Instead of the gentle sipping rise of a trout feeding on *Caenis*, I was faced with bold head and tailing fish which were basically taking fly with gay abandon. I had gone out that morning expecting to fish to a *Caenis* hatch. That would have been predictable, but instead I was presented with an unexpected hatch of fly.

Olives are unpredictable. The above event reminds me of another more recent occasion when we witnessed a heavy hatch of fly out of season. It was early October 2008 and the trout season had closed. I was out for the day with Larry McCarthy and Rod Tye. They were fishing Lough Corrib for pike and I accompanied these two intrepid voyagers in their quest for *Esox lucius* as an impromptu boatman. It may be uncharitable of me, but it is my firm belief that they were desperate for someone to row them around the hot spots.

The first area we tried off a river mouth produced a rapid succession of fish to both rods. Pike up to about 14lbs came thick and fast for about one-and-a-half hours and then the sport died. They had either fished out the area or the pike had gone off the feed, for when the sport died neither Larry or Rod could stir a fish. A change of scenery was in order so we then moved to a shallow reed-fringed bay. In late April and early May the bay can come alive with olive hatches, but that is when they are in season. The deepest water, about six to seven feet, lay in a channel towards one side adjacent to the reeds and this is where we expected to find the pike. It was early afternoon, and a light southerly was blowing across the bay. As I positioned the boat for Larry and Rod to begin throwing their ironmongery over the side, we noticed that the olives were pouring off and interestingly trout were moving to them. It was for me the most interesting part of the day, I became totally absorbed in watching the trout taking the olives one after another. I was so engrossed with what was happening that I may have neglected my duties, but then as my two rods kept informing me I didn't know what my duties were anyway. The fish were not put off by Larry and Rod throwing out their spinners. If a spinner fell by a rising fish, the trout would go down and then re-emerge a few yards further on. As the activity increased, Larry ceased fishing and joined me in just watching the fish moving to the fly. They came with such confident rises, you just knew that if the fish were in season there was a bag of trout in the offing. Flotillas of fly swept past the boat by the breeze were mopped up by the marauding trout. Leisurely rises, heads and tails could be observed slowly breaking the surface for as far as the eye could see. Larry and I were enraptured by the sight of the trout moving, and yet Rod oblivious to our attentions kept on throwing out his spinner in the hope of connecting with a pike. He was more interested and more engrossed in the pursuit of pike, than watching those lovely fish moving to surface fly on that October afternoon. Unexpected, but delightful, but I was glad that I went with them.

I can think of several instances where unexpected phenomena have produced positive behaviour by the fish which has led to me taking a bag of trout. The bloodworm on Sheelin, *Asellus* floating to the surface on Farmoor Reservoir, a fall of oak fly, a fall of flying ant, masses of ladybirds on Farmoor. They were all instances of which I had had no previous experience, and I might add they are events which subsequently have not repeated themselves. So the information learnt from the experience has really been of no further use to me. And yet as an angler, I can't help feeling that these one-off experiences make one more rounded, as we have to deal with the situation as it occurs, there and then, or the opportunity is lost. All the above concern situations which involved a mass of food. This season, 2009, towards the backend, I had an experience which again will probably be a one-off, but it didn't involve a mass of food. It had more to do with the positive response of the trout to a particular pattern of fly. What makes this experience interesting was that there were no natural insects on the water which the successful pattern imitated. Fish can be contrary at times.

It was early September, and although I had made no plans to go fishing the day was just too good to miss. By mid-morning I had the car packed and was away. The wind was a light south-westerly with good cloud cover, and it was warm. An ideal day for the dry fly, and it would suit the location on Lough Corrib toward which I was heading. I pulled the boat out of the mooring and headed south toward a vast area of shallow water. There was an archipelago of offshore reefs off the western side of this watery desert, and to the east of the reefs for about 400 yards some good trout were holding. I had located these fish earlier in the year, and they had been holding in the vicinity of those reefs for a good part of the season. They had received very little attention from other boats, so there was no reason why they shouldn't still be in the same location. The depth of the area where the fish were holding was about eight to ten feet deep and the bottom was covered in *Chara* weed. With good cloud cover overhead it looked deeper than it actually was.

I started off with two of my favourite sedge patterns, a Fiery Brown Sedge and a Chocolate Drop, both size 10. These are big fish flies, and I was hoping that they might just appeal to one or two of the better trout which I knew from experience would be present. There were a few olives and the odd buzzer on the water but nothing significant, certainly not enough to feel excited about, and there was no suggestion of, nor did I expect to see, a hatch of fly of any note. After about forty minutes or so I had a fish come up under my point fly, the Chocolate Drop. It hovered below the fly, dropped away and then came back again. I thought the trout was going to take, but then he made a half-hearted swirl at the fly and disappeared. He hadn't touched the fly, although the sight of the swirl would have convinced a lot of anglers that he had. I

Dee and Holly have all the angles covered in Lough Carra

thought the fish was line shy, so I tied on a length of 0.152mm tippet to my leader and connected the point fly to the tippet. This is a fine leader for this size of fly, but I was experimenting as I had been fishing with finer leader line for a lot of that season. About twenty minutes later another trout showed some interest in my point fly. However just like the first one, this fish did not take the fly.

As it was the point fly the fish were refusing I was not convinced that my leader was the problem, especially as I had dropped to a finer tippet. It is my experience that when a trout refuses a fly, nine times out of ten the presentation is at fault, and in most cases this means the leader. That is why if we are subjected to a bout of short rising, most of the refusals will come to the

171

droppers. Often, the dropper will twist around the main leader, or the fly will fall close to the main leader. In both instances there is a greater chance of the fish seeing the line and hence coming short. Whether or not my leader was the problem I will never know, because following the second refusal my train of thought shifted. The biggish fly was dragging the fish up, but there did not seem to be enough of an inducement to make them commit to taking. I could have tried moving the fly, as this sometimes makes the trout more aggressive and more committed to taking. My problem was that I wasn't attracting enough offers to make this tactic viable. These trout were cute and maybe they had seen just too many artificial sedge flies. With no serious amount of fly on the water, there was nothing to imitate to induce a more positive response from the fish, and yet I felt that I needed to change the flies. I could see no merit in changing to smaller patterns as the bigger flies had more pulling power, and with little natural fly on the surface I needed something which would draw the trout's attention. So I tied up a new leader using my usual line strength for size 10 flies, which was a 0.185mm mono and attached a daddy to the dropper, and a Ginger Mayfly to the point. I hadn't seen a mayfly for weeks, so there was no sound reasoning for this choice of pattern other than I wanted a big fly. At least the daddy was seasonal.

Shortly after changing the team of flies, a trout rose to the point fly. There was no warning, the fish just broke through the surface and took with a slow deliberate head and tail rise. It was one of those rises you could not miss. A fish of about 1½lbs soon came to the side of the boat for release. That was the most difficult fish; I had broken my duck. By the end of the day I had risen six trout, and landed them all. Four of them were real beauties between 3½lbs and 6lbs and they all fell to the mayfly. Even changing the daddy on the dropper and tying on another sedge pattern, could not break the spell, I couldn't attract a single fish to the dropper fly. For some reason they wanted that Mayfly. Why when there were no Mayflies on the water is a mystery. As usual, I returned all the fish, but even if I had killed a fish and spooned it, I'm convinced I would have learnt nothing, for I do not believe that the trout were locked into any single food item. There just wasn't enough of one species of fly on the water for the trout to zone in on, just bits and pieces. A few olives were scattered around, the odd adult midge, some daddies and even some sedges, but no great hatch or abundance of any one of them. To reinforce my opinion I saw a trout spasmodically rising along the edge of a slick. It took an olive, moved on a bit further and then sucked in a crumpled daddy which looked beaten up and lifeless lying in the surface film. The fish then moved further on and rose again, only this time it rose to my Mayfly. I just knew it was going to rise to me, from the way it was moving up the edge of the slick and the position of my fly in the skin of the surface film just on the broken edge of the calm water. The water exploded when I struck. It was a good fish.

It wasn't a classic solution, but the Mayfly was the answer to my dilemma. I wasn't fishing to trout which were rising to a hatch of fly, as I saw only the odd smattering of fly and even fewer rising fish that day. What I needed was a fly to pull the fish which were cruising deeper down in the water, but basically looking up for anything edible. Once attracted to the fly, it required the right trigger to deceive them in to taking. The sedges I feel had been over-used, and the fish were wising up to them. That is why those fish that did move to my artificial sedge patterns scrutinised the fly more closely. They were partially interested but at the same time were wary of them. Whether the trout took the Mayfly from memory feeding I do not know, but it did provide a welcome, if unexpected answer to my backend day on the Corrib.

Trout do not always conform to the rules, and because of this, it is my opinion that anglers miss out in certain situations purely because they refuse to accept that the fish might be behaving in a way which is contrary to the accepted mode of thinking. If a swarm of flying ants fall on the surface of the water on a hot sunny day in August, the trout will rise to them irrespective of whether it is sunny or not. Most animals prefer to feed in lower light levels, but this does not mean that they will not feed in bright sun if an opportunity presents itself. Many fly anglers can become caught up with dogma, and because they have heard that trout do not like the sun they automatically assume that they do not feed when it is sunny. It is true that trout do not like the sun. However, and believe me for I have seen it now so many times, if there is food present on the surface they will move to it.

Trout will seek the comfort of deeper water if it becomes too warm, and they will also hold deeper when it is sunny, but this is for comfort reasons only. Providing the temperature at the surface isn't too warm, trout will rise in bright sunny conditions if there is food present. In unbroken sunshine, do not assume that the trout have gone down because of the bright orb overhead. Be more open-minded and ask yourself 'Where has all the food gone?' It seems to me that most of our aquatic insects do not like hatching on hot sunny days, and if there is no food present, why should the fish remain at the surface? The stereo-typed angler will make the assumption that the fish go down in bright sun and do not feed at the surface. That is what he has been brainwashed into thinking. If you are open-minded however, there is always the possibility of the unex-pected.

Waiting for a fall of adult duckfly – Lough Corrib

Bright sun and good fishing do not marry well together, but a sunny day does not automatically mean that the trout will not rise. If it did I would never have experienced a rise to *Asellus* on Farmoor under a blazing sun, and I might add in very high temperatures also, a rise to bloodworm on Sheelin, a rise to the ladybirds on Farmoor Reservoir, a rise to snail trapped in the surface film on Rutland Water or some of the best rises to *Caenis* on the Corrib. In fact my biggest day for numbers of fish caught on the Corrib, came on a day of sun and a very light southerly wind. It was a day in early May 2001, when for some reason the olives poured off under an azure sky and bright sunlight. That day they defied all logic and hatched in huge numbers between the hours of 11am and 4pm, even though the conditions were far from ideal for this particular fly. An immense mat of fly had built up, caught in the flat water. Many of the flies were dead so the mat remained long after the main hatch had finished. Only the lightest of breezes, a zephyr of wind kissed the surface of the lough and the trout feasted oblivious to the bright sun overhead. Drifting from Clydagh to Annaghkeen I caught fish after fish on a Ginger Bits and a Grey Duster. You cannot write about such days, as it is just a repetition of catching and playing fish. As Sidney Spencer said 'the big days teach you very little' and he is right, for once you have the tactics worked out the hard graft is done. It then becomes a matter of how many trout do you want to catch before they either go off the take, or how quickly you become tired of catching fish. Trout are unpredictable, as is the food on which they feed. It is nice to think that the fish do not totally conform to the rule book, and more importantly, and I believe this is what a lot of anglers miss, the food on which trout feed does not always hatch or appear when we expect it to. Always be open-minded in your approach, as you never know when the unexpected may turn up.

14 Cursed in the Sun

In the light morning air the boat was lying idle on the water, marooned on the vast open waste of Lough Corrib. It was the 16 June, just after 6am on a clear fine morning in 2008. The mobile phone tucked away in the recesses of my fishing bag suddenly burst into life. I dislike mobile phones, and yet I'm told that I must have one, just in case. Just in case of what?

The ring tone cut through the early morning silence. It was annoying me. As it rang, my detestation for the modern piece of telecommunication which was rattling about inside my fishing bag grew. It became the centre of all my loathing. We must have lived sad lives, before the advent of the mobile phone and the internet. The phone kept ringing. Should I answer it? I knew who was phoning at such an hour. However, that didn't change the ring tone which kept nagging away at my cerebral well-being, just like the monster inside my head which was banging away denuding me of all rational thought processes. There was a time when I could be afflicted with a headache, a migraine headache, at the drop of a hat. They were so irritating because you just did not know when an attack might occur. The end of the week was a key time for an attack. As I relaxed, my weekend could be ruined by the onset of one of these headaches. Even the fishing suffered. The symptoms were such that you felt incapable of doing anything. All you wanted to do was to shut yourself off from the world, and hide away out of the light in a dark room. For about twenty years I suffered these debilitating headaches, and then for no discernible reason during 1994–95 they just stopped. Now after a long honeymoon period without an attack I felt as if I had a migraine headache coming.

The lightest of winds stirred from the west, but the boat hardly moved. Bang, bang, I could feel nausea coming on, and that bloody phone would not go away. From a cloudless sky the sun beamed down, its rays seemed to penetrate my skull, and then rebounded inside my head like the ball of a pin ball machine rattling around the table looking for a pocket in which to drop. Bang, bang, the phone and the headache were in competition, fighting it out for who could win the most loathing. I made a quick agitated grab for the phone. At that moment in time I could have easily thrown it into the lough, but I answered it.

Larry's voice came through clear and chirpy. 'Hello me old flower, it's a lovely morning the perfect morning for a fish,' my friend sounded so cheerful, and he was absolutely right. For a *Caenis* hatch it was a lovely morning, one of the few of that awful summer. The conditions were as near perfect as they could be. Without doubt it was the right morning for a fish. My problem was I was slowly being debilitated by the headache, and I was beginning to think I would have to leave. The sombre reality that I may not be well enough to take advantage of the morning conditions was beginning to dawn on me and this thought made me feel frustrated to say the least. Of all the mornings that I should feel so lousy, why did it have to be this one? All logic was lost to me, and I felt like venting my spleen on whatever came to hand. The mobile phone became the target of my anger and the vitriol poured forth: 'What is so good about the morning? That sun is burning a hole in my head, and I haven't caught a fish. It's useless, in fact it's more than useless it's ------- ----' I replied. I believe my friend was a bit taken aback by my reply, as were the two clients he had out with him. Vaughan Ruckley and John Cash were both professional people, and they were probably not used to such vitriol on the hallowed waters of Lough Corrib at that hour. I didn't consider the hour of the day; in truth at that particular time I didn't consider anything, I just wanted to curl up and hide away somewhere peaceful. Vaughan Ruckley and John Cash were probably looking up the lunar cycle to determine what the prognosis for my condition may be, and my good friend Larry was just trying to maintain a positive state of mind. 'C'mon me old flower, the conditions are good and you know it, and there is a hatch of fly coming off.' Larry was right, the conditions were good, but at that moment in time I may as well have been fishing in a bath tub. I just could not concentrate. It was reaching the point where I felt if my headache didn't clear, I would have to return home and try to sleep it off.

Larry could sense that all was not well with me and left me to my own devices. I could hear the distant drone of his outboard engine through the silence of the early morning air. He was a good distance off, at least several miles away, and then the engine fell silent. They had found some fish moving I reasoned. If there was to be any chance of me fishing I needed to shake off my headache. I had been on the water for over an hour and had felt muzzy from the start. Since then my condition had got progressively worse. It was tolerable to begin with, but now I was losing to the dull pulsing pain behind my eyes which would not go away. I needed to relax totally, shut up shop and hope the nausea and the headache would go away. There was a time when I would regularly take pain killers for the habitual headaches which used to stalk me every weekend, but now I rarely take them. This was an emergency. I searched for the box of pills which lurked in a small pocket inside my fishing bag. I found an unopened box of Paracetamol and noted that the use-by date had elapsed, but such was my need that I took two pills.

The fly rod was lying idle across the thwart boards of the boat as I slowly sipped orange juice and watched the trout feeding on the spent *Caenis*. The fish would come and go, occasionally the activity would die as a pod of fish moved off, but they were invariably replaced by a single trout or a group of fish. It would have been a rare moment not to have heard or seen some sort of fish activity within sixty to seventy yards of the boat. I was cursing my luck. There was a good hatch of *Caenis* coming off. My clothing was smothered with the empty shucks of the adult fly. Countless thousands of adult fly were on the wing all around me and the carpet of spent fly on the surface of the water was building. It was disheartening to see all the fly on the water and the trout feeding on them and not feel in the mood to cast. I felt vexed, but at the same time I found that without having a rod in my hand, my intensity of concentration had relaxed. Wearing a wide-brimmed hat which was pulled down over my eyes, and sunglasses to screen out the reflected glare was helping to reduce the negative effect of the sun on my well-being. Some high diffused cirrus cloud drifted over-head and across the sun, masking the sun's intensity of light. Under the subdued light I began to feel more comfortable and my mind began to drift. I became absorbed watching the countless flies returning to the water to lay their eggs, and the trout rising to them as they lay spent on the surface of the lough. A natural cycle was being played out before me in the warmth of the morning sun. The end, and the beginning of life. For an angler it was one of nature's great spectacles. I was no longer thinking about the headache – this was good therapy.

My mind drifted to the early morning start. I had been out for well over an hour and had unsuccessfully tried to cover a number of potential risers. *Caenis* fishing is very challenging, perhaps the most challenging fishing I have ever attempted. The fish look easy when you see a trout or a group of trout feeding on spent fly mopping up one morsel after another. But do not be deceived by their apparent lack of caution and the act of gluttony. These trout are high in the water and know how to frustrate one's attempt to catch them off guard. When they are fervently rising to the fly, one can easily be misled into thinking that the trout have thrown caution to the wind and will be a pushover. Believe

Ideal conditions for a Caenis *rise*

this at your peril, for the trout have an uncanny knack of avoiding abortive attempts to cover them with a fly. They make no sudden movement to avoid you, but if the fish are within thirty yards of the boat and you raise your arm to make a cast, they will invariably take evasive action. The trout will either change direction or they will bolt at the sign of the casting movement of your raised arm. On most occasions the fish just subtly change direction and avoid the area where your fly has landed. They can do this with uncanny ease and frustrate the best of anglers.

My earlier attempts that morning had been met with disdain by the trout as they thwarted any approach I had made to cover them. Every time they took evasive action and passed my fly with the contempt of an aristocrat. In one area I had located a group of big trout rising close to a small reef, which was just off the southern edge of an island. Twice I played cat and mouse with these fish in an attempt to move in well above them and cut them off, and both times they slipped out well to one side of the boat. At no time did they make a mistake, and they never once offered me an opportunity to cover them. My fishing was off the boil. I was not in tune with the fish. It may have been because of my headache, but I felt frustrated by the fish and my confidence slipped. The fine judgement of guessing correctly seemed to have left me. It was as if the trout could decipher which move I was going to make. It may have been due to the angle of the light or it may have been because of my condition, but either way the trout seemed to be one step ahead.

I have seen and been out with a number of anglers who have failed to make the adjustment required to take these difficult fish. Sometimes the trout will make a silly mistake but in the *Caenis* rise this does not happen too often. It is easy to underestimate trout which are rising willy-nilly ahead of you; the fish look to be a pushover but they are far from it. I have been out with several friends who have struggled to make the mental adjustment of fine judgement required to catch trout which are rising to *Caenis*. The principal faults appear to be one of judging the correct feeding line the trout are taking or fish-scaring movement in the boat. Either one of these faults will produce a negative result. Assessment of the feeding line will improve with experience, but the fish-scaring movement within the boat seems to be a more difficult fault to correct. At the sight of movement in the boat, or the rocking motion caused by the casting action of some anglers when they try to cover a fish, trout will either change direction or move off away from the boat. In a flat calm or very light wind, the rocking motion sends out little shock waves. These are alarm signals to the trout and the fish act accordingly. It is imperative to sit still in the boat as this avoids those little signals being transferred through the water. It is also a necessity to keep a low profile, and whilst keeping a low profile to be able to cast a long line accurately so that the fly falls where you want it to fall. This prevents the fish detecting any fish-scaring movement above the water. If one can present a fly on the feeding line without the trout detecting the angler's presence the game changes, and fish which were impossible become vulnerable.

When Larry and I first fished the *Caenis* rise on Lough Corrib there were far more fish rising then than we find today. The stocks of fish appear to be lower now, but lower numbers of trout are not the only problem. When we first fished the early morning rise the fish were more confident and came in closer to the boat. Now they veer off well ahead of the boat, and you have to make your assessment of the line they are going to take much earlier if you are going to cut them off with your presentation. This judgement is the fine line between success and failure. And for the first part of the morning my judgement had been off.

The trout were still rising, but the main hatch of fly had come to an end. However, there was a good carpet of spent fly lying on the surface of the water. It had been a wet year in 2008. The summer had been awful, and this was a rare opportunity to fish on a good morning in ideal weather conditions. In early June I had been out for three mornings in succession with a good friend assisting him in catching a trout in the *Caenis* hatch. Although an experienced angler with many years of dry-fly fishing under his belt, my friend still found the adjustment that he had to make to catch these fish was quite a transition from what he was used to. On the third morning he finally caught his fish and I was so thankful. However, apart from my morning on the 16th those three mornings took up the best weather conditions we had in June. Unfortunately because of the way I had felt, the first part of my session had been wasted. On top of this I hadn't cast a fly, or picked up the rod for at least thirty minutes or more. I had just sat in the boat trying to relax and watched the fish moving. My mind had drifted and with my thoughts the headache had lifted too – the painkillers had kicked in. For once they were working.

Subconsciously I had been watching a lone fish moving a good distance off. He was slowly moving up towards me on a haphazard route. In the period that I had taken out I had probably seen thirty or more different fish moving at one time or another and had felt no inclination to pick up my fly rod. It was as if the fly rod had not existed. I was content to just sit and watch the trout feeding, but the lone fish feeding way off in the distance slowly making its way towards me had a different effect on me. I reached for the rod. My mood had changed.

The fly-line slipped from the spool of the reel onto the floor boards of the boat as I pulled off a workable length of line. Soft and pliable from the heat of the sun it lay on the floor of the boat as I worked my right arm to make a cast. Two false casts and the line flew out through the rod rings and onto the surface

Author with an early morning fish, lower Lough Corrib

182

of the water. There I let it lie until I could make my cast to the target which I was now focused upon. Judging by the distance between the dorsal fin and the tail, the fish appeared to be a good one. The tail lobe would occasionally break through the surface of the water and make a slow leisurely sideways movement pushing the trout on to the next group of flies. One, two, three or more flies disappeared as the neb of the fish broke through the surface film and took in the flies. These trout are so deceptive, they appear to be moving so slowly and yet when they are on you the pace seems like a sprint. Fast and furious, so there is no time for hesitation.

A lone fish in the *Caenis* is a much tougher target. When the fish are so high in the water the window of vision viewed by one pair of eyes is quite narrow. Because their window of vision is so narrow the trout can pass your fly without even seeing it. They pass it even when the fly appears to be close to the fish, and yet I feel certain that this isn't a refusal. The fish just haven't seen the artificial. For the trout to come onto the fly, it has to be right in the slot. Earlier that fine line of judgement seemed out of reach. As I watched the lone fish approaching me, some more flies disappeared. He was about thirty-five yards away, and the centre of all my attention. My headache no longer existed. The trout moved onto another group of flies and sucked them in one after the other. As he sucked in the naturals the distinctive sipping sound could be clearly heard as he worked his way in towards me. I studied his line intently watching for any change of direction. Which way was he going to go next? He carried on feeding, locked in to a group of *Caenis* which was in front of me.

Keeping my right arm as low as I could I lifted my fly-line, made one false cast and put the fly down on the path I judged the fish to be taking. One can no longer put the fly down in their zone of vision. If the trout sees the fly fall in, they will adjust their feeding line to avoid the fly. The fly has to be far enough ahead of the fish, that the trout comes on to it without the fish deviating from their course. This is the fine line of judgement that one has to be in tune with. Get it wrong and all you will see is a fish taking avoiding action. They need to come on to the fly naturally without detecting your presence or the delivery. The dry fly (a Bits pattern, size 14 with a tuft of cdc attached for visibility) sat among the natural flies. At such times my heart rate always quickens – the fish is close but he is not yet mine. Such moments fill me with intense excitement and the momentum builds up until the climax of ultimate deception or refusal. If the trout refuses, it is as if you have fallen off the edge as he passes your artificial. But whatever the outcome the moment is always exciting because we never know whether the fish will make a commitment to take the fly. The trout took in a natural fly. There was a brief pause, the fish then took in another and moved on to where it sipped in two more flies in quick succession, and then the artificial disappeared. The ultimate deception!

Fishing with a 0.150mm copolymer nylon leader I had to feel for the fish as I lifted, and then cushion the strike as the weight of the trout pulled my line up tight. Using fine nylon and fishing at twenty-five yards or more to the fly it is easy to break the nylon on the strike. As I lifted and the weight of the fish could be felt I eased off, avoiding any sudden shock to the leader. Everything held, the fish boiled on the surface and then made a long run diagonally across and away from me. The line stretched out into the water following the trout's movement. I did not want the trout to take too much line, as the increasing drag on the fly-line could break the fine leader or tear the hook hold. It was a bit of a dilemma because at the same time with a nylon leader of 0.150mm I could not put enough pressure on the trout to stop him running. Thankfully the fish stopped with my backing splice about ten yards beyond the tip ring and I gingerly recovered the line. Slowly the backing splice came towards me and then down through the rod rings and onto the spool of the reel. The fly-line began to build up on the spool of the reel and I began to feel more confident of landing my fish. Several times the trout made a strong powerful run. The fish still had plenty of strength in reserve and yet he never took me to the backing again. Eventually he rolled onto his side. I slid the net under the fish and lifted my prize. Droplets of water fell from his golden flanks, dripping from the mesh of the net as I lifted. It was just after 7am. I had my fish, and I felt good.

The trout was a typical limestone fish with a small neat head, thick shoulders and heavily spotted down the flanks. June fish are in tip-top condition and this one was no exception – it was a cracker. Hastily weighed in the net, it went 5½lbs. I then placed the net back in the water to allow the trout to recover. Within a short time the fish was ready to go, and I gently lifted the mesh for one last look at my prize. It leaves one with such a wonderful feeling to see such a fish at close range. I then inverted the head of the net, and with a thrash of its

Andrew Flitcroft playing a nice fish with the early morning sun on his back

tail my trout was gone. A trout rises, you stalk the fish with a dry fly and deceive it. Nothing can compare to this. Whoopee, now I was buzzing.

When I release trout I would normally unhook them by hand in the water. To do this I slide my free hand down the leader until I can grip the fly between my index finger and thumb. And then with a quick twist the fish is free of the hook. This takes but a moment to do and the fish is then free to swim away. However, when using fine nylon this method of release isn't possible, especially with heavy fish as they can easily break the leader when you lift the fish's head. With fine nylon and small hooks I find the landing net a necessity, but for most of my fishing I would rarely use one. I have boated some big trout by hand. It is an action which I have never found difficult to perform. But on this June

185

morning using a fine leader I was thankful for the net.

That first fish was the beginning of a fabulous run of luck. Two more trout quickly followed the first, and they were both about 3½ lbs. They appeared to be young fish cloaked in a silver mantle with large black spots and fine translucent tails. These two trout were taken from a large pod of feeding fish, which broke up after the second capture. The activity then died and I had to search around to find another group of trout.

Cruising about the open water with the outboard ticking over on low revs I scanned the surface for a moving fish. I came onto a group of trout feeding by an offshore reef. It was well out, a good mile or more offshore and the vast expanse of Lough Corrib stretched away from me on all sides. There was a large rock on the reef which was showing above the surface of the water. Water lazily lapped around the rock, which was the only feature for some considerable distance. At least it provided a marker to pin-point my position. The trout seemed to be patrolling a route from the reef to a small shallow which was about 200 yards to the north-west. They were constantly breaking the surface film along the patrol route as they sipped in the spent flies. The lightest of wind from the north-west caressed the oily calm surface of the lough forming a patchwork of rippled water, which reflected and magnified the intensity of the sun's rays which were now searing down from a cloudless sky. Although the wind was barely perceptible from the north-west it did have an effect on the way the boat was drifting. It meant that I would be facing the surface glare as the boat drifted towards the south-east where the sun was climbing ever higher in the sky. Thankfully my headache had cleared which was just as well as the bright light and reflected glare could not have been worse, especially as I would have to stare into the glare to focus on my dry fly.

A group of five or six trout came up towards me mopping up spent fly one after another. I tracked them and put my fly on to what I thought to be their line. The fish kept heading towards the fly, nebs showing all the time. They worked their way in until they were all around my fly, and then one, two perhaps a dozen flies disappeared. It would have been the easiest act in the world to have struck and said that I had missed one, but this would have been a mistake. I could clearly see that my fly hadn't been taken. Striking would have only spooked the fish. The fly rocked to the movement of the trout feeding all around it, they were that close. A succession of naturals disappeared, and then the neb of a fish broke the surface below my fly and the artificial disappeared as well.

A gentle lift of the rod feeling for the fish and then the rod took on its battle curve once again. This was another good fish and when the trout was boated it turned the scale at just over 5lbs. As it lay in the folds of the net I admired the quality of the fish. It was a beauty, a testament to the productivity of a great fishery. And just like the previous trout I had caught that morning when I inverted the net, it shot away in a flurry of spray. To think there are those who firmly believe that big trout will not rise to the *Caenis*. A 5lb fish is at the top end of the weight scale for brown trout which we can target with a fly rod on these loughs. On a small dry fly if you fish in the right areas in the *Caenis* rise, a 5lb wild brown is more than a distinct possibility. What more could any trout angler want?

By a little after 8am I had taken four trout. The temperature was rising and it was going to be a warm day, and yet in unbroken sunshine the trout were still moving to the carpet of fly which was beginning to peter out. I knew the duration of the rise was now limited and if I wanted another fish I would have to act quickly. Luck was running with me for a small group of trout began working a short distance ahead of the boat. They were about fifty yards out from the edge of the reef. Quietly using the oars, I dropped the boat down to where I could ambush the fish. As I slipped into position they worked their way in towards the boat unaware of my presence. Keeping well down in the boat, and with the rod low at an angle of 45 degrees instead of upright, I cast out the line and let the fly sit on what I thought to be the feeding line. But the fish did not come onto the fly; they missed it. By using the oars to keep in touch with the trout I attempted to cover the feeding line with a number of casts. It took several attempts before the fly fell on the right line and another trout fell to the deceptive charm of the dry artificial. A fish of about 4½ lbs thrashed on the surface of the water as I tightened, and then powered off. Applying light pressure, the trout was coaxed back towards the boat and the waiting net.

Within minutes of releasing that last fish I heard the distinctive sip of a trout rising. Scanning the water in the direction from which the sound had come I spotted another fish rising well over to my right. It is amazing how far that sipping noise can travel. The fish was a good way off moving on a diagonal course into the wind and away from me. I spent the next two or three minutes rowing, trying to head the trout off with the boat. Pulling well ahead of the fish to where I thought there was a chance of an ambush I stopped rowing and picked up the rod. With my line out on the water I waited for the trout to move in towards the boat. It wasn't difficult to track the fish as it was rising regularly, but the trout did not move in towards me, and instead continued moving across the wind. I had to use the oars to keep abreast of the fish which was moving about forty yards away. We had possibly covered fifty or sixty yards of water when suddenly he changed direction and headed straight towards the boat. It was a difficult cast across the wind which was on my wrong shoulder, my casting arm. There was no scope for backing off with the boat; I would either have to make my play or let the opportunity go. I cast the fly out and the leader rolled over presenting the artificial on a straight line. If the trout came onto the fly it would see no nylon, just an artificial sitting in the surface film. The sips, a sound not unlike that of small children kissing, grew louder as the fish moved onto the fly and then the fly disappeared to the sound of a kiss.

This fish put up quite a tussle before succumbing to the fold of the landing net. It was another lovely brown of 4¾ lbs, my sixth and last trout of the morning. I couldn't help thinking that I had been blessed to have enjoyed so much good fortune over such a short period of time. I'm selective about the areas I choose to fish i.e. areas of the lough that hold bigger than average trout, but this alone will not guarantee fish of the size I caught that morning. What a morning, and to think I could have so easily missed out on my best session of 2008 had I left earlier when feeling unwell. A bag of six fish on the dry fly in a *Caenis* hatch for a total weight of around 26lbs, was an incredible run of luck. After releasing the last fish, I could see that the trout activity which had lasted for a good four hours was falling off. They were going down for the day. It was around 9am. My fishing session was coming to a close, and sensing that it was over I sat back in a glow of fulfilment. It was then that I noticed a boat quietly creeping in behind me. I hadn't seen them earlier for I was so absorbed in my fishing, but they had watched me play out the last two fish. Larry called over 'Well how many have you now?' In a distinctly bright tone I replied 'What a morning – I have six fish.' Larry got his reposte in. He turned to Vaughan Ruckley and John Cash saying 'So much for the man who was at death's door a few hours ago.' He then called over to me 'And how's the ------- headache now?' What could I say. My headache seemed a distant memory, but then good fishing is the perfect remedy for an angler who is feeling out of sorts. The sun beamed down from an almost cloudless sky, and the lough shimmered with reflected light. It had been a lovely morning, the perfect morning for a fish on the *Caenis*. Lough Corrib had given me six of the best 'What ------- headache?' I replied.

15 Dad's Bay

Just a handful of anglers will know of Dad's Bay. It is a name we gave to the bay to give it some anonymity. There are those who will have heard of these golden acres but they will not know of their whereabouts. By giving it a pseudo name we could at least in some small measure protect this jewel from the ravages of over-fishing. Dad's Bay is a bay on Lough Corrib. It may not cover a large area of the lough, in extent no more than eighty acres, but this piece of water at certain times holds some big fish, such as big brown trout which will in the right conditions move to the fly. More importantly in the right conditions they can be taken on a dry fly.

For one who loves hunting big brown trout near the surface, areas like Dad's Bay are dream locations. Surrounded by meadow land, bog and heath it is a food rich area. Fringed by beds of *Phragmites*, the bay has all the right credentials for attracting large trout which are looking for an easy meal. Shallow, with a silty marl bottom blanketed in *Chara* weed, much of it is no more than five to six feet deep, and with a few rocky reefs and islands scattered about it is ideal habitat for all types of aquatic insects. Insects are present in prodigious numbers dominated by the midges beloved by trout. Dad's Bay is a haven for these two-winged flies. It holds unquantifiable numbers of them, and they are a principal food of brown trout on Lough Corrib. And where there is a bounty of food, predators will move in to feed upon it. Timing is the key to success for catching these fish; time it right and brown trout fishing of an unparalleled quality is there to be had if you are lucky.

My first introduction to Dad's Bay was on a day when the fishing rods had been packed away. Larry and I were out doing some reconnaissance and reconnaissance, it is said, is never time wasted. Never was this truer than on the day I first visited the bay. For as soon as I saw this piece of water I remarked to Larry that it was an area I would like to fish at the right time. It just looked so inviting. All my experience was telling me that here was a habitat that would provide plenty of fly and that the fish would move in to find it. Looking down into the water I could see that the bed of the bay was covered in soft *Chara*, with the odd patch of white marl left exposed where no weed had grown. I felt so positive about what we had seen that I just had to give the bay a go. Larry told me that it was an area where a local angler, Tom Murray (affectionately known to those who knew him well as Dad, hence the name Dad's Bay) used to catch big trout by accident when fishing for pike. He also told me that when he went out fishing with Tom they also used to catch good fish on Mayfly or Dabbler patterns from the outside fringes of the bay. This was a good few years ago and since then Larry had gone off exploring other areas of Lough Corrib. Like me Larry wanted to learn as much as he could about the lough. As it is a big area of water to cover this took a lot of time and effort so he hadn't fished the area for some time. I felt so confident that the bay would produce fish, and I believe looking at the bay that day Larry did too. All we had to do was wait; wait for the right time.

On a nice evening at the beginning of June six or more weeks later Larry rang me to see if I wanted to fish the bay. Although I dearly wanted to fish I couldn't make it, but suggested as the weather conditions were ideal that he should go. At a little after midnight I received a phone call. I just knew it had to be my friend and as he was phoning so late it meant that he had caught. When I picked up the phone Larry's voice came through, and he was very excited. Speaking very quickly, he told me of his epic evening. He had just finished fishing and had caught four cracking brown trout for nearly 20lbs. All the trout had fallen for the Cluster and he had caught them in the area we had looked at earlier in the year. The fish didn't move until late and as it was a dark evening it was difficult to see the rises. Larry said that he could only spot the fish in a certain area of light and that when he saw a fish rising they took his artificial fly confidently. Larry was ecstatic and rightly so for this was an exceptional catch of fish, and it confirmed that the bay had great potential. I just couldn't wait to try it myself.

Three nights later Larry and I were out along with a friend of Larry's who was sharing another boat. As the fish in Dad's did not move until late Larry thought it best to try elsewhere for the first part of the evening. We both caught fish and finished with three trout to the boat. They were like peas in pod,

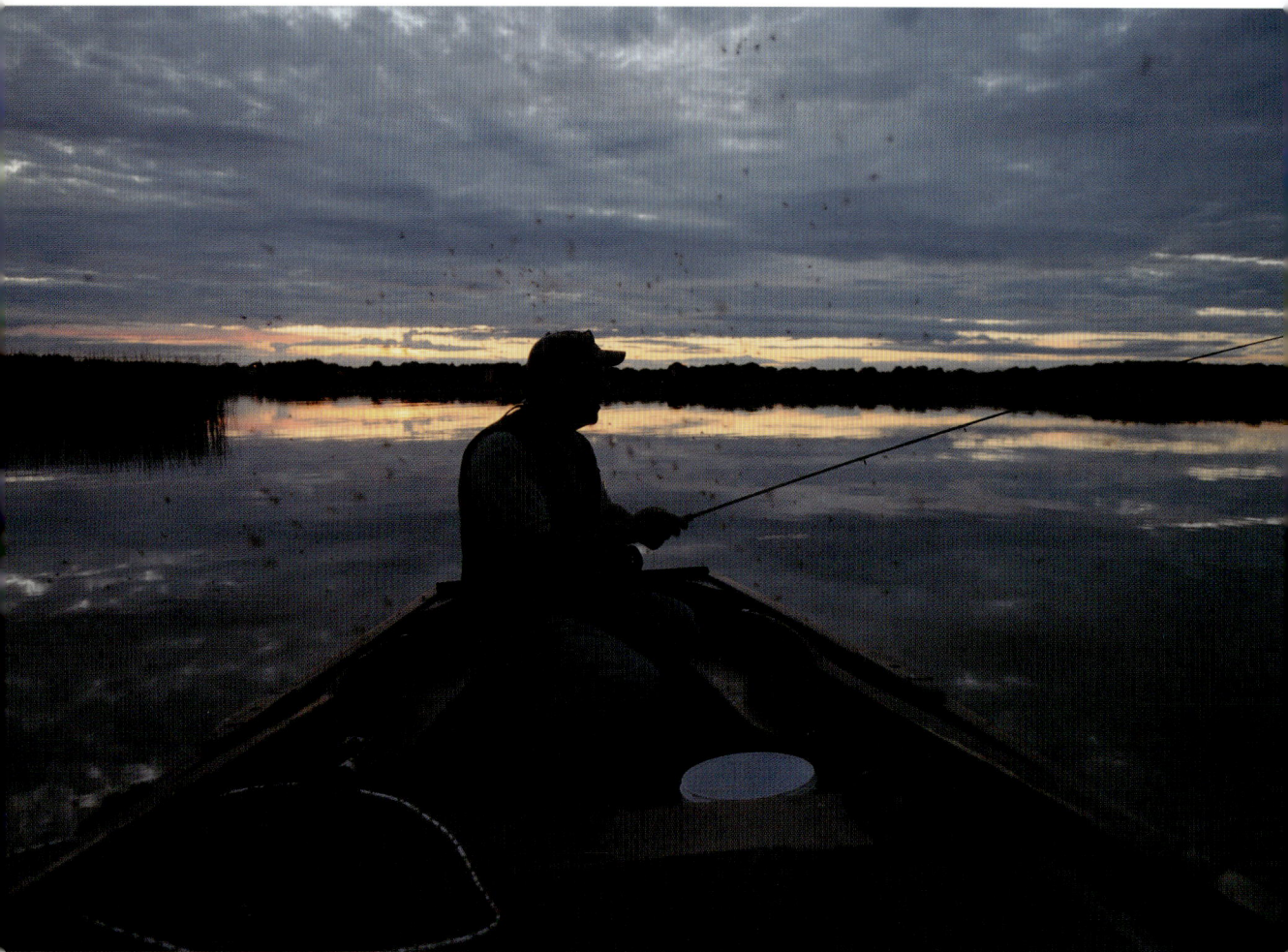

In the failing light sedges take to the wing, Dad's Bay, Lough Corrib

between 3 and 3½ lbs and as fat as pigs. Around 9.30 we ventured into the bay. It was a cool evening with little fly, and there were very few fish moving. We hunted down the side of a weed bed but saw no trout rising. Eventually we found a good fish moving in a corner of the bay, and both Larry and I agreed that the trout looked somewhere between 6 and 8lbs. We positioned the boat to ambush the fish. Unfortunately however, Larry's friend in the other boat came in across us and inadvertently disturbed the trout, putting it down. My

192

boat partner berated his friend for coming in on the fish, but I couldn't help feeling that Larry's reprimand was wasted, as his friend stared back towards us with a vacant look on his face. After the disturbance no other trout moved that evening, and as the conditions didn't look that promising we came off early.

The following day the weather took a turn for the worse and it blew cold with rain for the next two days. Late on the afternoon of 17 June the wind began to fall off and the cloud broke allowing the sun to peep through. The morning had been wet, windy and cold, but as the sun began to break through the cloud, the temperature started to rise. Conditions were improving. I hadn't been out on the lough for a few days but now with the improving conditions I felt a compulsion to go. All the signs were pointing to a nice evening and if the temperature held up there would be a good hatch of fly. If the fly came off there would be a real opportunity to take a fish. I just couldn't ignore the signs; my fishy barometer was telling me to give the bay a cast. It was my turn to phone Larry to see if he wanted to go with me. Larry desperately wanted to go fishing, but as he had been out guiding all day he said it would be difficult for him to find the spare time. At the time Larry was not only a guide on Lough Corrib, but was also a landlord of a local bar and he had no one to stand in for him that evening. So with such a commitment to work, he reluctantly declined. After wishing me good luck Larry told me that he would be working late and that I was to keep him informed if I caught any trout.

At around nine on that beautiful evening I found myself setting up my rod beside the lough shore. Blackcap and whitethroat tucked away in the surrounding cover were singing, backed by song thrush and the melancholic ballad of the blackbird. A vocal harmony of birdsong brought on by the improving weather made the evening feel vibrant and alive. There was still some heavy cloud out towards the north-east providing a backcloth of dark slate blue, but overhead and to the south-west the cloud was lighter and broken. Swans the colour of Dulux Brilliant White flew across the dark backcloth of sky. The contrast of the brilliant whiteness of the birds highlighted by the sun was unreal. After the cool wet start to the day the evening felt warm and sultry. The dampness rising from the ground and evaporating with the raise in temperature carried with it a heady mixture of scent-laden air. All around me the foliage on the surrounding scrub bushes and trees still had that lovely lush green of young leaves. They had not yet become tarnished by time. Startled by my presence, two redshank which had been feeding along the margin rose in unison, piping in alarm as they took off. Further along the lough shore, they alighted on some rocks with a typical upstretched wing movement. From the marginal cover behind me a grasshopper warbler was singing. The incessant chirr similar to that of an overgrown grasshopper, is sometimes likened in some bird books to the rapid click of an angler's reel. A myriad of insects were on the wing, the sunlight reflected off their wings giving the impression that the air was full of light down. Nature was busy all around me, and I could feel the infectiousness of the evening having an effect on me also. I felt excited at the prospect of fishing the bay and hurriedly threaded the fly-line up through the rings of my 6 weight rod and set up my cast. To my leader of 0.185mm copolymer nylon I tied a Post Hackle Midge to the top dropper and a Grey Duster on the point. All was now ready, it was around nine-thirty as I stowed my tackle in the boat and motored out of the mooring.

In the month of June in the west of Ireland the sun sets at a little after ten and as the main fly hatch would only begin after the sun had set I knew that there was plenty of time. It would be at least another thirty to forty minutes before the fly would commence hatching and hopefully with it, the fish would start rising. There was no need to rush. With the outboard at less than half throttle, I quietly motored into the bay with plenty of time to spare. The wind was from the west and dropping as the sun sank on the western horizon. I positioned the boat so that it was upwind of the most likely area for a rise of fish, and there I waited. My point fly was unclipped from the keeper ring, and my leader and some loose line was laid out ready to take advantage of a rising fish if a target presented itself. This type of fishing is a hunt. I'm looking for a target and when I find a rising fish I position the boat to take advantage of the situation.

Patience is the key, as these fish are easily spooked. If I fished the water blind I could waste a good opportunity by scaring any potential trout by lining them, and consequently putting them down before being able to see the trout feeding. Fishing before they can actually target a fish, especially a big fish, is an error that many anglers tend to make. They haven't the patience to wait and to let events unfold. Once you can see a trout moving near the surface, you know where your target is. More importantly by knowing where the fish is, you can avoid scaring the trout before it has seen your fly. Fishing the water blind would have been a grave error of judgement. I could sense that an opportunity was going to come my way, and it would be just a matter of time. Waiting without making any obvious fish-scaring movement would be paramount to success. As the evening deepened and the light gave way to the night, I sat patiently waiting for a fish to move. If you love nature and are observant, waiting isn't a problem, as it is all part of the game. There is always something to observe or hear if you are quiet while out on Lough Corrib.

Whilst silently waiting in the shelter of the reed bed, I lose myself to my surroundings. A cuckoo called from some shrub sallows before going to roost.

Evening is a good time for a big fish and Dee looks on with approval

195

Some people find the call boring but I never tire of them. To me it is the sound of late spring and early summer. It is a call I associate with settled weather, lovely evenings and quiet summer dawns. The sound of the cuckoo and good fishing seem to go together. As the cuckoo fell silent I detected another sound, that of a snipe drumming high overhead. Its partner was probably sitting on eggs in the boggy meadowland adjacent to the bay. The muffled strumming noise, created by a rapid movement of their tail feathers is part of a territorial display by the males. On quiet evenings it is possible to hear them drumming well into the night hours.

As I looked eastwards across the rippled surface of the water the reflected light from the western sky was behind me. Reflected light from the water's surface is of great benefit to the fisherman who fishes into the dusk period. The last vestiges of light upon the surface of the water make it easier for the angler to see a rising fish. This is why for the lake fisher, a south or an east wind is a good wind for late evening fishing. Looking towards the light we can pinpoint the late rises so much more easily in the illuminated water. With a west wind I did not have the comfort of looking into the illuminated water, and am facing away from it. The surface of the water is the colour of a wet basalt rock, but there is still light enough to see a fish.

Adult flies were leaving the shelter of the reed beds behind me and taking to the wing. One after another they came winging past me making a distinctive high-pitched whining noise as they flew out onto the open water, etching the surface of the water with their movement as they skated across the surface depositing their eggs. As the egg-laying is taking place, more adult flies emerged from their pupal shucks. Newly hatched flies crawled all over the gunwales of the boat, and the engine cowling was soon covered with olive green midge. Countless numbers of midge emerged and took to the air. All around me the air was filled with the whining hum of frenetically beating wings. All this activity would not go unnoticed; the optimum time for a trout was fast approaching. Fish which have moved into the bay specifically for this hatch of fly would be now hunting for food. These trout will hold in this bay for several weeks until the hatches of *Campto* buzzer come to an end. So for a few weeks while the trout have a well-stocked larder this is their home, but the fish will move on as soon as the food supply is exhausted. Knowing this we hunt these areas for a few weeks of the season for some of the largest brown trout we as fly fishermen can target with an artificial fly. This is why I'm here. You do not consistently catch these trout by aimlessly drifting the water casting blind in the vain hope that a big fish will come up and take your fly. To catch these trout consistently one has to hunt them down where they regularly come to feed.

What I find interesting is how do fish know where to find concentrations of food? Do they learn about these rich feeding areas simply by searching around or following other fish which possess prior knowledge of good feeding grounds, or do they acquire this knowledge from their parents? I find it interesting that shallow areas of bays can at certain times of the day or season come alive with feeding fish. In water which is only a few feet deep and mostly devoid of trout during the day the *Campto* buzzer, a fly which hatches after the sun has set can, as the light fades, draw fish into these fly-rich areas to produce some prolific rises. Some of these areas are so shallow one can see that there are very few trout present for most of the day, and yet at the time of the hatch, trout move in to feed on the glut of fly these areas produce. On the rich limestone loughs of Ireland, brown trout do not appear to be as territorial as the trout which live in rivers. River brownies, especially the larger fish, are very territorial. River fish will stake their claim to a good lie and defend this lie from all potential competitors. On the limestone loughs the brown trout move around to find food and the richer feeding areas always attract the bigger fish. It is interesting that even though numbers of big fish may be attracted to these feeding areas, there never appears to be any competition for a prime site. The fish may follow a patrol route and therefore it is possible to ambush them on this route. However, the line which the trout follow may be occupied by several or more big trout all feeding on the same food items. Over the course of the season, these trout may hold in a certain area in harmony with one another for a period of time while there is a good stock of food to be found, but once the food supply has been exhausted they will move on.

Some species of fish migrate over huge distances to find their food. Salmon for instance migrate over considerable distances to areas which they have never seen before, to find rich feeding. Would the same behaviour characteristic apply to brown trout within a large lough system, or do they acquire the knowledge by following other fish to far-off feeding grounds? They could follow more experienced fish and therefore over a period of time learn about the food-rich areas. If they do, what is interesting is we catch very few smaller trout. The bigger trout seem to know where and when to find the rich feeding, even if for a large part of the season they do not venture into the area to feed. At certain times of the season they will move into these areas to feed at key times, especially late in the evening and into the night. But for much of the day and a large part of the season, they move out to the comfort of deeper water even if they have to travel quite some distance. Whether it is instinct or learnt behaviour, it is uncanny how these fish know where and when to find this food, and how at a key time of the season which coincides with a hatch of fly they appear like clockwork to find the rich feeding. There is still much we do not know about the movement of brown trout within these large lough systems.

Searching the water for any sign of movement I heard the trout moving long before I saw him. The suck of a fish taking in fly from the surface film is such a distinctive sound, and in the silence of the late evening air the sound carries. Was it *the* fish, the trout I had specifically come to the bay for? The big fish I had seen when out with Larry a few days earlier? My line was out to one side of the boat. I lifted it to make sure the leader hadn't drowned, and put the line back down onto the water, and waited. Hearing another suck, well out to my left, I pulled with the oar to bring my boat into line and scanned the water for a sign, an indication of where the fish was located. He moved again and I had him in my sights, about forty yards out moving towards me. I willed him on to me, but the fish had other ideas and changed direction. One, two, three rises, and the trout swam out to the periphery of my sight. In the failing light the fish is lost to my vision, and yet I could still hear him feeding. Don't move out I begged. Turn, please turn. The next rise suggests that my prayer was answered, for the fish turned back towards me. Another suck, a gulp of air accompanied by a leisurely forward movement of the head as the neb of the fish broke through the surface film of the water. There were countless pupa stuck below the surface film, and the trout fed at his leisure. With plenty of food around the fish was in no hurry. He will feed until the food is either exhausted or he is disturbed. But the hunter was unaware that he too was being watched, and that he was also being hunted. The rises were getting closer. The fingers of my hand moved around the butt of the rod, testing the grip. Following a haphazard course, the fish moved in and across me, moving left to right. Around thirty yards out he rose again, the neb of the trout broke through the surface in a slow forward roll followed by the back of the fish and then the tip of the tail. As he dropped away, aided by the afterglow from the late evening light of the western sky, I could just make out a large brown shadow in the water. It was a big fish, and he continued moving in towards me and to the right. My hand tensed on the butt of the rod. With a smooth lift, I raised my fly-line off the water and up behind me. One false cast, and I put the point fly down where hopefully it was going to be in the window of vision of my target fish.

The fly sat on the basalt-coloured surface of the water and, hardly daring to breathe, I waited for the next rise, hoping it would be to my fly. As these trout, like all stillwater trout, constantly change direction when feeding near the surface, it can be difficult to judge the feeding line. Because of their erratic movement and critical eye, it is easy for negative thought to creep in. Will he refuse me, have I judged the feeding line correctly? These were the negative thoughts that were racing through my mind, and yet over the uncertainty I watched the fly expectantly. I had confidence in the pattern of fly, and the tackle I was using. It was a combination of fishing impedimenta which I knew well and understood. More importantly it was a combination which made me feel confident. Confidence is such a big factor, but there is always an element of uncertainty where fish are concerned. We just do not know how they will react to our offerings. It was but a brief moment in time, the time between the fly settling on the surface of the water and when the fly disappeared to the rise of the fish. And yet for all my confidence, for that brief moment I felt a little anxious. The moment transcended into an eternity of time, eclipsed only by the rise of the fish, and it is then, and only then that I knew the waiting was over. To the sound of a rising fish my fly disappeared and all my anxiety was erased. It is such a simple action, that of a trout taking a fly, but one which is for an angler so important if it is his fly which the trout has taken. I lifted the rod.

As the line tensioned I felt the weight of the fish. There was a large boil on the surface of the water, and then a solid weight moved away from me. The fly-line slipped easily through my fingers, and the few loose coils of fly-line lying on the bottom boards of the boat disappeared up through the rod rings. As all the loose line disappeared the reel sang – it was the song of a good fish running.

There can be no finer feeling for the dry-fly angler than when a fish is first deceived. It is the defining moment, but the sound of a singing reel crowns the moment with joy.

The fight is the part sandwiched between two greater events, the hooking and the landing of a fish. Of the two, hooking the fish after deceiving it with an artificial fly is the greater. I find it difficult to enjoy playing a fish, as not wishing to cause them too much stress I want to land them as quickly as possible. It is an odd feeling but I find playing a fish fills me with a mix of emotions. I'm filled with excitement from the prospect of landing the fish, anxiety from the thought of losing it, and I also have to deal with the stress of wishing to land it quickly. A melting pot of mixed emotions which are only sorted when the fight is concluded one way or the other.

My fish felt heavy, and with big trout there are usually no electrifying runs, frenzied changes of pace, or tight turns in the water. They are stolid creatures and try to muscle their way out of a problem. The fish bored away, and reluctantly I gave line. He took me to the backing but no further. Then by applying steady pressure I brought the fish in on a shorter line. He made several runs but never taking more than fifteen to twenty yards of line, and once I had him on a shorter line I felt in control. With the fish under the rod, the rod absorbs most of the shocks and saps the trout's energy. On a short line with the rod well bent we played out the ending. Eventually the fish rolled on its side and the huge golden flanks slid over the rim of the waiting net. He was mine.

Lying at my feet was one of the finest sights I could ever wish to see. A pristine fabulous looking fish of around twenty-four inches in length, one of Ireland's best. Staring in disbelief at my prize I felt ecstatic about my success. It had to be the trout Larry and I had seen four nights previously. If it wasn't, it certainly was a similar size to the fish we had seen. Filled with elation I quickly searched out the spring balance and weighed the trout in the net. Allowing for the net my fish registered 7lbs 2oz. I was tempted to kill the trout and have him set up, but decided against it. I took a quick photograph of the fish on the wet boards of the boat and then held him in the water for release. Happy with the thought that I had achieved my goal, I didn't need the body of my prize to make the moment any better. Wishing the trout good luck I opened my hand and released him. With a thrust of his tail which covered me in spray, he powered away leaving me with just a memory. After all that he had given me it seemed like a fair exchange – his life for a memory. I was happy with that.

With the fish safely released I checked my leader, and the fly which the trout took. After drying the fly I began searching for another fish. The light had almost gone but the conditions were good. The temperature had held up and there were still plenty of fly hatching. Bats flitted around chasing flies and I could hear snipe drumming as I quietly pulled the boat over to my right in behind another weed bed where I hoped to find another trout feeding. Upon reaching the weed bed I stopped rowing, and let the boat settle, taking time to look and listen. After several minutes nothing stirred, so I pulled over another thirty yards or more and stopped rowing. The boat glided to a stop on the outside of the weed bed, and again I repeated the procedure of looking and listening. All was quiet and the wind fell away as the night crept in. There was no sign of a fish feeding – I drew a blank.

As there was no sign of moving fish I decided to take the boat over to the other side of the bay close to a stand of *Phragmites* reeds which ran along the shore. Positioning the boat just off the reed bed I disturbed some sedge warblers and they began chattering. Not unlike the grasshopper warbler, only more boldly marked, the call is the distinguishing feature, as the grasshopper chirrs whereas the sedge chatters. The chattering carried on and I was reminded of nights spent fishing for carp or tench on the lakes of my native Oxfordshire. On summer evenings, these little birds would sing all night long into the grey light of dawn. Sitting beside the reed bed with little wind and no noticeable drop in temperature, I could have easily been by an Oxfordshire lake, but I wasn't. A different sound brought me back to my senses: the suck of a feeding fish and it was close by. I picked up my rod and stealthily let out some line. Making slow deliberate movements and very little noise I scanned the inky black surface of the water for the fish. Another suck and I could make out the ripples of the rise no more than fifteen yards away. In the darkness I could see the rise, but I could not determine which way the fish was travelling. I put the flies down close to the rise and waited for the next movement. Closer in and to the left, the fish came up again and sucked in another fly. I lifted off and dropped my flies in short of the rise. The fish moved again, but he changed direction and moved away from me. I lifted off and tried to head the fish, and again he changed direction. A game of cat and mouse, I covered the fish several more times without spooking him, but he didn't come to me. Then the trout moved in towards the boat. This time I just lifted the rod and without casting, dropped the flies in short. With only a yard or two of the fly-line out, the fish was very close to the boat. As is common with night fishing, I heard the suck before I saw the rise. It is as if the night gloom slows down the speed of light, but the truth is we never have enough light to see the rise as it actually happens. What we see is the disturbance after the rise has been made. The suck sounded as if it were at my feet, in the area where I had dropped my artificials, and this time I instinctively felt he had come to me. I could not see the flies or the rise, but I sensed that he had taken. Gently lifting the rod I felt for the fish, and a feeling of increasing weight came through. I raised the rod some more to set the hook and the rod pulled over, followed by a huge whorl in the water just yards out from the boat. Startled by the sudden movement, a chorus of sedge warblers burst into life as the fish made a strong run out from the reeds.

I was thankful that the trout ran out towards the open water, and I followed with the boat. There, with no obvious snags close by, I played my fish out. When he rolled on his side I could see that I had hooked another big trout. Not as large as the first, but in anybody's book it was a big brown. When I lifted the net I could tell the fish was over 5lbs, and on the balance he went 5lbs 4oz. I was over the moon. I just couldn't believe my luck. Either one of those two trout would have been reward enough, but to catch a brace of wild brown trout of that size was beyond my wildest dreams. I was filled with an overwhelming sense of elation. That was until May 2009 my heaviest brace of wild brown trout. It was a unique event which happened on an evening's fishing that lasted for no more than a few hours. And the fly which deceived those wonderful fish? A Grey Duster.

The hatch of fly was all but over after the second capture and with no other positive sign to lure me on I decided to come in. It was around 12.30am when I pulled the boat up. I do not remember any moonlight, the night was quite dark. The air was still, warm and humid. As I stood by the mooring I listened for any sound of birdsong. However the warblers which had been vocal all evening were silent, and there was no lively chatter emanating from the reed beds. Even the snipe had now fallen silent. After mooring the boat and putting

202

my fishing gear away I rang Larry. I could hear lively background noise in the bar. It seemed almost another world away, not at all like the silence I was experiencing by the side of the lough. Larry picked up the phone: 'Well?' and I related the events of the evening to my friend. '------- hell' he said, and after a few more expletives, 'Well done.' He also thought that the biggest fish had to be the same trout that we had previously seen in that location. Excited by the news of my brace and a need to go fishing he then said what about the morning. The morning? It is morning I thought. 'Are you serious?' I replied thinking it was a wind up. 'Never more serious' came the retort. Larry is a hard task master and he really has some drive, but this was bordering on insanity. He also has a tactic when persuading someone to do something they may not wish to do because it goes against their better judgement. His tactic is basically foolproof, as it works on the principle of not accepting no as an answer. I couldn't help thinking that we could be in danger of being sectioned for such an action. However, buoyed by my recent captures, an infectious madness to go fishing, and Larry's persuasive charm I agreed to meet him by the boat at 4.45.

After the phone call I drove home to grab a few hours' sleep. On arrival at the house I found it difficult to settle, as my mind was still racing, so I poured myself a glass of whiskey, opened the French windows and listened for any sign of outdoor activity. All was silent, only a gentle breeze came in through the opening, warm and fragrant. It carried the scent of meadowsweet and bog myrtle. Of birdsong there was none except for the lone piping of a distant wader calling from the shoreline of Ballynalty Bay. Through breaks in the cloud the odd star peeped through, bright shining lights gleaming in the pure air of Ireland's west. It had been a magical evening, and I didn't want the night to end.

Through my deep subconscious state I could hear a noise. Softly at first, the sound then came through harsh and noisy. The alarm brought me to my senses, dragging me from my deep slumber. I felt tired. It would have been easy to have turned the alarm off, roll back into the comfort of the warm duvet and let the weight of sleep take over. To hesitate would have been a mistake, and sleep would have won. I shook off the quilt and raised myself to my feet. Although it was early the grey light of dawn was already creeping in. In less than fifteen minutes, grabbing a carton of juice and a banana, I was back in the car driving to meet up with my friend. When I arrived at the mooring Larry was already preparing the boat to make a start. His rod was made up and lying in the boat. He was eager to go, so I quickly picked up my gear and stowed it in the boat, untied the mooring rope and stepped in. I could tackle up on the way out. To a floating line and a leader of around twenty feet I attached two small dry flies. Both size 14 and the leader diameter was 0.165mm.

After working the night in the bar Larry was keen to be off. He's always enthusiastic about going fishing. At the start of every session he enthuses optimism, such is his drive and determination. He is a good foil for those occasions when the fishing is tough, and with wild fishing we experience the tough as well as the good. Larry's resilience was severely put to the test once we were out on the open water, for we soon discovered that the conditions were far from ideal for the *Caenis* rise. We hunted several areas in the hope of finding a concentration of fish, but were thwarted by a nasty early morning breeze which had sprung up. It was warm and there was a good hatch of fly. However, the breeze was taking the fly away from the key areas and away from the fish. After several hours we had drawn a blank and it was looking as if we would come off fishless. The morning was not going to plan. With the carpet of spent fly blown off some of the favoured areas, we decided to have a look in Dad's Bay. Although we favoured the open water for the *Caenis* rise, the wind had been blowing in a direction towards the bay. So it made sense to go and have a look. We had this vain hope that perhaps some of the fish which had moved in the night before to feed on the midge, had remained there. But in truth I do not believe we were too hopeful.

The light for seeing my flies that morning had been difficult to say the least, and the combined effect of the poor light and the wind on the water had made it almost impossible to see them. Because I was having difficulty in seeing the flies and picking them up quickly, I decided to sacrifice my dropper and put on a much larger sighter fly. At least this would help me to focus on the point fly. In a *Caenis* rise, the point fly is the most important fly as it usually catches most of the fish. So sacrificing the dropper was no great loss, and the benefit gained from being able to pick up the point fly more easily would be greater. In my fly patch was a pattern which Larry had given me a few days earlier. It was a tying of the fly with which he had enjoyed such success earlier in the month, when he

A cracking early morning brown

had taken his big bag of trout from the bay. The pattern in my fly patch was a size 10, a big fly and easy to see. Ideal for a sighter pattern I thought. So I tied the fly to my dropper. At the time although I didn't know it, this was to prove an inspirational change.

We dropped into the bay, and found that the effect of the wind had been nullified to some extent by some outlying stands of reeds. From one of these stands of reeds a calm lane had formed the length of the bay. Slicks are always worth fishing especially if there is some fly on the water. There was still plenty of fly caught in the calm of the slick. It was the obvious drift to fish. Larry manoeuvred the boat so that it drifted down the calm lane. This meant that we could each cover a side where the calm met the ripple edge (always a hot spot).

Halfway through the drift, we came onto a group of three large trout feeding together. The fish were a good distance off and we watched them closely. Well ahead of the boat one of the trout came my way, and when he dropped down in the water, I made my cast. The point fly was in a good position for the trout came up and began feeding inches from the fly, but the trout passed it and carried on feeding. While the trout was up I left the flies before making another cast, as I didn't want to spook the fish by lifting off my line. The fish continued feeding right into the sighter pattern, and then much to my surprise the fly disappeared to a confident rise. As I tightened, 5lbs of very wild brown trout lifted from the water, and powered off. I boated three fish that morning for around 14lbs, all coming off the calm lane, and two were taken on the sighter. A Cluster.

The Cluster, as we named the fly after that particular morning, was I feel taken for groups of spent *Caenis* which can at certain times clump together to form small clusters of fly. Since that morning the Cluster has proved itself a worthy pattern when the bigger trout are feeding on clumps of *Caenis*, and because of its effectiveness we now tend to fish it on the point. The prime position. It is an easy fly to tie. One just basically ties in a Grizzle Hackle at the bend, and a Red Game Hackle about a third of the way down the shank of the hook from the eye. Then just wind the Grizzle Hackle up the shank of the hook to the position where the Red Game Hackle is tied in, and then continue winding the two hackles together towards the eye of the hook and tie off. A simple tying, the Cluster has proved its worth for both evening and morning fishing. Originally tied as a representation of the balling buzzer, it certainly works in the morning rise to *Caenis* when a size 18 would seem a more obvious choice.

In two short sessions I had taken three trout for 14lbs in the morning and two for over 12lbs from the previous evening. My introduction to Dad's Bay, was five wild brown trout for around 26lbs. It is an exceptional stretch of water, one of many in the vast acres of Lough Corrib. Since then the bay has given me many fish over 5lbs, three over 6 and two over 7. The second 7lb fish came while I was fishing with a friend of Larry's. He was so excited by the size of the trout, that when he lifted the fish in the net he exclaimed 'Bloody hell, would you look at the size of that trout, it is as big as a salmon!' As we parted the mesh of the net to look at the fish, his hands were shaking more than mine. I do not believe that we have abused this gem. All of my fish have been returned, and as far as I know of the other trout which have been caught there, only a handful have been taken out. Big wild brown trout are such beautiful creatures, we really should look after them better. They deserve more respect than many of the so-called fishing fraternity give them. We talk a good game but how many of us I wonder actually practise what we preach? Irish anglers do not know how fortunate they are to have open access to such fine lough fisheries and the wonderful fish they contain. To me, Dad's Bay is a little piece of Irish gold, and is there for all to enjoy. If you do happen upon this gem, do not abuse it.

16 Repeat Captures

One of the most contentious issues for game anglers in both the UK and Ireland is the issue of catch and release. Now I'm not going to raise an argument for total catch and release. I never have and never will. But what I do recognise is that some of our wild game fisheries need help. This particularly applies to the more popular fisheries, especially on the Irish limestone loughs which are basically free and open to all. Such is the popularity of loughs such as Corrib and Mask, there is always a risk of overcropping the stock, and if continued this will have a long-term detrimental effect on the sporting potential of these fisheries. The danger of overcropping is always open to abuse from anglers who selfishly will take advantage of the relaxed conditions which apply to these waters. A fertile system should be capable of providing a sustainable stock to crop. It is just a question of balancing the number of fish cropped to the productivity of the water, so that it doesn't impact on its sporting potential. Rules and regulation can be applied to reduce overexploitation, but this in some situations isn't or will not be enough unless the measures that are applied are very tight, and more importantly anglers adhere to the rules. On a lot of the Irish fisheries the protective measures are too relaxed, and it is on these fisheries where the angler as an individual needs to show some form of restraint. Take a fish by all means, but even if the rules permit it do we need to take four or six wild fish?

There are anglers who believe that fish will not survive the trauma of being caught on rod and line if they are returned. Catch and release has always been a contentious issue, and an issue which when discussed by some is fraught with dogma. When clouded by emotion people dig in and then all sensible reasoning is lost. I can accept that there are those who simply cannot justify catching a fish and then releasing it, and for these anglers I have a certain amount of sympathy. However, I have very little sympathy or time for those who try to justify killing a fish on the grounds that it will not survive if it is put back. Whilst we cannot say with 100 per cent authority that a fish which is returned after capture will

Larry preparing for a quick release

survive, the evidence would suggest that we can say that if a fish is quickly released back into its environment, it has a good chance of surviving the trauma of being caught on rod and line. If the fish survives after being returned, then it is possible for that fish to be caught again, and if the fish survives after being returned it is also possible for the fish to go on and breed successfully. How do we know that fish will survive capture by rod and line? There is a mountain of scientific evidence that proves this to be the general case. In addition, repeat captures, especially of coarse fish are well documented. Coarse anglers look after their fish and return them. Because they are returned and survive, the fish are caught again. This is proven beyond reasonable doubt. How traumatic the experience is for the fish we do not know, but it isn't enough of a shock to make them impossible to catch, and it isn't sufficient to kill them.

209

In 1959 an angler, Eddie Price caught a mirror carp from Redmire Pool weighing 40.08lbs. That fish stocked as a two-year old in 1934, was caught no fewer than nine times, spanning a period from 1959 to 1980. For most of that time the fish either maintained or lost weight. Then in the latter years of its life it began putting on weight again, until it was captured for the final time by Chris Yates (who incidentally had caught the fish before, seven years earlier weighing 38lbs) weighing 51.06lbs. The following year the fish died, and was buried beside the lake it had inhabited for forty-seven years. This carp, an identifiable fish lived for forty-nine years. It was anglers who mapped out the history of this extraordinary fish. From this information and the histories of other identifiable long-lived carp, we now know that these fish live for much longer (50+ years) than fishery scientists had originally led us to believe.

Until my nineteenth year, I never gave enough serious thought to how far a fish will travel or to how quickly they could be recaught when returned after capture. In the winter of 1969, a good friend, John Everard, caught a pike which weighed 20.06lbs from a gravel pit complex (Hardwick) comprising of two lakes totalling eighty acres which were joined by a narrow cut. Three weeks later, another angler, Fred Towns, caught a pike from the opposite end of the lake to which John had caught his fish. John who was very observant and present at the time of Fred Towns' capture, instantly recognised the fish to be the same pike he had caught three weeks earlier. At the time we found it difficult to believe that it could have been the same fish. We had no idea that a fish such as a pike would travel such distances, or that they would be gullible enough be caught again so quickly. For some reason which now seems a bit naïve, I believe that we always thought that the fish we caught were virgin fish. Of course like a lot of innocent beliefs, time exposes the truth. This was the first instance of fish recognition of a fish which had been previously caught, that I had witnessed. However, once alerted to the possibility of repeat capture, I was always open-minded to the fact and started to look for them. That fish came out again towards the end of the season as did several other pike which we recognised.

John Everard's observation on that late November day in 1969 was to me quite significant. For the first time I realised that it was possible to catch the same fish again after being caught and returned. If returned, I never doubted that fish survived the trauma of being caught, but it never entered my head that once returned they could be caught again. Up until that time I suppose, I thought that the fish after capture became impossible to catch, and we always wanted to believe that a fish we caught was a virgin, one which had never been caught before. The repeat capture of the pike by Fred Towns blew this myth away, and not only this, the event also showed that a fish could be caught quite soon after being returned. How soon we did not know, but with time and experience we now know that fish can be caught within hours or even less of being returned.

Once aware that it was possible to catch a fish which had been caught before, we began noting distinguishing features on the fish we caught such as scale deformation, distinctive colour or old scar tissue. By doing this we began to catalogue a series of repeat captures. I was nineteen years old, and although now such information is arguably old hat, at the time it was a revelation. Coarse anglers are now well aware of this. On some of the popular fisheries, the known fish have been given names, but what about game fishermen? Game anglers' opinions are I feel mixed when it comes to the issue of releasing fish. Attitudes have now changed, and there is a movement within game angling which is pro releasing fish, but there are those who are still totally against it and cannot accept that fish will survive the trauma of being caught on rod and line.

What I would like to see from the majority of game anglers is a more open-minded view of the subject. Also a lot of the game anglers whom I have questioned have a problem with coming to terms with the possibility of catching a fish which may have been caught before. If you do not look for it you will not see it. I firmly believe that the majority of game fishermen would never notice if a fish had been caught before. So for many of these fishermen the ideal of catching the virgin fish will never be broken. On the larger fisheries the probability of catching a fish that had been caught before, would be quite low. However a repeat capture is still a possibility, but the idea of another angler catching a trout which had been returned isn't the sole objective for catch and release. By returning fish, we at least provide an opportunity if they survive the trauma of being caught, disease and predation, to go on to reproduce. This is important for the long-term future of some of the popular fisheries, as it would help to maintain the pool of adult fish and the productivity of the fishery.

How many times could a fish be caught on rod and line before it succumbs

A beautiful brown from Lough Corrib. We should do more to conserve such fish

to the trauma of being caught or it becomes impossible to catch is open to debate. The big mirror from Redmire Pool was caught nine times. However there are a number of recognisable fish from Redmire which have been caught and returned and repeatedly caught again. One fish, a big leather carp, came out at least twenty times in its lifetime. Another example from a different fishery is a carp which was called Benson. This fish which inhabited the Bluebell complex from 1995 up until when the carp died in the summer of 2009, was caught no less than sixty times. All the above captures have been documented. It would appear that these fish never learnt to avoid capture, and carp are just as cunning if not more so than game fish. What is evident from an analysis of results of repeat captures, is that some fish are caught more often than others. Why this should occur is open to conjecture. Perhaps some fish are less intelligent than others, or perhaps they are just greedier or have a greater need for more food.

Since the recognition by John Everard of the repeat capture of the 20lb pike caught in 1969 I can now state that I have caught the same fish of a number of species, including trout, more than once. The two most interesting captures however, concern pike and barbel. The first was a pike which I caught from the upper River Thames. I caught this particular fish which only had one pectoral fin three times during the same winter season. The first capture was in November 1985 when I caught the pike from a swim just above New Bridge. Two months later towards the end of January 1986 I caught the pike again, just below the ford at Duxford and towards the end of February I caught the fish for a third time close to Duxford Weir. Duxford Weir is below the ford, so when I caught the pike for the third time it was dropping back down river. The distance by river between where I first caught the fish and where I caught it just below the ford, was approximately two-and-a-half miles. In all if you include the distance the pike had dropped back downstream, it would equate to a total distance of approximately three miles covered by that particular pike between November and the end of February.

The next fish of interest was a barbel, also caught from the River Thames from a section of river close to Folly Bridge in the city of Oxford. This fish, a very distinctive looking barbel with a twisted back weighing 7lbs 10 oz was caught four times over the period September to November of the same year, 1973. It was first caught in late September by John Everard. Later in October it came out again to another angler whom I knew, Geoff Barnes. The second capture was about 100 yards above where John had first caught the fish. Then in late November fishing an area of the river about 400 yards below from where it had been last caught, I caught the fish again. Fishing with John I caught the barbel from behind a bridge pile at around seven in the evening. Following the capture of the disfigured barbel with a twisted back, we fished a number of different swims that evening, roving up and down the river in search of fish. Conditions were good. After several days of rain, the river levels were high but falling. With heavy cloud overhead, and a mild night in store we knew that the barbel would be mad on if we could find them. However, after fishing several known swims without an offer I decided at around eleven to go back to the bridge pile for the last few casts before going home. First cast in behind the pile, I received a thumping bite and hooked another strong-pulling fish. When I lifted the fish in the net I noticed it was the same barbel which I had caught earlier. There was no possible chance for misidentification, as it was so distinctive. I had caught the same fish within hours of it being returned. The fish had travelled about fifty yards from a slow-moving eddy where I had returned it, back to the bridge pile from where I had first caught it. Not only had the barbel swum back to the same location, but the fish had also taken the same type of bait, sausage meat paste. This was also the type of meat bait which both John Everard and Geoff Barnes had used. I fished the same end rig for both captures, so the presentations must have been more or less identical, and yet the barbel was still prepared to risk being caught to eat the bait.

I have certainly caught the same trout more than once from both rivers and reservoirs. Brown trout can be very difficult sullen fish, but when they are mad on they can also be easy. If they are mad on, it is possible to hook and lose a brown trout, and then go on to catch it within seconds or minutes of the fish breaking free of the hook. It depends on how frenzied their feeding is. Give them enough time and they become catchable again. It could take days or longer. But once they start feeding, they are then potentially a target for an angler's fly. After being caught the trout, just like the coarse fish, will become more difficult to catch again, but just like the coarse fish they will not become impossible. Once they start feeding, we may have to work harder with our presentation to deceive them, but they will make mistakes, and with improved technique we will catch them. By limiting our kill, we not only guarantee the future of our sport by maintaining a sustainable population of fish, but we also help to maintain fish stock levels at a density where they will provide a high level of sport to the fly angler.

The above suggests to me that fish are not too traumatised by being caught on rod and line, and certainly it isn't a significant enough of a shock to deter them from taking the same food again. However, could the same reasoning be applied to game fish such as brown trout? There is enough evidence to suggest, especially from the USA that game fish, just like many of the coarse fish species, if returned do survive capture by rod and line.

In the book *About Trout* by Robert J. Behnke, there are numerous references to peer-reviewed evidence which supports the concept of catch and release on both rivers and lakes which are subjected to some intense rod pressure. In the chapter 'Limit Your Kill', Behnke cites data from a study of a section of a six-mile segment of Wyoming's North Platte River known as the 'Miracle Mile'. The data illustrates the significance to anglers of catching the same fish several times. What the chapter showed was that the brown trout being a more dour, obdurate fish are caught less frequently than rainbow trout. However, even though they are not so free-taking the catchable-sized population was turned over during the course of a season. Brown trout inhabiting the Miracle Mile were caught on average 1.2 times per season, and the wild rainbow trout were caught 6.3 times per season. This does not necessarily mean that every fish was caught the number of times quoted. Some may have avoided capture completely. However these catch rates do suggest that it is possible for anglers to exploit a population of fish to very low levels, levels which are not sustainable.

From another chapter titled 'Yellowstone Cutthroat', Behnke gives mortality rates for a three-mile section (Buffalo Ford) of the Yellowstone River which is subjected to some very intense angling pressure. During a six-week period from 15 July to 25 August, an estimated population of 7,500 trout provided an estimated catch of 72,698 during six weeks of angling. Each trout was caught and released an average of 9.7 times. The total mortality of trout during this period was estimated at 236. It would be highly improbable that all the fish died because of angler neglect but if all the mortality was due to hooking or handling mortality, it would equate to three fish killed per 1,000 caught and released, or 0.3 per cent (236 died from 72,698 caught). These figures show that game fish (trout) are pretty durable creatures, and are capable of surviving the ordeal of capture on rod and line if released. The cutthroat is a very free-taking fish. When compared with brown trout they are what you might call sucker fish. However, as gullible as they are they do show a high level of durability, and I feel certain that we could apply a similar level of survival to our brown trout also.

When it comes to vulnerability brown trout are not as susceptible to angler exploitation as the cutthroat, but they are still open to overexploitation. It would just take longer. On the South Platte River, Colorado, it took 1,900 angling hours per acre to catch each brown trout in the population, an average of two times. This level of fishing effort would suggest that the brown is much better at looking after itself, but even though they are less susceptible to overexploitation it is still possible to turn the population over. When we equate this level of fishing effort to loughs such as Corrib and Mask it seems impossible that anglers could have any effect on such large-scale fisheries. But then if we compare them with Yellowstone Lake (87,000 acres) it may not seem so extreme. Until 1970, angling regulations allowed three trout of any size to be creeled from Yellowstone Lake. From 1970–72 a minimum size of fourteen inches was initiated, and the bag limit was reduced to two fish per day in 1973. Despite these restrictions, the population in the lake drastically declined. A most astonishing fact is that this decline occurred when angling pressure was no more than four or five hours per surface acre per year.

In 1975 a new regulation was instituted requiring the release of all fish of thirteen inches and larger, a two-fish daily bag limit, with only flies and artificial lures allowed. This regulation was designed to protect the older, mature fish. By the 1980s the spawning run in Pelican Creek, a nursery stream of the lake, had doubled from 12,000 to 24,000. In another spawning tributary, Clear Creek, the spawning run had increased from 10,000 to about 70,000. These surveys showed a significant increase in the adult population. Trophy-sized trout (fish of more than 18 inches) rose from only three fish per 1,000 caught in 1973 and five per 1,000 caught in 1974 to eighty per 1,000 caught in 1983. The proportion of fish spawning for the second or third time (repeat spawners) increased from only a few per cent of the spawning runs to 25 to 30 per cent. When we release a mature fish, we are not only providing an opportunity for the fish to be caught again, but we are also giving it the chance to make the spawning run the following autumn.

In the UK and Ireland, I feel the biggest problem we have to overcome is the ingrained dogma associated with releasing fish. There are those who cannot accept the concept of releasing a fish they have caught on rod and line. Possibly they never will, but for the long-term future of many of our wild fisheries it is an issue that many of the non-believers are going to have to come to terms with if they wish to preserve their sport. If we study the information provided in Behnke's reports in the book *About Trout* it will be noticeable that a low population of wild trout can provide good fishing. Our wild stocks are never as

Hopefully released to spawn and perhaps provide another angler with the joy of capturing a wild fish

great as we would wish to believe, and this is what makes them so vulnerable to over-exploitation.

I have often heard it stated that fishing isn't just about catching fish, it is also about being there. Whilst I can agree with this sentiment to a degree, being there I feel isn't the prime reason for why many of us pursue fish with rod and

217

line. My love for the outdoors is such that I do not require an instrument such as a fishing rod to induce me to walk out into the wild. The wild is always there for us to enjoy, and I need no excuses to venture out and sample what wild places have to offer. Fishing takes me out into wild places, and this gives me enormous pleasure. However, my prime objective for carrying a rod and line is for the pursuit of and the catching of fish. The hunt, deception and the landing of a fish is an action which I enjoy, and it is one which I feel presents a problem for some anglers. They will use all sorts of excuses why they partake in a sport which could be perceived as being cruel, and will never openly admit that catching a fish provides pleasure. To me this kind of sentiment is a bit of a paradox where we can admit that we enjoy fishing, and we can enjoy being there, but we cannot admit that the pursuit and catching of a fish also gives a certain amount of joy. It would appear that to use the term 'catching' is a taboo subject, a hideous word and one we dare not mention for fear of condemnation.

Those who are conscious of this will even go to such lengths as feigning excuses to justify why they go fishing, and will use an argument such as they only partake to put a fish on the table. To me this type of argument is an admission to the fact that fishing is a barbaric sport, and that the only way they can justify their involvement is by killing the fish to eat. These anglers are not saints. They put up a shield in the hope that society will not castigate them for catching a fish. If this is the way these anglers feel, then all I can say is that the end cannot justify the means by which the fish was taken, and the use of a little bit of kidology doesn't hide the fact. If we are truthful, then I believe that the majority of open-minded anglers would concede that they enjoy catching fish every bit as much as being there. As well as the cost of travelling to our local river or lakes, or to different locations around the world, why else would we go to the expense of buying rods, reels, lines and all the 'must have' accessories which we anglers accrue in the pursuit of our passion if we did not want to catch a fish? No, it is more than just about being there.

If the pursuit and catching of a fish does provide so much enjoyment, why do we treat that source of so much joy the way we do? The limestone loughs of Ireland provide superb lake fishing for wild brown trout, and yet the quality of the sport these loughs provide is under enormous pressure and can be influenced by what we anglers do. We complain about water quality, loss of

218

habitat, even the pike and cormorants, and yet we do not consider what effect angler impact may have on these fisheries. There is no question that the level of sport that many of the Irish lough fisheries once provided has fallen, and this falling off isn't just related to poor water quality, loss of habitat and predator impact. If we were to take a look at these issues over the last ten years we would probably find that there has been no obvious increase in any factor other than angling which we could relate to the fall off in sport. The introduction of an alien species such as the zebra mussel or *Lagarosiphon*, are too recent to link to the poor catch returns on fisheries such as Loughs Mask and Corrib. These loughs were fishing consistently well, and I think we have to look closer to home for the problem many of these fisheries are now facing. Surely they are too precious to allow them to fall into decline through our own neglect. Although we may not like it, the problem lies on our own front door. We can all help. The next time you land that trout, pause and consider before making a rush for the priest.

17 Presentation

To catch a fish, location has always been the prerequisite for success. However, once located, presentation becomes mandatory if we are to deceive the trout. Some of our best anglers have written about this key element of our sport. Colour, fly pattern, or the size of fly although important are rendered impotent if the presentation isn't good enough to fool the fish. In other words the positive properties of these factors are negated when the presentation fails. There are always exceptions and there will always be the odd mug fish which will defy such predictions. However we should ignore these exceptions, for they will only detract from the real issue which is basically that none of the other factors can override the need for good presentation. Does this still apply today, or have we discovered new patterns of flies which are more potent and have such good fish appeal, that they limit the need for a well-presented fly?

If we consider nymphs or sunk fly methods, the depth at which we present the flies and the speed of retrieve will be key components of our presentation. The other factors such as fly size, the killing colour or fly pattern will become important but it is a sequence of importance which will only come into play once the optimum depth at which the fly is to be presented is established. So the type and size of fly pattern are of lesser importance than the prime key, depth. Once we have discovered the depth at which the fish are holding, we can improve the presentation by changing the density of fly-line, leader diameter, and even the weight of the hooks. If we logically consider fishing below the surface, it will become apparent that it makes sense to find the depth at which the fish are holding. Even in a river, fish which are feeding on nymphs or other water-borne fauna will not rise far above their holding station to intercept a morsel of food. So it is essential that we fish our flies where the trout will accept them. Having established the holding depth, we can then tweak the leader arrangement to improve the catch rate. One follows the other.

The same applies to surface fishing, only now we have only one plane to deal with. Dealing with one plane, the presentation should prove much simpler to solve. But is it?

With the sub-surface methods, leader diameter is not I feel so critical, unless we are dealing with trout that have been subjected to some intense angling pressure. When dealing with educated fish, leader diameter then becomes more and more important. The same principle applies to surface fishing, only with the dry fly we start lower down the scale of leader diameter. This is because the leader can be easily seen by the fish as they are looking up against an illuminated background. Even under a heavily overcast sky, the source of light will be coming from above the line which makes it very difficult for the angler to disguise the

Testing conditions calling for a fine leader and a small fly, Cong Canal

leader. To overcome this, for dry-fly fishing we fish with finer diameter leaders than we would for sunk line tactics, and the more educated the fish the finer we have to go. So fishing pressure and ultra fine leader are related, and how fine we have to go will be dependent on the level of pressure the fish are subjected to. On some of the popular Irish lough fisheries we are now fishing with much finer leaders than we did five years ago. At one time I would have been quite happy fishing with a 185mm leader for all my medium sized (size 12) fly fishing, but now I find that in some situations I have to drop to 0.150mm to fool the fish. For the small flies I have dropped to as low as 0.128mm and when fishing at range with leaders this fine the margin for error is very fine indeed. The biggest problem I have is the length of time we have to play the fish, but with such a light leader one cannot avoid the problem without risking a break. Thankfully, at the moment at least it would appear that we do not have to fish so fine for all the methods, especially for the larger mayflies and sedges.

Trout like any other fish will answer our probing questions with flies of different colours, sizes and pattern with their mouths. If the fish ignore, or swim up to and do not take the fly then we know that something is amiss. The reaction of the trout will provide a lot of information provided we are observant and take in the signals which are being sent. Providing they have not been put off by a clumsy cast or have detected angler presence, we have to assume that they are seeing something which makes them wary if they continually refuse a fly. To overcome this we have to eliminate certain elements of our presentation in the hope of finding a solution. If the fish completely ignore the fly, they have either not recognised the artificial as food or they haven't been deceived by the presentation. If it is the former then the simple solution is to change the fly pattern. However if the fish swim up to the fly and refuse or show some sort of reaction we have to assume that they are interested but are not prepared to take. As I said earlier the presentation is the prime key, so we have to be certain that this element isn't at fault before making adjustments to the end offering. With dry fly, providing the leader is in or below the surface film the only way that we can improve the presentation is by going finer. Sometimes the fish will be put off by a movement from the angler, a poorly sitting fly or some other obscure reason. We should not confuse these types of refusals with the situation where the trout consistently swim past the fly. In such a situation nine times out of ten the leader will be found wanting. What I do believe is that on some of the Irish loughs we are now experiencing leader line shyness, and the trout are now behaving more like the trout of some of the hard-fished systems in America. Unfortunately unlike many of the American systems, the Irish loughs do not appear to hold such high stock densities.

The trout in Lough Corrib for example have become more difficult to catch. Although impossible to prove conclusively, I would say that there are several reasons for this and that they are mostly related to angler pressure. Firstly I would say that there now appears to be fewer fish for the angler to work on. Assuming this is correct, a lower stock density makes it harder to locate the fish. If locating the fish has become more difficult, then it stands to reason that this will affect our catches. But location isn't the only problem with fewer fish. Once we have located them, they are not so confident as they are when the competition is greater from having plenty of companions around. When the competition amongst individuals is higher they are more eager to take the fly. Secondly, those fish which are present have now been subjected to some intensive angler pressure. They appear to be both boat and line shy which has made them increasingly difficult to deceive. Some may argue that the boat and line shyness are a result of the fish being returned, and whilst I wouldn't disagree with this assumption it doesn't, I believe, provide the complete answer to our problem.

How many anglers on the Irish loughs return their fish? Perhaps 10, 20 or 30 per cent. If we were to say that 30 per cent of the trout caught which are over the size limit were returned by anglers on Lough Corrib, and in my opinion this would be a high percentage for trout of a takeable size, could this level of return be the cause of the poor fishing we are now experiencing? If we consider the number of times that some of the coarse fish are caught, would returning such a low percentage of trout to what is considered to be a healthy stock pool of fish be a problem? I don't think so. Trout are no more intelligent than coarse fish and yet some coarse fish have been caught innumerable times. Many coarse fish are longer lived than trout, so there is a wider window of opportunity for the angler to exploit them. Some of the recognisable fish are caught quite often, even on the same bait. If the pulling power of a particular bait diminishes, the angler simply changes the colour or the flavour of the bait to renew its catching potential. If we are open-minded and apply a similar logic to trout, then I believe we would see that returning the fish isn't the cause of the poor catches on loughs such as Corrib and Mask. The trout is not as long-lived and because of this, especially with the Irish brown trout, I do not believe they are caught and returned often enough to avoid anglers completely. The window of opportunity to catch them repeatedly is much narrower, and many of the Irish fish are killed anyway. I would be highly surprised if the percentage of Irish trout which are returned and caught again is higher than a few per cent. They are simply not caught enough times in their lifetime to ever become so elusive that we do not see or catch them. If there were a lot of trout showing and we were finding them difficult to catch, then we would just change our flies or tactics, just as

Evening fish are generally more confident feeders and are therefore easier to deceive

the coarse angler would change the colour or the flavour of his bait. We do not have the opportunities to make such changes, because the fish are just not showing consistently enough. Why? Could it be that the fish are not there, and those that are there are not as confident because they do not have the influence of competitive companions around them?

We are led to believe that the stock of brown trout in loughs such as Corrib and Mask are healthy. If the stock of fish in the lough is as high as we are led to believe, then as well as the smaller undersized trout there should be a considerable number of fish which have not been subjected to a trauma related to angling. Yes, those fish which are returned will become increasingly difficult to catch. However if the stock is a healthy one, then the competition amongst the fish will always ensure that a percentage of the educated trout make a mistake, even for anglers who are not prepared to improve their presentation. If we then add the returned fish to the percentage which haven't even been caught before, and the stock is supposedly quite high what we should be experiencing is fishing to a small population of educated trout amongst a larger population of comparatively naïve fish. In such a situation we should be experiencing good rises of fish. Competition and a good stock of naïve fish would provide plenty of opportunities for the angler. We are not experiencing this. The problem isn't about trout becoming shy because they are returned; it is about numbers. On many of the American systems anglers are not fishing to a pool of returned educated trout amongst a larger pool of naïve fish. American anglers basically fish to a pool of educated trout, some of which have been caught more than once, and yet the rises remain good and the fishing likewise. What anglers here should realise is that the difference between many of the American systems, even if the fish are educated, and the Irish loughs is the stock numbers in the pool.

What we now have to contend with on some of the Irish loughs, is I believe a lower stock of trout which has been subjected to some intense rod pressure. These fish, even the ones which haven't been caught before, are more cautious because of the lack of competition from a near neighbour. Hence other than the periods when there is a hatch or fall of fly outside of the popular angling time of ten until six, the trout do not rise so freely. And even when they do rise, they are now far more cautious than the free-rising fish of the eighties or nineties. If there were more fish present, competition amongst the trout would ensure a greater window of opportunity for the angler to take them, but this isn't happening. It would be politically unacceptable to restrict the number of anglers who fish a water such as Lough Corrib. So the only way to ensure a continuation of the high level of sport the fishery has to offer is to give the stock greater protection. In 2008 a limit of four fish over thirteen inches was introduced to help conserve the stock. This was the first real measure of protection the brown trout of Lough Corrib had been given. Sadly I feel this is too little, too late, and I'm afraid that a four-fish limit isn't tight enough to counter the current high level of angler effort. As anglers we need to adopt a more responsible attitude towards these fisheries and show a little more restraint when it comes to taking fish over the size limit. Do not assume because the bag limit is four fish that this is the number of fish you should take. The pool of educated trout will increase if more trout are returned. But by returning more of our catch this will ensure that the stock density is higher than it currently is, and with more fish will come greater competition. Increased competition will guarantee that the fish will move more freely than they do at the moment, and for the anglers prepared to work on their presentation, their catch rate, just like the catch rates of anglers in America, will be related to the number of trout they have to work on. Angler catch rates will improve with increasing stock levels. The two are related.

In the last few seasons on Lough Corrib Jeremy Herrmann has pioneered the importance of fine leader and fishing from the shore for deceiving the trout. Fishing from the shore is one way to overcome boat shyness, and Jeremy's catches would support his theory. He has also made me think more seriously about using finer leaders for much of my top water fishing. I did not think it would be necessary on Corrib especially on some of the areas which I fish. But none of the remoter areas of the lough have now escaped the attention of anglers. Even the lower end of Lough Corrib now sees a lot of boats at key times, and this has made the trout more wary. Like any hard-fished water fine leaders are essential if we are to deceive the fish. The harder a water is fished, the finer the angler has to go to deceive the trout, but there are limits to how fine we can take this. As far as boats are concerned for a lot of top water methods I can't help feeling that the standard 19ft boat could be now a disadvantage. There is no question that in many areas on Lough Corrib the fish are detecting

A setting sun and a flat calm. Dick Yorke will hopefully exploit the fading light to his advantage, Lough Corrib

the presence of a large boat. The observant anglers have noticed this. It isn't unusual now to hear the statement from anglers noting the reaction of trout feeding near the surface in light ripple conditions, that they see the fish veering off to the left or right well ahead of the boat. These fish are now exhibiting an increased awareness to the trout of only a few years ago, and they are reacting to the presence of a boat much earlier. To overcome this increased awareness we are going to have to give more thought to the size of the boats we use. Such

227

adjustments to our way of thinking may take time but I can now foresee a movement towards smaller boats, and other alternatives to the standard 19ft craft for fishing to educated trout on the Irish loughs.

Should we consider making our flies more lifelike? Would close imitation help to deceive the fish any better than a suggestive pattern? There is a school of thought that believes if we offer the fish a pattern which closely resembles the food they are eating, the lifelike appearance of the fly will overcome any suspicions the trout may have about taking the fly. Whilst I can accept that the trout may readily accept the lifelike appearance of the fly, I do not believe that the close copy could ever override the need for a good presentation. With many fish, a well-presented bait has always been the key to consistent success, so why should trout be the exception? If I had the choice of fishing a close copy on a coarse leader or a suggestive pattern on a fine leader, I would always choose the latter. This is because I believe that for a trout or for any other fish to take a bait from the surface, that lure needs to be seen behaving naturally and unattached. Wary fish will look harder at a food item, and the more wary they are the greater the need for a finer line. It is all about presentation. Coarse anglers will know this, and if you study the reaction of coarse fish to loose offerings you will see what I mean about the importance of the way a bait is presented.

Certain baits have a long life when it comes to catching coarse fish. Whether this is because the fish like them, or because they are easily accessible and freely available I do not know. Sweetcorn and boilies are two classic baits. Neither of these baits are naturally occurring, so the only way the fish find them is because they have been introduced by anglers. You would think that the fish would become suspicious of these unnatural baits. Well, they do in time but not enough to stop eating them. The way the angler overcomes the suspicions of the fish is by improving the presentation of the bait. The bait has to behave absolutely naturally, and in no possible way should it arouse the fish's suspicion before it takes the bait. I have observed carp and tench feeding on loose offerings thrown in by anglers. The fish sucking in one loose offering after another and completely ignoring the bait which is attached to the angler's line. These fish will do this time after time. It isn't a fluke that they do not take the baited hook. Coarse anglers have a big advantage over fly fishermen: 1) they can throw more loose offerings in to hold the fish, which gives the angler time to play around with the presentation: and 2) they are fishing a bait which lies on the bottom. With a bait which is lying on the bottom, line diameter isn't such an issue. What is essential is that the fish come onto the bait without detecting the line, so that they find only the bait. Also the bait has to behave naturally. Even the weight of the hook can make a bait misbehave. So although the bait may be attached by a hair to the hook the angler sometimes has to counteract the weight of the hook by adding small amounts of a floating substance to the bait to overcome the suspicions of the fish. It is vital to produce a natural movement to the bait so that the fish cannot tell that the bait is attached to a hook. If the angler can achieve this the hook-bait will be taken along with the loose free samples. The presentation and not the bait has been perfected to fool the fish.

What does the above tell us? That fish will continue feeding on the loose offerings of unnatural little round baits scattered around a bait which they are suspicious of, and they will continue feeding until all the loose offerings have been eaten. They are not put off by the presence of a bait of which they are suspicious, and until that bait behaves like one of the loose offerings they will not take it. It isn't the bait which is so important, but the presentation. The angler can change the colour, flavour and even the size of the bait, but basically they are just little round balls and the fish eat them even though they may be suspicious of them. Now if we apply this logic to dry-fly fishing and for trout which are ignoring the fly, we have to establish whether they are ignoring the fly because the presentation is poor, or are they ignoring the fly because they do not recognise it as food? If they recognise it as food, I cannot believe that in most situations, a trout, especially a wary fish, would take a fly attached to a thick leader no matter how close or lifelike the imitation may be. I believe they would behave just like a suspicious coarse fish taking in all the loose offerings around a bait which is attached to the angler's line, and thus the trout would continue feeding on the naturals and ignore the artificial.

Then we have the issue of close imitation verses suggestive patterns. A close imitation will deceive a trout once it comes onto the fly, but will a close copy deceive the trout any more than a suggestive pattern? This is a difficult issue to prove. However I do believe that if trout readily accepted a suggestive pattern, then they would recognise that pattern as food and they would, just like the coarse fish with the unnatural little round baits take that fly again, if the presentation is good enough. Certain flies can, just like a coarse fisher's bait, be exhausted through overuse. If the shelf-life of a suggestive pattern of a certain tying was exhausted through overuse we would then need to try another pattern. It is just like the coarse angler changing the size, flavour or colour of his boilie in order to find a bait which the fish will accept. The only way that a fish can try the new boilie or pattern of fly is to take the pattern into his mouth, and if he takes it in then we have achieved the deception. And the only way we will achieve that deception is through a good presentation.

If a trout were to swim up to the fly without taking it, then I would suggest that the trout has made a deliberate movement towards the fly with the intention of taking it. If it hasn't taken, then the fish has seen something suspicious with the leader and this is a clear indication that the presentation is at fault and the angler should react to this accordingly. This doesn't mean that all rejections are related to a fault in the way the fly is presented, but most will be. Once we have eliminated that presentation is at fault, we then work on the other variables of size, colour and pattern.

I do not believe that healthy feeding trout could ever become impossible to catch. Trout which are feeding and growing in a wild environment will, just like the coarse fish, be open to being caught by anglers, and like the coarse fish which are repeatedly caught they will become more wary. The more difficult they become, the harder we will have to work with our presentations to deceive them. Brown trout, especially Irish trout do not live as long as some species of coarse fish. In their lifetime, I do not think they could ever be caught and returned sufficient times to make them immune to angler methods. They would become more difficult, yes; but impossible? No. What is essential for good fly fishing, even if a percentage of the trout are well-educated fish is a good stock density for the angler to work on. This and a good presentation will guarantee the thinking angler sport in the future.

18 Dry Fly – The Variables

Having established an acceptable leader line diameter, one which will consistently deceive the fish irrespective of the direction from which they approach the fly, we then have to consider such matters as the colour and the mode, such as whether the fly should be sitting on or in the surface film of the water. Fly pattern and colour will usually be related to the conditions or the type of food on which the trout are feeding. On windy days the trout sometimes prefer a high-riding fly. If they are looking for this type of presentation, a well-hackled fly that sits high on the water is ideal. The problem with a high-riding fly is that they can produce a lot of abortive takes. If the trout start coming short and you know that they are not leader shy, then you need to fish a fly which sits lower in the film. For the majority of presentations a fly which sits low in the film is usually the answer, and this will cover most of the adult midge and spent fly rises. When trout are looking for emerging flies, or a fly which is either penetrating or sitting below the film, patterns such as a Klinkhammer, parachute style tyings, or those suspended by a bunch of CDC or foam are ideal.

Before we make the first cast if we observe what type of fly is hatching, or is lying spent on the surface, or if we consider such factors as the time of day, season etc, we can usually make an informed decision about size, colour and type of pattern we should tie on to our leader. These variables, fly colour, pattern and size will usually be dependent on the type of food the trout are feeding on. It is all a question of elimination; make the correct moves and you will arrive at a fly which the fish in most situations will regularly accept. Once we achieve this level of deception I do not believe we can take it any further. We will not raise every fish which we cover with a fly. Like it or not some will ignore the offering, but then I have never seen a trout which takes every natural either. This occasional 'blanking' of a fly, even the natural insect, by a trout seems to be part of their psyche. Perhaps it has something to do with a defence mechanism or perhaps their digestion. Who knows? What is evident is that a feeding fish will not eat every fly. In the *Caenis* hatch I have seen fish take in spent fly one after another and then stop feeding, even though there are countless flies on the surface, only to re-emerge and commence feeding again. Whilst down, the fish has passed a number of flies without taking them. So do not always jump to the conclusion that a trout is refusing, or be put off if they sometimes swim past the fly, even if they have seen it. Very often when you have a fly which is working, a trout which has previously ignored the same offering will take if you have time to cover the fish again. If a fly has been working the occasional refusal never deters me. This is a different scenario to covering several trout with a fly which they repeatedly ignore. Then the message is clear.

It is also important to be able to cast the fly to a trout so that the fish will come onto the fly without being scared by a clumsy cast, or by the action of casting. In other words the fish hasn't detected our presence, and therefore should not be suspicious when approaching the fly. Accurate casting is a must, but on still water we are casting the fly to a position where we believe the trout is going to go. This is all about intuition, and feeling in tune with the fish. Even though we cannot see them, we need to put the fly where we believe the trout will come onto it. Observing which way the fish was moving after the last rise will greatly assist the angler when it comes to determining where to put the fly. There was a time on the western loughs of Ireland when one could cast the fly to within inches of a rise and not put the fish down, but this is no longer the situation. Put a fly down too close to a fish, and it will now boil away from the artificial in alarm. This is learnt behaviour from too much exposure to anglers. If the trout see the fly arriving they make the association with a bad experience. We now have to put the fly down with sufficient lead, so that the fish comes onto the artificial without seeing the lure enter its window of vision from above. With sufficient lead we avoid spooking the fish or alerting it to our presence. The fish will then remain feeding in a confident manner and will be not at all suspicious when it finds the fly on its patrol route. If the presentation is good, and we have chosen our pattern of fly wisely, then there is no reason why the fish shouldn't take.

Time and experience will help with our decision making, and as we build up a catalogue of information we will, over the course of a season, instinctively

This angler chose to fish from the bank to deceive this fine brown from just over the drop-off along the shore Lough Corrib

Lovely conditions on Carra. Wave and light are ideal for deceiving fish

know which flies to select to cover certain hatches of fly or a specific time of the
year.

The seasons and the hatches of fly repeat themselves every year. Flies which
worked at a certain time of the season, or in a particular hatch of fly will work
again when the cycle is repeated the following year. What is important is to
recognise when the cycle repeats itself, and to remember the successful patterns

234

of fly and the method used at that time. If we can remember such information, then we can make an informed decision about which flies to tie up, and the method we are going to use. The good anglers will remember this information and know when to apply it. This takes a lot of the guesswork out of deciding which flies we are going to use or which method to apply on the day. It is all a question of logic.

Colour and the way the fly fishes (whether the fly is sitting in, on or penetrating the surface film) are the important points to remember. In the early season when duckfly hatch, we know that the grey and black coloured flies work well, and for the olives, ginger, and olive green. As we progress into late April–early May, for the large spring buzzer, olive green, grey and even claret, and for the mayfly ginger, grey, olive green and claret. During high summer the muted browns and claret for the sedges and colours such as red and hot orange come into play. For the back end, dark browns and claret. This is a simple for-mula for a range of key colours to cover a fishing season on a wild limestone fishery, but it is one which works and a good base to work from.

As well as the colour, at certain times during a hatch of fly we need to consider the footprint our artificial patterns make on the surface of the water film. Even with suggestive patterns it is important that we represent certain features which cover the various stages of a hatch. For example do we wish our artificial to represent the emerging stage of the fly cycle? If so then the Klinkhammer or shuttlecock type of flies are two excellent dressings to imitate this stage of the hatch. With these two patterns most of the body of the fly penetrates through and below the surface film, a mode of presentation which is suggestive of the hatching insect as it is about to emerge from the pupal shuck. Crippled or spent flies can be represented by 'Bits' patterns. With a few turns of hackle, they sit low in the surface film and this is the important element of this representation. We want the fly to sit in a shallow hollow in the film, and the Bits patterns perform this function admirably. Isn't it funny how some of the simplest dressings can be so deadly! The biggest drawback with this type of fly pattern is seeing them at a distance. In poor light they can be very difficult to see. For the duns and the adult midges the fly needs to sit a little higher on the film. A high-riding fly also allows the angler to move the fly without it digging in when inched back across the surface. Moving the fly during a hatch of lake olives or when the adult midges come back onto the water to lay eggs late in the evening, can sometimes make the difference between the fish taking whilst ignoring the static fly. I find that in the majority of situations the static fly works best, but for those occasions when the trout want the fly with a bit of movement, we need the fly to hold up and not sink below the surface when we inch it back. For this type of representation a buoyant, well-hackled fly works best.

19 Favourite Flies

If I were asked to name my favourite flies for wild brown trout on the Irish loughs, I would not find it difficult to draw up a short list. What is interesting is how my list of all-time favourites has changed in the last twenty years. Before 1990, wet flies would have dominated my short list for the wild fish. Even for the reservoirs of England the wet fly and imitative subsurface patterns would have filled my top ten. But from 1990 on the wild loughs of Ireland, I began to use the dry fly and imitative nymph patterns which I had found so successful on the English fisheries. It happened slowly at first, but with an increasing tendency towards the more imitative approach as time moved on, and so much so, that by 1995–96 dry flies and nymphs dominated my boxes of favourite patterns. Such was the success of these patterns, that it changed my whole outlook about fishing for wild brown trout. From being a favourite, the wet fly now had become a third choice, and basically a method for the wild windy days or the late season. And if I were to take a critical look at my returns to wet fly methods, I would note that I caught far fewer big fish to wet fly even though I fished them almost exclusively for twenty years. Since 1990 I have caught upwards of 100 wild brown trout over 5lbs, and I can only account for six of those fish falling to wet fly. The majority have been taken on dries. Now if I had to choose a top ten the dry fly would totally dominate the list. There would be only one sub-surface pattern in that list and it isn't a wet fly. Isn't it funny how time changes our way of thinking? Is it the fish which change or is it us as we grow older (or more likely is it the environmental conditions, including angler pressure)?

Apart from the early season nymph fishing and the late season wet fly, I would not feel at all restricted if I were limited to dry fly only. When I look back over the seasons, it is clear to see that the dry fly has given me my best days especially with the bigger fish. And now, with time and experience, it is easy to see why the dry fly has produced the quality fish. It is a presentation which if you get it right will fool the bigger trout, and of all the methods, dry fly, nymph and wet fly, the dry fly is the easiest presentation for the angler to achieve. So my box of all time favourites now would be a box of dry flies with one nymph pattern. Yes, there will times in the early buzzer season when I will fish a team of nymphs and not consider a dry, but as the season wears on I will fish the sub-surface patterns less and less. Even in the early season duckfly hatch, our earliest buzzer hatch, there will be periods when I will fish a dry fly with all the confidence in the world of taking a fish. I now rarely start my season before St Patrick's Day. However, before the month of March is out I know I will have taken my first trout on a dry imitation.

So what flies would make up my list? All the flies listed have taken 5lb+ fish. If I had to place them in order of merit, highest status awarded to the fly which has taken more trout over 5lbs than the next, the Chocolate Drop would be top of my list and the Claret Bits would come bottom. However, the Grey Duster has taken more quality trout than any other fly in my box. It is a good suggestive pattern which covers a longer season than some of the flies listed, and it has worked on just about every limestone lough fishery I have fished in Ireland. The flies which have produced my biggest browns are the Mayflies and the Sedges. But then one would expect this. These are big flies which in their season will bring up the big trout. However this to me doesn't paint the whole picture, for I'm not looking for the fly which has produced my biggest trout, I'm looking for a fly which offers the best prospect of taking quality fish at specific times of the season. A Mayfly is no good to me in March or early April. So I will list my flies as they come into season and not by order of merit. To choose by order of merit would be a much harder task, because one would then have to choose between a fly which has given some exceptional days, against the fly which has produced the largest trout. I do not know how you could measure one against the other and say which is better.

Grey Duster – In my book, *Trout From A Boat* I described how I came upon the killing powers of this fly. It was basically a fluke. I had tried numerous patterns for some fish which were rising in shallow water just off the main boat channel on Lough Corrib. It was early May and the conditions were a clear bright day of light wind following an overnight frost. I remember the grass still white with ice crystals as we drove down to the mooring. In the prevailing

238

Grey Duster

conditions I had reservations about a dry fly working, but the trout were rising to surface fly. It was just a question of finding a pattern they would take. Lunchtime was approaching and all four of us were blank when I tied on a fly which I had left reposing in the fly patch of my waistcoat. It was a river pattern which I had used on my last trip to a local river in Oxfordshire, the Windrush. It had a few tail whisks, a light grey body of seal's fur and a few turns of badger hackle. The fly was my tying of the Grey Duster. I had deviated from the original tying by substituting a light grey seal's fur body for the original mole's fur. The reason for the substitution was that the seal's fur remained lighter in colour when wet, and it also had better buoyancy. Within minutes of tying on the fly an opportunity presented itself and a good trout came up and took me, a fish which I lost at the side of the boat. Following the loss of the fish we then went in for lunch. No matter how frustrating it may be to move away from rising trout, and I found it tough believe me, especially when at long last it looked as if I may have found a solution to a difficult rise, I felt committed to meet the arrangement we had made prior to going out that morning to meet up with friends for a break. That said I couldn't wait for lunch to finish and to go back out, as I knew that I was going to catch fish. What was in question was how long would I have at them before they went down. There was no need to worry as the trout continued rising until about 6pm before they went down. In the afternoon session I caught eight trout. No other member in the party had a fly to match mine. It was the only pattern I had with me as I had left my river flies at home, and as it turned out I was the only member of the party to catch fish; the others all came in blank.

Since that early May day the Grey Duster has taken numerous trout over 3lbs for me, and it has proved its worth time and time again. If I were restricted to one pattern for the spring fishing this simple fly would be my choice. Now I would never be without it, and come the early season it will still be up there with the best of my patterns.

Post Hackled Midge – Like many of the best flies, this pattern was produced from an evening at the fly tying desk as an afterthought when I had completed tying the flies which I had listed to do that evening. With time to spare I began experimenting, tying some proto-types for testing. I wanted a fly which I could fish with confidence in a hatch of emerging buzzer. Nymphs I felt offered a solution, but there are situations where I thought a dry fly could be a better bet. It was a question of finding a pattern which the trout

Post Hackled Midge

would accept in light winds or flat calm situations, when a lot of the natural fly struggles to emerge through the surface film. When such conditions prevail, we can experience some good but frustrating rises, as the trout rise in a determined fashion and yet refuse many of our offerings. Sometimes towards the end of the rise we would tie on a fly and catch a few fish. We then thought we had found the answer, only to find that when similar conditions prevailed again the trout treated the latest new-found solution with disinterest. It was evident that we needed a fly which we could fish static. The washing line offered a solution, but I felt we really needed a fly which would sit in and just below the film. Shuttle-cocks and Footballer type patterns have all worked, however on the evening when I was experimenting at the fly tying desk I tied up some flies with a herl body, a thorax and a post hackle for floatation on some sedge hooks. They were similar to the Klinkhammer only using different materials. One of the flies was a pattern I now call the Post Hackled Midge, with a rib of black tying silk, Canada goose herl body, thorax of peacock herl and a grizzle hackle tied around a post of white polyester.

I didn't have long to wait to put some of the new creations to the test. On

240

a late afternoon and evening in early April the wind dropped away to produce ideal conditions for a hatch of fly, just the type of conditions I wanted. Fish soon began showing and I tied up the new patterns. The Post Hackled Midge was on the top dropper and three fish took the fly in the first twenty minutes of the rise. As it was going so well I tied the fly to the point of my leader. Of the eleven trout I caught in that session nine fell to the new fly. The only change I have since made to the original pattern is that I now tie it on grub hooks, instead of the sedge hook.

Dog Fly – The only sub-surface pattern in my top ten. I first tied this fly over the Christmas period of 1996. It was the result of improving an already successful nymph pattern. When I tie a fly which replaces an old one, I normally discard the former for the new pattern. This is one of the few patterns where I have not followed that rule, but in truth I rarely use the older fly now. The progression to what is now the Dog Fly took a long time, but like all good things it was worth waiting for. I now have a dropper pattern which I feel when the conditions suit it is hard to beat.

The seed for what is now the Dog Fly was sown on a June evening back in 1973. We were fishing Farmoor Reservoir when an angler, Philip Lowe, showed me a fly which he was using. He had just taken a nice trout and was keen to show me the fly which had accounted for the fish. The tying was tail: badger hackle fibres; body: natural ostrich herl ribbed with copper wire; thorax: peacock herl; hackle: badger. Philip called the fly a Magnet Nymph, a name which to me sounded rather catchy. It was a transgression away from the wet fly and a step towards a more imitative tying. We used to do well with the Magnet Nymph fished as a top dropper during a hatch of midge, when there was a light ripple on the water. Fished just below the surface of the water for the last couple of hours in the evening, the fly could be quite productive, especially for the brown

Dog Fly

trout for which Farmoor was well known at the time. I didn't make any changes to this fly until the late seventies, when I substituted the ostrich herl with the Canada goose herl, and replaced the copper rib with one of silver. This and another pattern with a tail of furnace hackle fibres; rib: gold wire; body: Canada goose herl; thorax: dark olive seal's fur and a furnace hackle became two of my top patterns for the English reservoirs. They really scored on Rutland during the eighties when we caught a lot of good sized overwintered rainbows.

Then in the early nineties I began using the Magnet Nymph for the wild brownies in Ireland. I had reservations at first about using the fly for wild fish, but then I reasoned if the pattern was acceptable to the acclimatised fish of the reservoirs why should it not work with the wild browns. My lack of confidence in the fly proved to be unwarranted, as just as on the reservoirs its killing power could deceive the fish. However over the Christmas of 1996 I felt that the tying could be improved. I was also doing well with the Grey Buzzer which was tied on sedge hooks and I felt that this profile with the curved body offered possibilities for the improvement of the Magnet Nymph. So I dispensed with the tail fibres and tied the fly on the curved sedge hook. The only other change I made was to include a wing of badger hackle fibres tied in under the thorax.

We visited the Corrib in early April 1997. This would be the first time that my late wife Cathy visited the lough. We were staying at a rented house beside the lough which was owned by a Tommy Carey. The house was tucked away beside the shore of Ballycurrin Bay and it was close to a good duckfly area. On the first morning we called into the local shop to buy provisions and on leaving the store Cathy looked a little puzzled. Her pained expression begged an enquiry to which she replied 'Dennis are there flies down by the lake which bite?' I could see that Cathy was concerned and was in need of reassurance that her family were not at risk of being bitten to death. So I tried to explain that we were at no greater risk of being bitten than at any other house we had previously rented by water. Our own house in England backed onto the River Windrush. Living close to water there was always a risk in certain weather conditions of being bitten by midges. The house we were renting was close to water, but in a limestone area, so the risk was no greater than living at home, and it certainly would not be as bad as some of the houses we had previously rented in Scotland. 'Why so much interest in flies that bite?' I asked. Then Cathy explained to me how the woman on the till in the shop upon hearing her accent realised that we were most probably on holiday and had enquired where we were staying. When told about the house we were renting the till attendant warned about the flies. Cathy said that the woman had warned about dog flies which were down by the lake. For a moment I was puzzled. Dog flies, dog flies. I thought it was a wind-up, as there are no dog flies on Lough Corrib. Then it clicked and I burst out laughing, Cathy had misheard the pronunciation of the word – it wasn't dog flies the woman was warning us about, it was the duck flies. Then I explained about how at that time of year huge hatches of non-biting midges hatched from the lough, and that the flies had a generic name: they were called duck fly. I found it amusing, but Cathy didn't! 'Not a word' she said.

The weather wasn't at all favourable for most of our stay, and it wasn't until the Thursday towards the end of our holiday that the conditions changed. In the late afternoon the wind began to ease, and by evening I thought that I might be in with a chance of seeing a rise. It was still windy but nothing like as strong as it had been. At around seven in the evening I pushed the boat out from Tommy's mooring. That evening I took five fish, four on the new fly. The following morning I was out early and caught nine trout before the wind freshened putting the fish down. I came off just before noon, five of the nine having been caught on the new fly. It has since then taken some wonderful bags of fish, and in a light ripple if the trout want a sub-surface fly it takes some beating. The original tying is still my best pattern, but I also tie this fly with different body and thorax colours. An olive body with a gold rib and a Greenwell hackle is also another good colour combination. As the fly had proved to be such a winner I had to give the new pattern a name – it had to be the Dog Fly I thought, but 'Not a word....'

Cluster – This is a great pattern to fish late in the evening when adult midge are on the water. It is the most recent fly to join my top ten, but it is a fly which has given me in a short time some very big trout. It is a fly which is easy to tie, and with its well-hackled body of Grizzle intermingled with red game for the top third it doesn't look at all like a natural midge. However, when well oiled, it rides high on its haystack of hackle tips and when twitched across the surface of the water it comes to life. Then you can see an action not unlike that of an adult egg-laying midge.

Larry McCarthy first introduced me to this pattern, but the first time I used the fly was quite by accident to a hatch of *Caenis* in the early hours of the morning. I could not have had a better introduction to a new fly pattern. Tied on basically as a sighter it looked so out of place amidst all the spent *Caenis* when the unthinkable happened and the fly was taken. As I tightened, 5lbs of very wild brown trout exploded from the water, and powered off. It was no fluke as I took another big fish on the same fly a little later, and finished

Cluster

with three trout for around 14lbs for the session. The Cluster has since proved to be a good fly for big browns when the *Caenis* is clumping together.

As a morning fly the Cluster proved to be a revelation, but its true vocation is as an evening pattern when the adult midge is on the water. When the conditions are right for a big fall of adult fly, it can be deadly when inched back across the noses of feeding fish. In late April and May when there is a chance of fishing to the balling buzzer, this is a must-have pattern that I would just not like to be without.

Ginger Bits – The true colour for this fly is like a faded golden olive. I bought a batch of seal's fur from an old tackle shop in Oxford. It was labelled light ginger and was supplied to the shop by Veniard's. Looking through the colours that the shop had in stock, the light ginger looked to be the right colour for some Mayfly patterns which I wanted to tie. As the Ginger Mayfly turned out to be such a good fly especially when there were plenty of duns around, I thought I would tie up some Bits patterns in the same colour and try them for the trout feeding on lake olives. On the Corrib in a hatch of olives this fly turned out to be a killer. With a few turns of light Greenwell hackle and a body of light ginger seal's fur it could not be simpler to tie. And just like the Grey Duster a good fly for the spring fishing.

Some anglers cannot make the Ginger Bits work but I believe this is because they have not perfected the colour. As I said earlier the colour was labelled light ginger and was supplied by Veniard's, but I feel that it was the product of a mistake with the dying process. All the ginger furs I have since seen are either too orange or amber in colour. It should be more like a faded golden olive. Worried about the future stocks of this fur, along with a few close friends we decided to buy the entire stock of light ginger from the shop. I'm glad that we did.

Ginger Bits

Claret Bits – This is a non-specific pattern, which basically imitates nothing in particular and yet it is good all through the season, even at the back-end. I have never found it a fly which consistently takes the bigger trout. However I have found it a productive pattern and one I would not like to be without.

Claret Bits

In sizes 10 and 12 it has taken a lot of fish from a number of different waters, especially Loughs Sheelin, Mask, Carra, Conn and Corrib. Why claret should be so attractive to brown trout I do not know, but even in the Mayfly claret can be a killing colour. A very good fly for high summer when there are small sedges on the water. Body: claret seal's fur; hackle: a few turns of red game.

Grey Mayfly – Tail: grey squirrel; body: grey seal's fur; wing: grey squirrel; hackle: well-marked badger.

I first fished with this fly on Irish waters in 1991, and on both Sheelin and Corrib the fly proved to be a winner. Since then I have taken trout from most of the major Irish Mayfly fisheries with it, and such is my faith in the fly which produces oodles of confidence, I feel that if I can put this pattern in front of a trout feeding on spent gnat it will be taken. It is so important to have that belief in your patterns, for then you fish with a certainty that invariably brings success. The Grey Mayfly has given

Grey Mayfly

me many memorable days, days of quality and days when a cricket score of trout came to the boat, but most memorable of all was my first 5lb fish from Corrib. That fish was the most beautiful creature, and I think it sealed my fate. Success is not only a great motivator, but it also has addictive powers which lure you on in the hope of achieving more. The sight of that first big fish totally captivated my mind, and I wanted so dearly to catch another one. I was caught in a spider's web from which there was no escape, I had to learn about this enigmatic water and hopefully solve some of its secrets. That quest brought me to the shores of Lough Corrib where I now live, and although I have since caught some wonderful fish, I still want to catch another one. My yearning for another big one still burns, perhaps not as strongly but it is still there. Would it have been different I wonder, if I had not fished the Grey fly on that lovely day in May, when the shores of the lough were blooming with yellow of the gorse and showing every shade of Irish green?

Ginger Mayfly – Tail: grey squirrel dyed yellow; body: light ginger seal's fur; wing: grey squirrel dyed yellow; hackle: light greenwell. A fly from the same stable as the Grey Mayfly, tied in the same manner but using different colour materials to represent the dun phase of the insect's cycle. I caught my biggest trout from Lough Corrib using this fly on a day in late summer, so the season for this fly isn't solely restricted to the month it is named after. This fly now has

Ginger Mayfly

a strong following and quite rightly so, but it would be a hard choice as to which fly I consider the best, the Grey or the Ginger. The Grey has given me more fish over 5lbs, and yet it is the Ginger which has given me my biggest fish from the wild waters of the west of Ireland. These flies are big mouthfuls for a trout, and they will bring up some big fish. So always be prepared for a whopper.

Chocolate Drop – This fly has probably accounted for more wild brown trout over 5lbs than other patterns in my box. I tried it as an experiment on Sheelin in the early nineties and it was an instant success. If you tie a pattern and it catches fish then you try it again, and if it then catches you know that you are on to something. Sometimes we do not always get it right with the first pattern, and we have to do a bit of tinkering to perfect the tying. With the Chocolate Drop I have never felt a need to change the original tying. When this fly is on, the fish take it and that is good enough for me.

So many big fish have fallen for the seductive power of this pattern, that I find it hard to single out any one of them. If I had to select a particular experience it would have to be when I flew over to Ireland to fish Sheelin when the bloodworm were up. Having received a phone call from Stuart McTeare, I flew to Ireland at short notice to fish for three days over a long weekend, in the hope of catching the rise of bloodworm which occurred on the

Chocolate Drop

lough during hot weather. The first day saw perfect conditions, warm and sunny with light winds. The bloodworm came up as Stuart had predicted. It was a unique experience, a natural event which I had never seen before. Bits patterns in red, orange and claret did the damage on the first day, but then the weather changed. On the second evening I was fishing to trout that were rising to sedges. At the very end of the rise I noticed a good fish rising close to an exposed reef. It rose three times and took three Peter sedges in quick succession. While it was rising I cast my artificial in the hope of cutting the fish off, and the fourth rise was to my fly the Chocolate Drop. The fish weighed a little under 6lbs, and Stuart had said that if I caught a good fish that evening would I bring it in as he wanted one for dinner the following day. So I killed the fish.

On my return to the lodgings which were then at Finae, Stuart was waiting, so I gave him my brown. He weighed the trout and then placed it in a Belfast sink. The fish basically occupied the base of the sink. It was a lovely trout, perfectly proportioned with a small neat head. 'What did it take?' Stuart enquired. 'A sedge,' I replied. 'What type of sedge?' another enquiry. 'A Chocolate Drop' I answered, and with this I then showed my interrogator the fly. Stuart was interested in the fly, and as he examined the pattern I told him about the little cameo of how the fish had risen and taken three Peter sedges in quick succession before taking mine. Upon hearing this little snippet of information my questioner thought that an autopsy was in order. Stuart found a marrow spoon, and took a stomach sample from the trout. A quick examination of the spoon revealed that there wasn't a sedge to be seen, and he placed the content in a saucer of water. The fish was full of *corixa*. Stuart was now up for a bit of mischief and in a mocking tone he begged another question: 'I thought you said the fish had been taking Peters before you caught it?' I couldn't believe that there were no sedges in the stomach content, and I was beginning to question myself but replied 'that I had definitely seen the fish taking Peter'. Stuart was already waiting with a reply and quickly suggested that I should get my eyes tested. Why I questioned the content of that saucer I do not know because the answer was there in front of me, but I had to take another sample. I opened the fish's mouth and was about to insert the spoon to take another sample, when I noticed something inside its jaw, infact I noticed three some-things. They were well crumpled but there was no mistaking them. I suggested

248

that Stuart should take a look inside the mouth of the trout. On doing so, his mouth opened – Stuart's not the fish – and there was a moment's silence. 'Well did you ever!' Another momentary silence, then 'What about a whiskey?' 'That would be nice' I replied.

The body colour for this fly is produced by first dying the fur with hot orange, and then dying it again in a mixture of claret, black and fiery brown. It should have a colour of dark chocolate brown, but when you hold it up to the light the orange should show through. Body: dark chocolate brown seal's fur; wing: deer hair leave the butts protruding out over the eye of the hook; thorax: same as body; hackle: furnace. Trim the wing butts so that a stub of fibres is left protruding above the eye of the hook.

Fiery Brown Sedge – Sedges, especially the larger sedge flies are specialist patterns for big fish. Just like the mayfly, a Murrough or a Peter is a big mouthful

Fiery Brown Sedge

for a trout. It doesn't take too many of these flies to fill a fish up. When they are on them the trout feed for short periods at key times. One of the best times for the bigger sedges is just before the light fades in the evening. Choose your area carefully. Select a sheltered bay or a mark where you know concentrations of the fly will come off, as at the key time the trout will move in to feed on them. The Fiery Brown is an alternative to the Chocolate Drop, as is another sedge pattern I use with a body tied from the fur of a hare. The fur for the Fiery Brown should be a rich fiery brown colour. Body: fiery brown seal's fur; wing: as for Chocolate Drop; thorax: dark brown seal's fur; hackle: red game or furnace.

20 Mayfly Box

We all have favourite items of tackle. For most fly anglers it will most probably be a rod, but it could be any item from a rod to a Swiss army knife. One of my favourite pieces of fishing impedimenta is a fly box, a dry-fly box made by Wheatley & Sons. The box is made from pressed aluminium, with individual compartments which are covered by spring-loaded see-through lids that aid fly selection, and easy access to the individual cells. The box was one of a limited run, and it is unique because it has large Mayfly-sized

compartments on one side and standard-sized compartments on the other. It is ideal for all my Mayfly and Sedge patterns, and will fit into a jacket or waistcoat pocket.

I have used Wheatley fly boxes for both wet flies and dry flies for many years, but I did not know of this particular type of box. The standard dry-fly boxes were fine for most of my dry flies, however the compartments of the standard size were too small and tight for my larger Sedge and Mayfly patterns. I needed a box with larger compartments. With this in mind I made an enquiry to Wheatley, and put my request to a Brian Guest who was working for Wheatley at the time. He informed me that Wheatley were working on such a box, about twenty-five years ago and kindly sent me one of a limited run of boxes. The box was part of a pilot scheme to test whether there would be a market for such a product. I do not know whether the box made it into full production, but I have never seen it advertised as part of the Wheatley range of boxes.

When I first received the box from Brian Guest I wasn't that sure about it. The configuration of the cells looked odd, and I thought it too big and bulky, but with time I have grown to love that piece of pressed aluminium. The box is ideal for all my Irish dry-fly patterns. It measures 6" x 3.5" x 1.5", has six large compartments, plus four smaller compartments in the base and sixteen smaller compartments in the lid. With twenty-six cells there are sufficient to cover all my needs.

Fashions change, and anglers follow fads with equipment just as the high street shopper keeps up to date with all the latest trends. Many anglers, especially boat anglers now prefer a large open-leaf fly box. This gives them quick access to a greater array of flies. For those who like to keep a fly box in their pocket, as I do, the plastic fly boxes have become very popular. But I much prefer aluminium to the plastic fly boxes, especially for my dry flies. Where the dries are concerned the individual compartments of the Wheatley boxes are a boon. One can keep several flies of the same pattern in a compartment, and with a see-through lid you can clearly see what the cell contains. There are a lot of plastic boxes on the market which have individual compartments, but they do not have the separate hinged lids to each compartment. On windy days when you open a plastic box, the flies are exposed to the elements, and are easily blown out of the little cells. This isn't such a problem with the individual compartments which have a clear lid. You can see which pattern of fly you want, and open that cell only. The risk of the flies being blown away is then minimised, as you have greater control of the contents. For boat or bank anglers fishing in windy conditions this is a big advantage. Even in a howling gale I rarely lose a fly to the wind from an open cell.

For dry flies, other than the Bits patterns I much prefer a box with individual compartments as they do not distort the hackles or the wings. Dry flies stored in individual cells are not crumpled or flattened like the flies kept in foam boxes. The worst offenders for spoiling a fly are those boxes which are shallow with a narrow gap between the sheets of foam. When closed the contents of such boxes look like they have been pressed between the pages of a book. Sometimes the

The sun sets on the end of another season 30 September 2007, Lough Corrib

252

Mayfly spinners dancing over lough-side foliage beside Sheelin. Their last act in life to ensure the continuation of the species

flies come out looking like pressed dried flowers, and require a bit of TLC to bring them back to shape. So for all my river fishing, standard dry patterns and the larger dry flies I have a Wheatley box for each discipline. All the boxes will fit into a standard pocket on any fishing garment, and I do not have to worry about transferring flies from a large open-leafed box to a smaller container if I choose to go bank or river fishing. At least this way I avoid the risk of leaving an important pattern behind, as they are already in the relevant box. One just chooses the box or boxes which you think you will need.

We all have our fancies, flies which provide a lot of confidence. If I were to forget and had to borrow someone else's fly-rod or fly-reel it would not bother

253

me unduly, but for the type of fishing I pursue, I would never want to be without my favourite box of flies, as to me that box is indispensable. All the boxes have a sentimental value, and they are more important to me than any of my rods or reels. My smallest box contains all my river and *Caenis* patterns. I have owned it for about thirty years, but it is much older than that. A friend, Stewart Hamilton bought this little gem for me for a pittance at an auction. It was a snip, a bargain buy that has served me well. My favourite, however, the largest of the trio, is the box I have discussed above and it is my favourite because it contains a selection of flies which have given me my biggest trout, and some of my very best days on the water. A lot of very fond memories are associated with that box, many of which will be of unforgettable days of cracking sport out on the Irish loughs. Each winter when I replenish my stock of flies, I look through the little windows of each compartment to check on the contents. The contents of some of the cells will be well used: the Chocolate Drop, Fiery Brown Sedge, Hare's Ear Sedge, Cluster, Ginger and Grey Mayflies; they are all in there, and they could tell so many stories of big wild brown trout. That box is almost like a diary, and with a glass of whiskey in my hand it is nice to reflect on a cold winter's evening about the battered contents contained therein. Open a window to a cell and the images come flooding out, each battered fly telling its own story.

21 Return to Arrow

In the opening page of our family photo album, the first print on the front leaf is an old black-and-white photograph of my eldest son, Ben, at the age of nine months. He is sitting on a section of elevated ground surrounded by wild grasses and flowers. Behind him is a backdrop of a lough and a distant hill. The year is 1977 and the lough in the background is Lough Arrow. Although I had visited Ireland previously, I had never up until that time fished the limestone loughs for brown trout. There was so much to see and experience in Ireland, the country being new to me and the fishing largely unknown. My previous sojourns to the Emerald Isle were taken up with fishing for salmon and sea trout. Now as I look at the old photograph of Ben, I'm taken back to a little boreen set amongst rolling limestone hills that lead down to the lough, and a chance encounter with a local farmer leading his horse and cart back from the fields. We passed pleasantries as one does in the country, and fishing came into the conversation. Upon hearing that I was interested in fishing, the man, a certain Barney Ballintine, was only too willing to offer advice about the lough, and subsequently showed me hospitality as only the Irish can. As our conversation concluded he suggested that I should call on him later at around 9pm that evening.

This little story is told in my book *Trout From A Boat*, but basically I called on him at the appointed hour. He invited me in to his small farm cottage and we drank tea until nearly ten. Then he took the old cane rod with a cast already made up from its rack, and we walked down the little path to the boat. The boat was clinker built; there was no outboard engine, just a set of oars. We stowed our rods across the thwart boards and stepped in. Surrounded by copper rivets, oak ribs and larch planking, Barney rowed to the chosen bay. With every stroke of the oars the boat glided silently across the water and when we reached the chosen spot, we sat and waited for the rise to begin. The boat was wedged on a bed of *Potamogeton*, and mature trees which grew down to the water's edge sheltered the bay from the wind. A screen of reeds filled the margin behind where we were positioned, and all around us were clumps of aquatic weedbeds. Some of the weeds were just emerging through the surface of the water; it was ideal sedge country. There was no hurry; everything happened in Irish time, at a leisurely pace, until the trout began to move. As soon as the fish began to rise, Barney pulled the boat off the weed and we drifted. Then the time flew, the fish came with aggressive rises and hit the flies with a wallop. The trout we caught that evening were not enormous, but they were all quality fish of 2lbs or over with the best pushing 3lbs. As quickly as the trout came on, so they went down, and once the rise had finished, we continued to fish well on into the night, though we had no further offers.

I do not remember if Barney was a good angler, however I do know that he knew his lake and where to go at the right time to catch a fish. Still water fly fishing for wild fish isn't about chuck and chance it, or just about luck either. That evening taught me more in one short session about fly fishing for wild brown trout on the Irish loughs, than a multitude of sessions since. It wasn't luck that he took me to a certain area of the lough, it wasn't luck that the fly hatched when they did and it wasn't luck that the trout rose to the fly when they hatched. We may have been lucky with the conditions: we are all blessed with that type of luck. The rest however, was down to one man. What I experienced that evening was about having the knowledge and applying it at the right time. He may not have known it, but Barney gave me a classic introduction to fishing for wild brown trout on a lake. And what he showed me that evening would have a huge bearing on the path my fishing would take in the future. What I learnt in a few short hours all those years ago, still applies today. Techniques may have changed, tackle may have improved, but the principle of how and where we apply it is still the same.

That first evening was over thirty years ago. The Peter fishing on Lough Arrow then was of some repute; its reputation was such that anglers from all over the country used to visit the lough just for the sedge fishing. Then like so many of the Irish lake fisheries, Arrow fell into decline. Whenever I planned to visit Ireland for an angling holiday I would occasionally make a tentative enquiry about the fishing on the lough, but the word was that it wasn't worth visiting. Time passed, and there were other fisheries to visit. The limestone loughs of the midland plain, and of the west of Ireland were still to come. They were to provide me with some great fishing, applying the principle which I learnt on that summer evening in 1977. Such were my catches that all my energy and attention was centred around them. Lough Arrow became a long-lost gem. Then over the last few years news came filtering through that the fishing was improving. We made plans to go up and fish it, but time and weather conspired against us. This year I had planned to visit the lough in July, but again I was thwarted by the weather as we were hit by a deluge of rain throughout July and August. Lough Arrow it would seem, would remain just a memory. The season was moving on; we were well into the back end. Then, in mid-September, and quite out of the blue, Larry McCarthy asked me if I would like to go up for a day to fish the lough. It was the week before an inter-provincial competition was due to be held on the water. Larry was fishing in the competition for Connaught and he wanted to do a recce before the match. After two months of almost continual rain the weather had at long last settled, and although it was later in the year than I would have liked, I agreed to go.

Regions change as time passes, especially in modern Ireland. New house builds and farming practices are mostly responsible for these changes. Some areas that I know in the west of Ireland have altered radically in the last fifteen years. The Celtic Tiger has come and gone, leaving an aftermath of social and environmental scars. We tend to be negative about the changes, when in reality life has improved for a lot of people in modern Ireland. I did not know what to expect as we passed through Boyle and traversed the southern edge of the Curlew Mountains. After so many years without seeing it, would the lough now look different with the passing of time, or would it be just as I remembered it? If the area had changed a great deal, would I feel negative about it, and about coming back? They say one should never go back after a long absence, and this concerned me, and I began to feel anxious. As we neared the viewpoint, I wanted to look away, and yet I felt drawn to it. I should not have been concerned, for when the lough came into view, my first impression was that it looked just as beautiful as it did all those years ago. The distant spread of water stretched out towards the north, surrounded by the wooded limestone hills. There were no high crags, or exposed buttresses of stone topping the hills, just rough moorland and some weathered limestone. Yes, there was some development on the surrounding slopes of the hills, but apart from one hotel development far away from the shore, there appeared to be no radical changes. It was hard to believe that it had been such a length of time since I had last seen Lough Arrow, and it was even harder to believe that I had never seen it in all that time on my travels around the country.

Lough Arrow lies in Co. Sligo, a county synonymous with that of the poet William Butler Yeats. The lough has a mature appearance, similar to that of a large English lake. There are no weathered and exposed shores, or rocky islands of rough stone. It is surrounded by rolling limestone hills. The slopes of the hills were densely wooded with a good mix of mature trees, and scattered amongst the trees and on the slopes are various houses. Typically Irish, the houses were brightly painted, with no clumping of housing development. There are a number of islands scattered about the lough, some of which are quite large in size, and are verdant with tree cover. They break up the open tracks of water, and offer good protection to the boat angler from strong winds. Lough Arrow is said to be around 2,000 acres in extent, but it looks much larger than this to me. An incredibly rich limestone lough with good mayfly and sedge hatches. It isn't so surprising that it is a noted water for sedges, as with so much marginal protection from the tress, and well-weeded bays, it has all the classic features for a good sedge fishery. The spring buzzer is also said to be good, but the best time to visit Arrow would be from mid-May to late August. It is during this period, when the mayfly and sedges are at their peak that one is in with a chance of taking a big fish on the fly.

There were four in our party: Larry, his father John, and a visiting angler from Andorra named Xavi, as well as myself. After parking beside the boat mooring on Dodds' shore, we unloaded a heavily packed vehicle of two outboard engines, two fuel tanks and all the necessary fishing equipment for four anglers. How we fitted all the bits and pieces into Larry's motor I will never know. He's a past master with plenty of experience at making use of every available inch of space. It was a bit like putting your hand into a lucky dip box – you just did not know what was going to come out of the back of the vehicle.

With all the gear unloaded we made up our rods beside the boats. There was plenty of banter exchanged between the other members of the group. As I assembled my rod, I felt subdued and dropped out of the conversation with the

It was a day of light wind and cloudless sky

others. My mind kept drifting back to an age when Ireland was new to me, and how it was here on this lough on whose shore I was now standing that I first fished for wild brown trout in Ireland. The lough gave me such a welcome then, and such an insight into fishing for wild brown trout on the Irish limestone loughs. With such an engaging friend as my boat partner, there wasn't a chance of being left to my thoughts for long. My reverie was broken, with the sound of someone's voice, and it broke the thread of my reminiscence. Abruptly, I was back in modern Ireland. 'What flies are you fishing Denny?' It was Larry. I looked up at the sky. We may have been battered by wind and rain for two

259

Playing the big fish on Arrow

months, but now an Indian summer had descended upon Ireland. We were faced with an almost cloudless sky and merely a light wind. The weather had moved from one extreme to the other. Will we ever have suitable conditions for fishing? This was Lough Arrow, the home of sedge fishing, and I wanted to fish sedges, but the light wind conditions were calling for a smaller pattern. I chose to start with Dark Brown and Fiery Brown Bits on the droppers and a Claret Bits on the point. All were size 12.

Rods set up, we headed off across the lough to Brickeen Bay. The margin was fringed with emergent reed beds, and a grassy field on the north shore of the bay ran down to the water's edge. Cows came down for a drink. They looked at us with those large soulful eyes, water dripping from their noses as they raised their heads. The wind, if you could call it that, was a very light north-westerly, and where it caught the surface of the water it left a light ripple. It would be blowing out of the bay, and as it was the only area as far as we could see with a broken surface, we thought this would be a good place to begin. We started our first drift which would take us out from the bay, and down onto an area known as The Thumbs, situated just north of Annaghgowla Island. The water level was high, and as it was the backend of the season, the weed beds were dying back. However, even though it was late in the season, we could still see the remnants of old weed growth pass below the boat as we slowly drifted along. With a bright sun overhead, this was going to be a tough day. We knew it, but on a fishery like Arrow you just never know.

We had seen no fish rising, however, our confidence was buoyed by the sight of several nice trout pitching in the vicinity of where we were drifting. As we were just leaving the bay, a good fish came to me. It was on the blind, and totally unexpected. I could see that it was a big one, and it took the Claret Bits with a lovely head and tail rise. The rise was so slow and confident, it left me with all the time in the world to time my strike, but as I tightened no resistance was felt. Where I expected to feel a solid heavy weight at the end of my line, I was left pondering over a missed rise. It looked unmissable, and yet I was left with nothing but an apparition of a fish taking my fly. We continued with our fishing. Larry was in good form and the stories were well embellished, so I was never going to get bored. As we neared the end of the drift, we came close to a shallow. Here over water about four to five feet deep, Larry spotted a fish rising, and he covered it with one of his Sedge patterns. The trout came with a quick slappy rise, not always a good sign that a fish has taken properly, and when Larry tightened there was nothing there. Two rises, and no fish to show for them.

It wasn't the best of starts, but we were not put off by this failure. However, I had been considering the trout which I had missed. It was a big fish, I had had a clear view of it. Why the hook didn't find a hold was a mystery. There was no question about the fish coming short, as the rise was so leisurely and confident I could see that it had taken the fly in. My mind was filled with a vision of the trout taking, and I couldn't help feeling that perhaps I should be fishing with bigger sized flies. When we made up our rods earlier I had intentions of fishing with Sedge patterns, but the conditions put me off. Now I was having second thoughts. With this in mind I broke down my leader as we motored over to a new mark to start the next drift, and tied up a fresh one, with one dropper. Two flies would be easier to turn over in the light winds. On the dropper I tied a Fiery Brown Sedge, and on the point I tied a Chocolate Drop, both size 10.

The next drift took us down onto Annaghgowla Island. We started from the edge of a large reed bed, and as the boat inched its way down towards the island some cloud passed overhead to mask the sun. It was during this period with the sun clouded over, that I had another rise. Again it came on the blind. This time as I struck I met with firm resistance, and a lovely trout of about 2¾ lbs leapt from the water as the line tightened. The fish sped away taking line on several powerful runs before he came in on a short line and bored away beneath the rod. With the rod well bent, it sapped the energy from the trout which was played out and boated. Fixed firmly in the corner of its jaw as we lifted my prize into the boat, was the Chocolate Drop which had brought about its downfall. The first fish, especially on a tough day, I sometimes feel is the most difficult to catch. I had my trout; at last my duck was broken. After releasing the trout, the sun came out, and as we made slow progress down the lough we had no further action until we neared the end. As we passed the Thumbs, Larry missed two fish in quick succession, both coming short and not taking properly. The sun then broke through and in the light fluky winds there was an air of hopelessness, and what little action there was died.

As the doldrums set in, it seemed like the right time to take a break, and we went ashore to meet up with John and Xavi. It was always going to be a difficult day – late season, light fickle winds and plenty of sun. Considering the conditions, I was pleased to have caught a fish. The first fish can be as I said earlier the most difficult, but once you are on your way it is funny how the run of luck can shift in your favour. Of the two other members of our party, Larry's father John, had momentarily hooked a fish which then came adrift, but otherwise they had nothing to report. We had seen very few free-rising fish, but we had seen a number of good-sized trout pitching. This provided some encouragement, for at least we knew there were trout in the vicinity, and if the conditions were to improve, hopefully we could fare better in the late afternoon.

Following the break we drifted down to Ballantine's Point. We slowly crept along over several shallows on this drift, and as we neared the last of the shallows a lovely trout of at least 4lbs+ rose just outside casting distance from me, and off to my right. I immediately lifted off and covered the fish, or so I thought, but he never came to me. It was either a refusal, or he hadn't seen the flies as they remained unmolested on the oily surface of the water. As we neared the end of the drift, my gaze was drawn towards the mooring just off the point bearing the surname of a man, a man whom I had met many years ago. With eyes fixed towards the shore, I was hoping to see an old clinker-built boat pulled up in a little quay, backed by an unkempt little corner of a field with a rough path leading up to a small farm cottage. Wishing for the ravages of time to have spared this particular part of Lough Arrow, I longed for it to remain unchanged. The contours of a landscape hardly ever alters, it is what is on the face of the landscape which changes. Take away a mature tree or an outcrop of rock and what we knew is changed forever. I was absorbed with my quest when modern Ireland clicked in, and Larry's phone began to sound; it was a call he had to take. The timing could not have been worse, and yet Larry's phone conversation did not break the spell. His voice just faded away as I continued to concentrate on the area where I knew the boat would be.

I felt haunted by memories. Images came flooding back of an angler, an English angler in his mid-twenties who had not fished for wild brown trout in an Irish lake before. Raw and inexperienced, and although he did not know it at that time, the man had so much to learn, walking down the path on a late summer's evening to the lough with the older, more knowledgeable Irishman, who would teach him so much. For the English angler this was the beginning of a journey, an Irish odyssey pursuing enigmatic fish from the vast wastes of the Irish limestone loughs. The Irishman was going to sow the seed, the beginning of the journey, and show the novice angler the ways of wild trout. With rods in hand, and the flies already tied to the cast, they would walk down to the wooden clinker-built boat pulled up in the little mooring. There was no engine, just a set of oars. And as they quietly sailed out, there is a vision of a man wearing a well-worn tweed jacket pulling on the oars, an old cane rod laid across the thwarts of the boat and of being surrounded by oak ribs and larch planking.

As the daydream faded, I was struck by a strong recollection. I dearly wanted, the boat I was looking for, that was hidden from me by the last of the outgrowing branches of the shoreline trees, I dearly wanted it to be made of wood. As we cleared the last of the cover which was hiding the boat from view I could then look in, but as the view opened, the spell was broken. Pulled up and lying where the old wooden boat used to nestle, was a fibre-glass boat. Even worse there was a boathouse built to one side, and everything was clinically tidy. With a wistful sigh I looked away. We all move on; the man whom I once knew has now gone. The new replaces the old; it is the progression of man's stain on the wilderness. I felt disappointed, but my feeling of disappointment didn't spoil the memory.

The boat continued drifting down the wind. I said nothing to my friend about my thoughts. I put them to the back of my mind and concentrated on the fishing. We rose no fish on that drift, and as we neared the end Larry quipped that he was going to make a captain's decision. It transpired that the phone call he had received was from a friend who had fished the lough a few days earlier. His friend had suggested we should try a drift off the island of Inishmore, and so that was where we headed. As we rounded the headland to Inishmore the wind picked up a little, and it clouded over. If nothing else, at least the conditions were improving. The change of drift was to prove an inspired move. We had seen no sign of fish activity for some time. However, as soon as we began drifting the island shore, we saw trout pitching, and an occasional rise. The increase in activity could have been because of the improving conditions, but we couldn't help feeling that we had moved to an area where there were some trout on the move. Our confidence was improving and it wasn't ill-founded, as a little way down the drift a trout rose in front of me. I covered the area where the fish had shown, and was rewarded with a confident rise. My resultant strike met with that lovely feeling of weight at the end of my line, and the second fish of the day, a trout of about 2¼ lbs, was brought to the side of the boat and released. Perhaps things were picking up.

We continued drifting on down the island shore. Ahead of the boat and about mid-way down the island a reed bed grew out some distance from the

264

The 5lbs brown showing autumn colour

shore. The light breeze was pushing off the outer edge of the reed bed and out across a more open stretch of water. With the cloud holding, the conditions were the best we had experienced all day. As we drifted outside of the reed bed, a big fish moved far off to Larry's left, about fifty or more yards away. Larry marked the spot where the trout had shown, and pulled the boat over. We had no idea of exactly where the fish was. There was no option, but to cast out and

265

leave the fly sitting. We were hoping that the fish would betray his presence by moving again, as this would then give us a better idea of his position. I scanned the water for a sign of the trout. Whilst scanning the water for a moving fish, it is important to keep your own flies in your peripheral vision as a trout may take. I'm glad that I did, as I just noticed my fly disappear to a barely discernible rise. It just vanished; there was hardly a break in the water. Instinctively as the fly disappeared I tightened, and everything went solid. The rod was wrenched down, the tip almost touching the water as the trout tore off line in a strong run away from the boat. It shot off at breakneck speed taking me into the backing. Some fish fight and others don't; why I do not know. It has nothing to with condition as some of the best-looking trout will come in like a lamb. However, this fish was no lamb; he was a fighter. The line sped off the reel as he made several long runs. Normally a brown will come in under the rod and fight it out boring away below the boat. This fish was different; he wanted to keep his distance and stubbornly refused to come in close. Larry suggested that I enjoy the fight, as I had waited long enough for the take from such a fish. There were no apparent snags so I had no problem there, but I like to keep my fish on as short a line as possible. It not only minimises the risk of being snagged, but on a short line you have greater control over the fish, and the bend of the rod will quickly sap their energy. This brown however never came in until he was beaten. Pound for pound he pulled as hard as any fish I have caught. Eventually the trout came up on its side, and Larry did the honours with the net. Hoisting the fish aboard, he opened the meshes of the net and then with a wry smile said 'I don't know how you do it, I'll give 5lbs for that one.' Then he put out his hand and at the same time said 'Well done'. It was a superb late season cock fish, with the colour of autumn glowing off the sides of his flanks. A big wild brown is a truly magnificent fish, and this one was no exception. After taking some quick photographs, I held the trout in the water for release. The fish soon recovered, and I could feel the strength returning to his body as he tried to push forward. With a strong thrust of his tail, he broke away and the bond between us no longer existed, he was no longer mine. Wild and free as he slipped away disappearing below the mirror of the water into a dark void of nothingness, I wished him well for the winter to come.

Inishmore was being kind to me, and as we continued drifting down the

The sun sets on a memorable day

shore towards the bottom end of the island I picked up a fourth fish. It was another nicely conditioned trout of about 1¾ lbs. I was having a run of luck in what were testing conditions. Why it should have gone my way I do not know, but the fickle phantom of luck had stayed with me. After this, the sky cleared and the wind dropped altogether, conditions which in the autumn are never that productive. In the season of mellow fruitfulness, a clear sky and lack of wind are usually indicative of a temperature drop. As the shadows lengthened the flat surface of the water reflected back the evening light, every detail of marginal foliage was mirrored in the surface. We knew it was over, and so it was. Larry had had one of those days. His luck was out, he rose the same number as me, but never connected with any of them. Why none of those fish stuck will remain a mystery. He said you know when your luck is out when a fish rises in front of you and then moves over to take your partner's fly. Of the other members of our party, John caught the only other fish, and this was after I had given him a pattern of my successful fly. The Chocolate Drop had accounted for all five fish.

267

Co. Sligo that evening was bathed in beautiful evening light, and as the sun went down I took some photographs of Larry fishing into the last of the western light. The aurora of illumination touched the surface water of the lough, a jamboree of soft and yet bright light spread across the western horizon. Above, the night sky was already setting in, and much of the surrounding environs were in deep shadow. It was the end of the day. We can try to capture a moment and photograph the sunsets and sunrises. Artists can portray the scene on canvas. In my opinion the artist captures the mood of the event better than the camera; however, even then I feel the artist fails, for I believe it is all about atmosphere, and atmosphere is about being there and experiencing it for oneself. My return to Arrow was one of nostalgic reminiscence, a pilgrimage of a kind, and I was touched by the mood. My eldest son, the little boy smiling in the black-and-white photograph is now thirty-three, and on reflection, I know that I cannot leave it another thirty years before I visit again. The biological clock is against me. Plans are already afoot; next season is time enough to wait.

21 Borne out of the Wind

Some of my most exceptional fishing days have come as a result of planning. By being selective about the venue and the season, I try to time my visits to certain areas to coincide with key times. Occasionally however a good day may happen just by chance, when you least expect it. My best fishing day of 2009 came in what was perhaps the worst mayfly I have experienced in a long time. The mayfly hatch on Corrib had been a good one. Even the conditions for once were better than they had been for a number of seasons, and the fish were showing but the larger trout were proving to be elusive. Then fate took a hand, and just by chance on 29 May I had an exceptional day. There was no pre-planning, my decision of where to go was one of circumstance made because of a number of incidents which occurred prior to that fateful morning. And so it was on the morning of the 29th when I made a decision that would give me one of the best days of wild fishing I have ever experienced, and my biggest trout of the season.

Before I made my decision I had spent the last four sessions prior to that morning fishing big water, and when I say big water I mean fishing in rough windy conditions on a big rolling wave. On the Corrib we were catching fish, but it was a struggle to catch a trout over 2½ lbs. Most of the trout were in the 12oz to 1¼ lb bracket, with a sprinkling of larger specimens, but I had nothing over 2½ lbs to show for my efforts. This would be unusual for me as some of the areas I fish consistently produce trout bigger than the average Corrib fish. But even these areas in 2009 were failing me. So three rough days on the trot and no sizeable trout to show for my pains left me feeling a little bereft of enthusiasm. On the evening of the 27th I received a phone call from Jeremy Herrmann asking if I would like to go to Sheelin the following day. Now I wanted to fish Sheelin, as it is a lough which produces some exceptional fish to the fly, and I had planned to go in late June. As the Corrib was giving me a hard time, the idea of fishing Sheelin appealed, but I hadn't seen the weather forecast for the 28th.

The forecast was for 30 kilometre winds, and suddenly the idea didn't appeal so much. I have never found the lough that productive in a strong wind, and for the gnat the conditions would be totally unsuitable. As soon as I saw the forecast I rang Jeremy back to cancel the trip. Jeremy brims with confidence and he is so enthusiastic about his fishing, it is sometimes hard to say no. He had never fished Sheelin before, and was very keen to go. So against my better judgement I agreed.

I have always held the highest respect for Sheelin, and I know that it can be a tough water especially when the conditions don't suit it. On our day the mayfly hatch was magnificent, the lunch was wonderful but the day was awful. It blew up and the wind didn't drop off, not even for the last few hours in the evening. We returned from that trip, tired, wet and fishless. When I arrived home which was around 1.30 to 2.00am I felt exhausted. Clothing, tackle bag, camera bag were all soaked. Drained of energy I just spread all the impedimenta out on the study floor, hung the wet clothing in the utility room, had a hot shower and went to bed.

The following morning was one of sunny periods, giving way to the occasional shower, but the wind was still fresh. I walked my dogs down to the lough shore. A fresh west wind was blowing into and along the shoreline. Great mounds of foam had collected on the windward shore, a sign indicative of a windy night. The conditions were not impossible, in fact they were far from it, but I couldn't help thinking about the great rolling waves one would meet if one went out. After the previous day, and those which had preceeded it, I wasn't at all attracted to the thought of going out in a boat. Luckily I hadn't planned to go out with anyone, so I never felt committed to go. Now as I studied the conditions any thought of my going out was expiring with the wind. Did I really want to face another day of mountainous waves crashing over the gunwales of the boat, or the thud, thud, thud as the bow cut into the wave? No, this wasn't for me today, the thought of going out did not appeal at all.

Back at the house I poured myself some coffee and in a thoughtful mood took in the vista of the upper lough and its environs from the comfort of an armchair. My house overlooks Lough Corrib, and the view is one of water and islands with a backdrop of distant mountains. The waves were breaking as the great rollers crested; it didn't look at all appetising and I was glad that I had made the decision not to go out. Two boats were going out from Inishmica-treer. Spray broke all around the head of the boats as they pounded into each wave. They appeared to be heading toward Inchigoil four miles distant, and I thought of how many waves they would strike before they reached the fishing grounds. With each wave would come that jarring thud as the bow cut into the wall of water. It did not look like fun, but I'm sure the occupants of the boats were oblivious to it, and enjoyed their day. For me I was glad to be sitting in the comfort of the house watching, and not out in that turmoil with them. However, this was the mayfly season and I dearly wanted to go somewhere. What I could not face was another pounding out on the big water.

I needed an alternative to the boat fishing, a river or some shore fishing perhaps, but where? The rivers were more than likely full with run-off from recent rains, so didn't offer too much promise; it had to be a shoreline. Where could I find a shoreline which would offer protection from the keen west wind and the chance of a fish in the mayfly? This would have been a much easier decision to make a few years ago, however now it isn't so simple as many of the areas have been fished out. The more I thought about it, the less Lough Corrib seemed to offer. Mask offered more potential in a west wind, but Mask wasn't fishing. Was this too risky? It was a decision which in a way I made out of convenience, and yet the more I thought about it, the clearer it became. Even though the lough wasn't fishing, I decided to fish a bay on Lough Mask.

My waterproof clothing was dry, but the rest of the bits and pieces strewn over the study floor were still damp from the previous day. As most of the impedimenta was still damp I chose to take just a few essential items with me. I picked up a reel loaded with a WF6 floating line; a couple of spools of leader material; my Mayfly box; some floatant and a small tape measure, and secured these essentials in the pockets of my jacket. To this I added a 9½ ft rod, some chest waders and boots. Apart from the waders and boots which I would be wearing, my entire kit, all the essentials which I needed were in my jacket. The only item which needed carrying was my rod – a landing net I thought was a luxury and I rarely take one when bank fishing anyway. One could not have travelled lighter, than just a few basic bits of kit and a rod. To this was added some sandwiches and a bottle of water. The time was around twelve noon when I left, and it takes approximately thirty minutes to drive to where I would park the car. From the car it would take at least another thirty plus minutes to walk in and up the shoreline of the bay to the top of the wind. On the shore of the bay at the top of the wind I could eat my lunch before starting to fish, and then work my way back. This was the theory, and if I caught a fish that would be a bonus. One thing for certain, I was not going to be buffeted by the incessant wind and wave in a boat that day.

As I left home and turned out of the little boreen which leads down to the house I couldn't help thinking that perhaps I had made a mistake. For several weeks the angling grapevine had been reporting that Lough Mask was struggling to hit form. My anxiety dissipated as I passed Ballynalty Bay on my drive northwards towards Ballinrobe. Even Ballynalty Bay which is normally well sheltered didn't look that inviting; waves were breaking for as far as the eye could see. The sight of the cresting waves set my mind at rest, and at least I now felt more comfortable with my decision to fish from the shore, even if I had chosen the wrong lough!

The Partry mountains lie along the western flank of Mask, and when viewed from the eastern shore of Mask they stand out as a long flat ridge. They are not particularly high, and yet because of the low-lying limestone terrain they could be seen for a large part of my journey, an ever-present guide to the whereabouts of my lough. Lough Mask is said to be over 20,000 acres; it is hard to believe that such a large spread of water lies in the bowl at the foot of the Partry's, and yet hidden away from the prying eye of the passing motorist lies a sheet of water which contains some very big trout. If you drive around the north or the west shore you will basically see all of Mask, and yet if you drive up the east side, you never see it until you are beside the lough shore. With the mountains to guide me I drove in and parked the car. My bay was in view but distant and the main body of water was lost behind a mosaic of limestone outcrops, stunted trees, heath and wetland. This is a part of Ireland which hasn't been ravaged by the sharp claw of the Celtic Tiger. It hasn't been subjected to the scarring impact of modern land-clearing machinery, and is to me a wild paradise, a haven for wildlife, where flora and fauna abound unmolested as it has seen no development as such or change of land use, and I hope that it remains that way for many generations to come. It is a unique part of County Mayo, and it is an area which I love.

A drift on the east shore of Lough Mask

With the car parked, I donned my waders and boots, put on my jacket, picked up my rod and prepared to walk out. It could not have been simpler, and I headed off in the direction of the distant bay. Walking out I could hear the background noise of the main lough; she was angry and it is a sound which in the silence of the west of Ireland carries. At my house on the shores of Lough Corrib I can hear when the lough has built up a head of steam, a sound like a strong wind blowing through the leaf canopy of trees. A background roar made by the sound of the breaking waves made me feel smug when I thought of the boats out on the main lough battling with the elements. At least it made me feel positive about my choice of venue, and my decision to fish from the bank. The walk was easy, with no steep gradient to test heart and lungs. In the low-

273

lying areas the ground felt soft and forgiving underfoot. Around me a mixture of wild grasses, and exposed limestone was interlaced with the striking pink and purple flowers of early purple and broad-leaved marsh orchids. The sloping grassy banks beneath the limestone outcrops, were studded with late flowering primrose. Marsh marigolds filled the margins of wet land pools, and amongst the fissured limestone, burnet rose and bloody cranesbill added a riot of colour to a wild garden. If you look there is so much to see. It takes no more time to take in what wild beauty lies around us, and enjoy the best of what nature has to offer. And if I stop and linger to admire some natural beauty, what is it going to cost me? A few minutes of time.

I dropped down over a rough stone wall, and crossed some wet land. Just before I reached the shore of the lough, a snipe flushed a short way ahead of me from a patch of coarse marsh grass. Cautiously I moved forward, watchful of where I put my feet and parted the grass from where the snipe flushed. There in a shallow nest of a few dried grasses, and neatly arranged with their pointed end facing inwards, were four eggs. The markings on the eggs blended in with their natural surroundings. If I hadn't seen the bird flush I would never have seen those four little gems. One misplaced foot could so easily wipe out the new life forming within those fragile calcium shells. Taking careful note of where the nest was situated so that I could give it a wide berth on my return journey, I carried on down to the edge of the bay. Much of the shoreline is exposed lime-stone, firm underfoot and easy walking. The head of the bay is just over a mile away and eighteen minutes of brisk walking, a pace which is made easier with the wind in your face.

At the top of the bay I laid my rod down beside a large flat rock, took off my jacket, picked a suitable place to sit and eat my sandwiches whilst at the same time keeping a careful eye on the water in front of me. It was just after 1pm. The cloud was lifting and the sun was breaking through for longer periods. Apart from the wind it was a lovely May day, and sitting in the lee of a rock out of the wind it felt quite warm. It would feel quite different however, once I was out on the water exposed to the true strength of what was a fresh blow from the west. Out on the water the wind would be blowing hard onto and just off my right shoulder. For a right hander this direction of wind wasn't ideal. It would make casting uncomfortable, but it was ideal for fish working into the wind and along the shore. As I sat in the comfort of my protective rock some flies, both mayfly and olives, were hatching from a band of water about twenty yards out from the shore. I watched them, ethereal wings proudly erect, bobbing along on the waves. They sailed down with the wind, along the shore and off out across the bay. I expected to see a fish rise but none came. Thoughts of the angling grapevine news about Mask that it wasn't fishing came flooding back to haunt me; perhaps it was correct after all. I put this negative thinking to the back of my mind, as it was too late now to worry about how the lough was fishing.

Feeling refreshed I picked up my rod and assembled it. With the reel attached and the fly-line threaded I made up an 18ft leader of 0.205mm copolymer with one dropper about seven feet from the point. To the point I tied a Ginger Mayfly

Larry returns a big Lough Mask brown

and to the dropper a Grey Mayfly both size 10. The leader was degreased and floatant was added to the flies. All was now ready. Moving forward towards the water's edge I pulled off some line from the reel, and made a few false casts as I waded out into the lough. The flies had been hatching from a band of water about twenty to twenty-five yards out. This I thought would be the productive area and so I concentrated on this band. My flies went out and across the wind to cover the water. The wind was pushing down the shore so I took a step downwind to keep the flies fishing for as long as possible. By keeping the rod just upwind of the flies I could keep them sailing down the wind for a distance of four or five yards before I lost control of the line. When too much of a bow formed in the line, control was lost and my artificial Mayflies did not float down with the natural movement of wind and wave. Putting an upwind mend in the line helped, but it did not solve the problem completely. As soon as the flies began to drag I lifted off and cast again, repeating the process of stepping downwind to maintain control of the flies' drift as I worked down the shore.

About thirty yards downwind of where I first began, there was a large slap of rock breaking the surface about twenty yards out on the inner edge of the band of water which I was covering with my artificial flies. Behind me a heavy bank of cumulus cloud was building and as I worked down to where the rock was positioned, the sun disappeared behind the bank of cloud. With the change of light the water looked more appealing. Where previously when the sun was shining it was the colour of a faded denim blue, and reflecting a lot of harsh light, the surface now appeared to be much darker and softer. The wind hadn't abated, but with the change in light the conditions were now more favourable for a fish. Flies continued to hatch, not in great numbers but enough. I had been fishing for about twenty minutes when I came to the rock. Lifting off and casting so that the line fell just downwind of the rock, I took a step forward so that the flies would drift on unhindered. Just after stepping forward and planting my foot, a fish came up to my top dropper, the Grey Mayfly, and took with a classic head and tail rise. Lifting the rod, I felt that satisfying sensation of weight at the end of my line. It is such a good feeling, the moment when you lift and feel living resistance at the end of your line. The trout jumped and bored away. He was a spirited fighter, refusing to give in until he came to hand. A lovely fish of about 2lbs was admired before being unhooked and returned. I had seen no rises to the natural flies, and yet this fish had come up and taken my artificial fly. They are funny creatures, trout.

After releasing the fish I quickly dried my fly and resumed fishing. Casting, shuffling forward, casting, shuffling forward I worked my way down the shore. The shoreline on much of Mask and Corrib is difficult to wade. Sometimes you may come onto a section which is made up of gravel or shale, but most of the time you are feeling your way over rocks which are planning to upend you at any moment. It isn't easy, however the fishing can at times be rewarding. As I worked down the shore, carefully feeling with my feet at every step to make sure my front foot is placed securely, I scanned the water for a sign of a moving fish. About ten minutes after releasing the first fish, a group of mayflies hatched at more or less the same time just out from where I was standing. Five or six flies popped up and sailed off with the wind. Their wings turned like the sails of small yachts, as they swiveled in the air current. One, then several more take off to run the gauntlet of swooping swallows and martins and other avian predators. Two of the flies stubbornly sat it out. I watched them intently, and was just beginning to wonder how on earth the trout could resist them, when the fly nearest to me was taken. For a moment the ephemeral queen was there on the surface of the water, the proud queen of May, and then without warning dethroned by a heavy slashing rise. Without hesitating I lifted off, and covered the area just upwind of where the fly had disappeared. The rise was aggressive, leaving a great whorl in the water. Whatever made such a swirl, looked heavy. I would like to make the acquaintance with whatever dethroned the queen I thought, as my Mayfly imitations settled on the water.

My flies were out on the water for no more than a few seconds when the tail fly, the Ginger Mayfly was taken. It too disappeared in an aggressive boil. I raised the rod and felt the line tighten against the fish. As soon as I felt the increasing weight on the end of my line, the surface of the water erupted, and the fish made a strong run out and away from me. In no time at all the loose fly-line was ripped through my fingers, and the reel was making a merry tune. Although I hadn't seen it, I knew that the fish at the end of my line was something special. There wasn't only a strong feeling of power, there was also a feeling of weight. This fish was heavy. The backing splice was just outside the tip ring when the run stopped and the fish kited round to my right. I gained a lot of line, and then the trout tore off again in another strong run. After this my fish came back in towards me and then I played the trout out on a shorter line. He cruised up and down in front of me, and on a short line, my leader line as tight as a violin string whined in the wind. Then the trout came up, and I saw it for the first time. I'm pretty confident when it comes to landing a fish by hand, but on seeing the size of the trout to which I was attached, I had my doubts. I would beach it, I thought. So backing off towards the shore, I led the fish in. As luck would have it, there was a grassy shallow incline behind me, and this is where I led the fish, and keeping the pressure on, the trout came in towards the grass on its side. The rod was bent double, but as soon as the fish was beached I dropped the rod and with, a sigh of relief, grabbed my prize.

The joy I felt when I had the trout in my hands, words cannot describe. It was big, and it was beautiful. Heavily spotted with golden flanks it was possibly the best-looking trout I have ever caught. My hands were shaking with excitement as I gazed down on my prize. Trying to be rational I tried to judge the weight of the trout. I'm usually a pretty good judge of a fish's weight, but I did not want to judge this one as I was too excited and might overestimate the size. So I took out my tape measure and put it across the fish. It was twenty-six inches in length, and in tip-top condition. As a friend of mine would say, when describing the condition of a fish with flanks as tight as a barrel, it could not have crammed another ounce of weight into that frame. A twenty-six inch Irish lake trout would weigh around 8lbs in my book, and that is the weight I gave my fish. Kneeling in the water holding that beautiful trout, was a moment to savour. Gently holding the fish by the tail, it quickly recovered its strength and then kicked away sliding off into the deep. All connection between us severed, the fish no longer mine was wild and free.

On seeing the fish swim away I picked up my rod, wandered back from the water's edge and sat on a nearby rock. From here I could see most of the bay. The waves were still rolling down the spread of water in front of me, as they had done before my encounter with the big fish. They betrayed none of the drama that had just occurred but just rolled on by as if nothing had happened. Two sandpipers came flitting past and alighted on the shore. They were no further than a good cast from me, their bodies continually bobbing as they moved along the margin of the water searching for food. My mind had been racing with images of kneeling over a big fish, and the sandpipers were a calming diversion. For a few minutes they searched for invertebrates washed up along the water's edge, and then they took off and flew further down the bay. Having settled down I retied a new leader, and attached the same flies to the line. Satisfied that my flies were securely tied I waded back out into the lough, and resumed fishing.

Step by step I worked down the shore. Two more trout followed, both around 1lb in weight, and then I went through a long period without a fish. For at least an hour or more, I didn't move or see a trout rise. I had worked my way down to a rocky section of the shore. Below me the rocks jutted out into the bay for at least thirty yards. Huge slabs of rock worn by the action of wind and wave protruded above the water. The mayfly were still hatching, coming

Vaughan Lewis fishing down the shore of the bay on Mask

off at regular intervals and I began to see an odd fish rising, but none were close enough to cover. Although I could not cover a rise I was half expecting a trout to come fishing blind, but nothing materialised. Then a fish moved just out from me and well within range. A lift of the rod and I put the flies down to cover the rise. The flies sat drifting on the waves, and then the fish came with a wallop. Before I could raise the rod fully, the line was snatched through the fingers of my hand, and for the second time that day the reel sang. Again I felt and heard the backing splice fly up through the rings of the rod. With the rod well hooped over, the strain told on the fish and he came back in a wide arc as he kited in. Once I had the trout in closer to me I felt in control, and tried to play him out on as short a line as possible. The line strummed with tautness as the fish bored away from the pull I was exerting. Eventually the pressure told, and my fish came up turning on his side. As soon as the trout was on his side, I backed off towards the shore and led him in. On the measure he went a good twenty-two inches, and I put this one at 5lbs+. My luck was really in as I knelt over another lovely trout in cracking condition for the second time that day. The wind was ringing in my ears, and all around me was the sound of the waves washing onto the rocky shore as I released him. He powered away, and I wondered to myself whether this was really happening.

In what was the worst year I have ever experienced on Lough Corrib for big fish, I had just taken two fish for over 13lbs. And that was from a lough which wasn't fishing. They say that fishing is largely about luck, and well in a way we all need it. That is why we have days when nothing seems to go wrong, and everything is basically perfect. But there is another kind of luck, a run of luck which we create for ourselves, and if it passes my way I like to think that I make the most of it. Some of my friends just seem to miss out where the bigger fish are involved. Blighted by misfortune, they will either make a hash of the rise, break the line or simply lose the fish in play. I can't help feeling sorry for them when they miss a big fish, as these opportunities do not happen that often and it is sickening to see a chance go begging. In a season I may have anything from half a dozen to a dozen chances of taking a trophy fish. If I miss one it makes a big dent in my prize list. One should really make the most of such opportunities. Iron out the little glitches. Tune up the reflexes with some easier fish, be totally comfortable with the leader line, and practise playing fish firmly. Firm pressure maintains a constant pull on the hook hold, so apply this without breaking the leader and there is little scope for the hook to drop out.

I was on a high, the day could not have been going better, and I had a feeling that there was still some more fish to come. The wind kept driving in on my right shoulder, short gusts scudding across the water, and scratched the surface as it raced away from me. Overhead the cloud thickened and as the cloud base grew heavier the light changed. With the light change, I could see creamy coloured tramlines of foam etching their way down the bay, for as far as the eye could see. And the mayflies were still emerging, popping up to the surface and sailing down with the wind. As the cloud became heavier, the flies seemed to stick for longer. They were finding it difficult to lift off, and were a great temptation for a fish. My slow methodical crab-like movement brought me down to where the rocks jutted out into the bay, the outermost rock being perhaps thirty to thirty-five yards away. A huge slab of limestone which showed golden brown beneath the marching waves was just sub-surface, but in the trough of a wave the water broke over and rolled around it. Inside it was a jungle of more rocks, some protruding well above the surface. The wind was throwing wave after wave against the exposed faces of the protruding rocks, and as the water broke in a creamy foam with the rise and fall of the swell. My attention was drawn to the edge of the maelstrom, where a fish had moved. Although difficult to see in the cauldron of broken water, it was definitely a rise, and then the trout rose again. It was coming my way, and it was coming fast.

I put the flies down, just above where the trout had last risen. I was confident it was going to take, I just knew it. The flies were bobbing down with the waves, when a nose came up and my top dropper, the Grey Mayfly disappeared. When I tightened lifting the rod to make contact with the fish, there was a great whorl in the water. Something heavy and invisible beneath the waves, powered away from me on an unstoppable run. About forty-five yards of line ran out into the bay, before my unseen adversary came to a halt. Then the fish changed direction, and began running upwind to my right taking a lot of drowned line with him. I had no control over the trout; it ran as it pleased, and I could do nothing about it. Well upwind to my right it turned and came in towards me, and as it did so I gained a lot of line, and then it swung across me and began heading towards the rocky jungle on my left. It felt powerful and heavy; there was no hope of turning him. This fish for the moment at least was in charge. I applied all the strain I could, but it was bit like having a horse tied to a kite string. As he passed me and headed towards the rocks I knew that there was no hope of stopping him, and that the inevitable smash was looming. And then I couldn't believe my luck as the trout changed direction of his own volition, and charged back out towards open water. The line was strumming at it cut through the waves, running up just inside the jungle of rocks. Hope was rising as the line neared the point to where it was directly in line with the outermost rock, and I thought the fish was going to clear it, and move out to the snag-free water. There was just the slightest hesitation, then a great swirl over the golden coloured slab of limestone, and my line fell limp.

Big fish which are lost, sometimes eclipse what has gone before. This one wouldn't, for the day had been too good. Parting company with the trout was infuriating, which left me with a mixed feeling of emotion. Both excitement and disappointment were sweeping through my mind, jostling for the top position. But I think overall I was too excited to feel too down about the loss. It was a day which was reminiscent of a day on Lough Corrib, fifteen or more years ago when I had five fish which took me to the backing. That day I landed four beauties from a bag of eight fish. It was an exhilarating experience of reel-screaming runs, a rod well bent and heavy fish. But there was a fish in particular which ran me well into the backing, an invisible force of power and strength which I didn't land. After several strong runs he came in under the rod, and I thought that I had the beating of him. But I hadn't bargained for the incredible strength of that fish, he was stubborn and he was heavy, I just could not bring him up. Something had to give. Eventually the strain proved to be too much for the hook hold, and the hook pulled out. I never saw him, but I know that fish was big, very big. And yet that day, even though I lost what was undoubtedly a big fish was etched in my memory as one of those unforgettable days. Losing the big one, couldn't take away what had happened before or after that day. It was a day of pure joy and pleasure and this day would be the same.

The trout which I lost in the bay was the only trout to break me in 2009, and in a season when I fished with leader line that was finer than I have fished for some time, I find it ironic that that particular fish should break me on what I consider to be my standard leader diameter for the mayfly. Even with the

0.205mm nylon I couldn't pull that fish off course. It was just too powerful, and the power was such that I was left wondering with the nagging thought, just how big was that trout – it was big there is no question about that. I can hypothesise all I want, for in truth I will never know, and perhaps that is how it should be. These things happen, and like it or not, it is part of fishing. If we knew all the answers, hooked every rise, and banked every fish would there be any pleasure, I wonder, in what we do?

After recomposing myself I set up a new leader and tied on two new flies: a Grey and a Ginger, the same patterns of fly as I had been using before; there was no point in changing. Knots tested and the flies oiled, I went on with my business. Moving about forty yards down the shore, I resumed fishing just below, and downwind of the outcrop of rocks. I worked the water as I had done previously, punching out the flies across the wind, and walking down with the natural drift. Within minutes of resuming fishing, a trout came to me with a quick splashy rise. Missing the rise, I put the flies back down smartly and he came with a wallop. This trout spent more time in the air than any of the others, a real acrobat, cart-wheeling and throwing himself into the air in a wild frenzy of jumps. When I eventually brought him in, the fish filled my hand with the depth of his sides – a lovely trout of about 2¾lbs. Shortly after this another fish around 1½lbs was added to the bag, and then it went quiet. I must have covered 100 yards or more of shore without moving a fish.

The wind was easing. Casting and control of the line became much easier. Even the cloud base was lifting a little to allow the odd glimpse of watery sun to break through. Mayfly were still hatching, emerging in little bursts of activity, but the fish seemed to be going off the take. Well down the shore towards the bottom of the bay, the limestone gave way to a softer muddy-marl bottom. Wading became more of an effort as my feet stuck in the soft glutinous mud. No longer did I have the problem of being up-ended by treacherous uneven rock, now I had to contend with the suction of the bottom mud as I lifted my feet to take a step forward. A billowing milky cloud of fine silt rose up around me with every foot-step. In places soft weed grew over the mud, and scattered around were beds of *Potamageton* and water milfoil. There were no dense beds of weed, so they was never going to be a problem, but they did suggest a change in the characteristics of the bed of the bay.

On the gentler wave it would be easy to see a rising fish, however I could see no sign of activity. As I was scanning the water a trout rose to one of my flies, and I missed it. He went on his way unhindered, as did the next trout that rose to me. Two in succession, and up until that point I had only missed one rise. I concentrated more on my flies, and less on the scanning. It appeared that even though there were no signs of fish moving to the natural mayflies, they were coming to my artificials. Why they should rise to an artificial fly, when there was no suggestion of activity to the natural flies on the water was a mystery. But rise they did. The next time one of the flies disappeared I made contact, and again for the fourth time that day, something heavy moved off and out into the bay. With the rod well hooped over, and the line strumming through the water, I played out another good trout. All the big fish were a similar shape and colour. In colouration and shape they looked like peas in a pod, as if they had been produced by the same set of parents and had lived in the same environment all their lives. On the bank the fish measured just under twenty-one inches, and I put him at 4½lbs. It was just before seven in the evening and shortly after this I caught another, a much smaller fish around the 1¼lb mark. This was to be my last trout of the session. Having fished all the water which was available to me, it seemed pointless to continue, as it would mean going back over ground I had already covered. More than fulfilled with the fish I had already caught, I walked away. It was time to call it a day and bring to a close, an unforgettable Mayfly day.

Feeling an inner glow which comes from having had a good day, I was in an exuberant mood as I walked back towards the car. And as I walked back across the wetland lapwings rose on broad wings, agile flyers they turned and wheeled in the air uttering that distinctive call, pee-wit, pee-wit to warn their young of an intruder encroaching upon their territory. Curlew called and the snipe drummed overhead. Willow warblers sang from every thicket. The trees, birch and alder, willow and hazel were portraying their best colour, a vibrant green of new leaf growth showing fresh and lush, the emerald greens of Ireland on every bough. It was such a wonderful evening, and feeling in such a joyous mood I purposely drifted off course to traverse some higher ground of the peninsula which protected the bay. From my vantage point, I could see the main body of water and the range of mountains along the western side of Mask. Dark masses of billowing cumulus cloud rumbled in from the west. They loomed over the mountain ridge, the colour of deep Wedgwood blue, the paler fibrillated edges of the cloud mass like fibrous cotton wool merged with an over-wash of grey hues. Small breaks where the cloud base thinned and opened up, showed a bright illumination of gold and the palest blue. The surface of the lough was a reflection of the overhead sky, dark and forbidding, but where the illumination cast its light upon the water each wavelet which caught the light was reflected back like shimmering sequins on a dark robe. It is a wonderful view looking westward towards Maamturk, and in the right light it is stunning. In the words of Keats from the opening lines of his poem Endymion: 'A thing of beauty is a joy forever.' I could see nothing, but natural beauty all about me.

On the drive home my head was spinning, going over the events of what had happened that day. Through the mirror of recollection, thoughts of heavy fish running against the strain of rod and line filled my mind. As I pulled into the drive I could see Lough Corrib spread out below the house, and I wondered how the boats had fared in the strong wind. Parking the car, I unloaded my few bits and pieces and took them to the study. Spread over the floor was all the other tackle which I had left behind earlier that day. Everything was as I had left it, spread out to dry after the last session out on a heavy wave; it was as if time hadn't moved. Feeling hungry I made myself something to eat and poured a glass of wine. The evening was well set, and through the window I could see the spread of Lough Corrib, just shutting down for the night. The last vestiges of evening light caught the surface of the lough, the Maamturk mountains out to the north-west were dark in silhouette. With the sun down and behind them, the mountains lacked colour. They look so different when exposed to, and bathed in morning light. Then you can see every fold and bit of relief in the hills. The day was coming to an end. It was a day in May to remember. Deep in thought, my mind turned to the tackle spread out on the floor of the study, tackle which had been soaked from too many days out on the big water. And it reminded me of a decision made just before noon that day, a decision borne out of the wind.

Footnote

For those who believe the bay is easy, I would like to say that I went back the following day and caught one trout around 3½lbs. After this I fished the bay on five other occasions, and endured five blank sessions. I never moved a fish, and except for a couple of big trout pitching never saw another fish rise. With much of my fishing I make a point of fishing areas which hold a greater percentage of larger trout. Many of these areas are rich shallow bays with a low density of fish. Rich feeding and the lack of competition produces some of the biggest trout one can catch on a fly, and that is why I go to these areas. But with fewer trout around they tend to be moody, and it needs the right conditions and a good hatch of fly to bring them up. If they are not rising you will have a very tough day, as searching for them on the blind is like looking for the proverbial needle in a haystack. That day on 29 May the fish were on, and it coincided with a decision that wasn't pre-planned, but when I realised what was happening I made the most of my run of luck.